WELCOME TO...

PC Sound, Music, and MIDI

by Tom Benford

MIS: PRESS

A Subsidiary of
Henry Holt and Co., Inc.

Copyright 1993 by Management Information Source Inc.
a subsidiary of Henry Holt and Company, Inc.
115 West 18th Street
New York, New York, 10011

First Edition—1993

ISBN 1-55828-316-1

Printed in the United States of America.

10 9 8 7 6 5 4 3 2 1

MIS:Press books are available at special discounts for bulk purchases for sales promotions, premiums, fund-raising, or educational use. Special editions or book excerpts can also be created to specification.

For details contact: Special Sales Director
MIS:Press
a subsidiary of Henry Holt and Company, Inc.
115 West 18th Street
New York, New York 10011

Trademarks

Throughout this book, trademarked names are used. Rather than put a trademark symbol after every occurrence of a trademarked name, we used the names in an editorial fashion only, and to the benefit of the trademark owner, with no intention of infringement of the trademark. Where such designations appear in this book, they have been printed with initial caps.

ACKNOWLEDGEMENTS

There are many individuals, too numerous to list individually by name, who all contributed in some way to make this book and CD-ROM possible. I'd like to take this opportunity to thank them all, and especially the following people who really "went the extra mile" in assisting me:

First and foremost, a very special "thank you" is in order to Les Paul, Jay Chattaway, Suzanne Ciani, David Arkenstone, John Archer, Bob Fowler and Steve Branca for taking time in their busy schedules for my interviews and for the permission to use their words and/or music here as well.

Kudos are also in order for Sue Shroeder and Michael Sullivan at Narada Productions, Joyce Greenawalt and Jim Presley at Yamaha, Mike Holiday at Freed International, Paul "The Guitar Guy" Unkert, Steve Reed at Musician's Friend, and all of the hardware and software companies who so graciously provided their products and technical support for coverage in this work.

DEDICATION

This book is dedicated to:

Liz Benford — my wife, business partner, and photographer for her support, encouragement and patience;

Tim Benford — my brother and earliest supporter who also acted as my "roadie" in producing my first demo records some 25 years ago;

Carl William Lesch — my boyhood choirmaster (now deceased) who first kindled and stimulated my interest in music;

Vince Occhino — my guitar instructor who couldn't have had the slightest idea of the monster he was creating by teaching me a few simple chords as a teenager;

And to all of my readers — may you find the joy and beauty that comes from producing music yourself!

CONTENTS

LESSON ONE:

Off to a Sound Beginning

An introduction and overview of sound:

- What it is and how it is produced

- Noise and tone

- Basic terminology

Welcome

Sound is around us constantly. It is so pervasive, in fact, that we take its presence for granted and scarcely give it a second thought during the course of our daily lives. Sound, however, is really quite a marvelous phenomenon, and how it is created, heard and perceived by humans is fascinating. How it can be produced, processed, altered, and used with a personal computer is absolutely amazing.

You're about to embark on a sonic adventure into the world of sound, music, and MIDI on IBM-compatible personal computers, and I'll be your guide and mentor. While my primary goals are to make this experience educational and informative for you, I also want to make it fun. Along the way I'll introduce you to new terms and concepts that will help you understand and get the most from PC audio, decide what hardware and software will be right for you and your computer system, and how to get the most use and enjoyment from your existing equipment.

I hope this book stimulates your interest and piques your curiosity about the musical aspects of PC audio and MIDI, since these can be extremely rewarding and satisfying. Above all, I encourage you to be inquisitive and experimental—your own discoveries about sound and music will undoubtedly be the high points of this adventure, and these can be a perpetual source of wonder that continues long after you've finished reading this book.

So let's get started by answering a fundamental question...

What Is Sound?

Sound is the result of vibrations that produce waves of rapidly changing air pressure. This definition is as true for the sound produced by the cry of a newborn infant as it is for the sweet strains of a concert violin or the rumble produced by a Space Shuttle launch. Regardless of its source, sound is produced as the result of vibrations that affect the air pressure.

To understand the process more easily, let's use a drum as an example. When a drum is struck by a stick, the drumhead vibrates the air around it. These vibrations travel in waves that are called, logically enough, *sound waves*. Inside your ear, the eardrum (also called a *tympanum*) vibrates when sound waves come into contact with it. The auditory nerves send this vibrational signal to your brain where it is interpreted and identified, producing what we recognize and call sound. This is the nitty-gritty of sound and sound perception and, though simplified, applies for all sounds, even those beyond our range of hearing (dogs, for example, can hear sounds that we can't).

Sound vibrations are transmitted through matter, and matter is made of molecules. The molecules in the air vibrate to transmit the sound waves. You can hear sound under water, because water molecules also vibrate to transmit sound waves, and sound can also be transmitted through solids. Conversely, in outer space there is no sound, nor is sound possible—space is a vacuum that doesn't contain any molecules that can be used to transmit sound.

Sound can travel at approximately 742 miles per hour, but this speed is greatly affected by temperature, altitude, and density of the air. To give you an example of the speed variation, the exact velocity of sound in air at 32°F (0°C) is 1,089 feet per second, but at 68°F (20°C) it is increased to about 1,130 feet per second. Sound travels slower through gases (such as air) than it does in liquids, and it moves slower through liquids than through solids. The more densely packed the molecules of matter are, the better and faster sound can travel through it.

Figure 1.1 *All sounds are produced by vibrations that cause changes in air pressure. These changes make your eardrums vibrate and send signals through the auditory nerves to your brain where they are identified as sounds.*

By recording sound waves, their characteristics can be graphically displayed so we can see what the sounds look like, literally, in diagram form. The characteristics of sound waves are called the sound's *attributes*, and these are what give sounds their own particular identities. These attributes include how high or low the sound is (*pitch*), how loud or soft the sound is (*intensity* or *volume*), and whether it is tinny or mellow (*quality* or *timbre*). The presence or absence of these attributes in different amounts are what determines whether a sound is noise or a pitched sound, also called a *tone*.

In a tone, the vibrations that compose the sound wave occur at regular intervals and repeat themselves. Conversely, noise sound waves have irregular, nonrepeating vibrations, as you can see in Figure 1.2. This is what distinguishes a tone from noise.

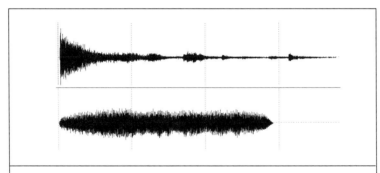

Figure 1.2 *Noise sound waves, such as the sound of a glass breaking (top), are irregular and nonrepeating. Tone sound waves, like a voice singing aah (bottom), have regular, repeating wave patterns.*

The frequency with which these vibrations repeat themselves determines the pitch of the sound, and these vibrations are measured in *cycles per second*. A *cycle* is one complete waveform from its beginning to end, as illustrated in Figure 1.3. One full wavelength of a wave represents one complete cycle representing one complete vibration in each direction. All waves are referenced to an imaginary synchronous motion in a circle. Thus, one complete cycle is divided into 360 degrees. The phase is that part of the cycle, expressed in degrees, that is completed at a certain time. The various phase relationships between combining waves determine the type of interference that takes place. The frequency *n* of a wave is equal to the number of crests (or *troughs*) that pass a given fixed point per unit of time. The period *T* of a wave is the time lapse between the passage of successive crests (or troughs). The speed v of a wave is determined by its wavelength and its frequency according to the equation $v = ln$. Because the frequency is inversely related to the period T, this equation also takes the form $v = l/T$.

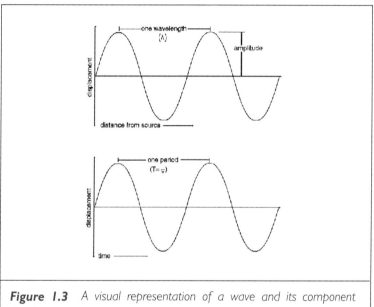

Figure 1.3 *A visual representation of a wave and its component structures.*

The amplitude of a sound wave is the distance the wave rises above and dips below the imaginary median line running through the middle of it. A cycle is measured from the crest of one wave to the crest of another, and the time it takes to complete an amplitude cycle is called one *period*. The number of periods (cycles) is called the *frequency*. The rising and dipping portion of the waveform is its *modulation*, which is illustrated in Figure 1.4 on the next page. *Modulation* is the process in which some characteristic of a wave (the carrier wave) is made to vary in accordance with an information-bearing signal wave (the modulating wave). *Demodulation* is the process by which the original signal is recovered from the wave produced by modulation. In modulation the carrier wave is generated or processed so that its amplitude, frequency, or some other property varies. *Amplitude modulation* (AM), widely used in radio, is constant in frequency and varies the intensity, or amplitude, of the carrier wave in accordance with the modulating signal. *Frequency modulation* (FM) is constant in amplitude and varies the frequency of the carrier wave in such a way that the change in frequency at any instant is proportional to another time-varying signal. The principal application of FM is also in radio, where it offers increased noise immunity and greater sound fidelity at the expense of greatly increased bandwidth. In pulse modulation the carrier wave is a series of pulses that are all of the same amplitude and width and are all equally spaced. By controlling one of these three variables, a modulating wave may impress its information on the pulses.

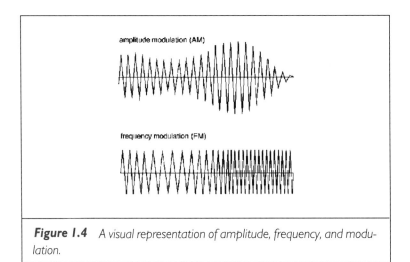

Figure 1.4 *A visual representation of amplitude, frequency, and modulation.*

Low-pitched sounds have fewer cycles than high-pitched sounds. This is illustrated in Figure 1.5, which shows the sound waves of two C notes played on a violin an octave apart. Cycles are represented in hertz, abbreviated *Hz*, a frequency measurement unit invented by Heinrich Rudolf Hertz (1857-94), a German physicist who succeeded in producing the first artificial radio waves. A "concert A" note that vibrates at 440 cycles per second is therefore written as *440 Hz*.

The human hearing range is between 20 Hz and 20,000 Hz, although this varies somewhat between individuals. Sounds below the lower threshhold (under 20 Hz) are called *subsonic*, while sounds above the range (over 20,000 Hz) are *ultrasonic*. Many insects and some animals have hearing capabilities that span from the subsonic through ultrasonic ranges, so, in comparison, human hearing is confined to relatively small range.

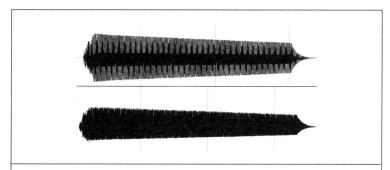

Figure 1.5 *Low-pitched sounds have fewer cycles (vibrations) than high-pitched sounds, as shown above. The upper waveform is a low "C" note (131Hz), while the one at the bottom is also a "C" note but one octave higher (262 Hz). Notice how the low "C" has deeper wave cycles (vibrations) which are spaced much further apart than the smaller, shallower cycles of the higher-sounding note.*

Cycles increase their frequency linearly rather than geometrically. This means, simply, that the C note one octave above the low C in the illustration is vibrating 262 cycles per second, or double that of the low C, which is vibrating at 131 cycles per second. *Timbre* gives a tone its own distinguishing sound. *Sustain* is how long a sound's vibrations continue. Both the clavinet and guitar have longer sustain times for the note, while the marimba's note is of very short duration, as shown in Figure 1.6 on the next page.

The volume or loudness of a sound, also called its *intensity*, is measured in *decibels*, abbreviated dB. The sound's volume is determined by the strength of the pressure of the radiating sound waves. Human hearing responds to intensity in a range from zero to 120 decibels, and any sound with pressure over 120 decibels is painful.

Timbre is the quality of a sound that distinguishes it from other sounds of the same pitch and volume, and it is timbre that gives distinctive tone to a musical instrument, a voice, or a voiced speech sound. Simply put, it is timbre that gives sound its tonal "coloring."

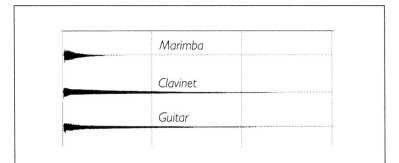

Figure 1.6 *All three of these instruments played the same note, and the resulting sound wave pictures for each graphically display the tonal differences that distinguish them—they each have their own unique timbre.*

A sound's timbre or tonal quality is determined by subsidiary tones called *overtones*. The number and relative prominence of overtones produced by any instrument is what determines the distinctive timbre it has. A trumpet, for example, produces different overtones than those produced by a violin, and the overtones give each instrument its own distinguishing timbre. Many factors are involved in producing overtones, including the type of material producing the initial sound vibrations (such as vocal chords, a drumhead, or a guitar string), the resonance of the sound source (the brass bell on a trumpet or the hollow body of a guitar), the velocity or force producing the vibrations (how hard a key is struck or a string is plucked), and other factors.

Summary

What we've covered here are the basic building blocks of information that will provide you with a good foundation for understanding the dynamics of sound. In succeeding chapters you'll find this information valuable in helping you to understand how computers process sound and how to get the most out of it for your own particular requirements or desires.

Glossary

amplitude	How much a sound wave rises above and dips below the median line of a waveform. The amplitude determines the sound's intensity or volume. (See Figure 1.4 on page 6.)
cycle	One complete iteration of a waveform measured from peak to peak. (See Figure 1.3 on page 5.)
decibel	A unit of relative measurement commonly used in audio and electronics technology. Abbreviated *dB*, a decibel is one-tenth of a bel, named after Alexander Graham Bell. Measurements in decibels fall on a logarithmic scale, since they always compare the measured quantity against a known reference.
harmonic	A tone in the harmonic series of overtones produced by a fundamental tone. The term harmonic also describes a wave whose frequency is a whole-number multiple of that of another.
intensity	The loudness of a sound, determined by the amplitude of the waveform. Also referred to as *volume*, intensity is measured in decibels.
modulation	The variation of some characteristic of a waveform (the carrier wave) in accordance with an information-bearing signal wave (the modulating wave). Demodulation is the process by which the original signal is recovered from the wave produced by modulation. In modulation the carrier wave is generated or processed so that its amplitude, frequency, or some other property varies. By controlling one of these variables, a modulating wave may impress its information on the pulses of the waveform. (See Figure 1.4 on page 6.)

noise

A soundwave that has irregular, nonrepeating vibrations that usually produces an unpleasant sound.

overtone

A harmonic produced by a fundamental tone.

pitch

How high or low a tone is, as determined by its position in a musical scale. Pitch is determined by the frequency of the vibration, measured in cycles per second.

timbre

Also called *tonal color* or *musical quality*, timbre refers to the sound characteristics that allow us to differentiate one sound from another and refers to the qualities that make sounds unique. Timbre is what makes a saxophone sound like a sax instead of a guitar. Timbre is determined by the overtones (subsidiary tones), and the distinctive timbre of any musical instrument is the result of the number and relative prominence of the overtones it produces.

tone

In music, a tone is distinguished from noise by its definite pitch, caused by the regularity of the vibrations that produce it. For a sound to be called a tone it must possess the attributes of pitch, intensity, and quality.

tympanum

Also spelled *timpanum*, this is the eardrum. It also refers to a membranous external auditory structure in certain insects.

waveform

The mathematical representation of a wave, especially a graph of deviation at a fixed point versus time.

L E S S O N T W O :

Fundamentals of PC Sound

- How PCs process and use sound
- Analog versus digital sound
- Sound synthesis
- Some audio terminology

Analog Sound in a Digital Environment

People live in an analog world, computers exist in a digital realm. What this means, in simple terms, is that computers deal with digital logic—everything is broken down to a series of *true/false* or *yes/no* or *on/off* or, ultimately, *one/zero* conditions. We humans have qualitative degrees in our sensing and decision processes, rather than the stark one/zero digital logic computers conform to. While this makes our lives more interesting and enriched, it presents problems for digital devices like computers that rely on absolute rather than qualitative data.

To illustrate the difference between analog and digital, let's use a clock. An analog clock has a minute hand, an hour hand, a second hand, and numerals on its face. A digital clock, however, relies on digits to display the time rather than hands sweeping around a dial.

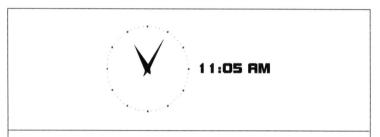

Figure 2.1   *Both clocks are showing the time as 11:05, but the one on the left is an analog display, while the clock at the right is digital. Analog measurements have qualitative degrees, whereas digital measurements are absolute and rely solely on digits. All digital computers use the digits 1 and 0 to represent on/off, true/false, or yes/no conditions.*

With an analog clock, it's possible for the minute or hour hand to point to the space in between two numerals; a digital clock is absolute in the time it displays, with no *in-between* times.

For computers to process analog sounds such as speech or music, they must first be converted to digital format. This is accomplished with an *analog-to-digital converter* (ADC). To playback the digitized sound from the computer, it's necessary to convert it back again. This is done with a *digital-to-analog converter* (DAC). The ADC and DAC conversions are handled by a PC sound card that is usually capable of a great deal more, including the ability to play music, synthesize sounds, and provide interfacing to other devices including CD-ROM drives and MIDI equipment. We'll explore each of these areas in more detail as we progress through this and subsequent lessons.

But first, let's take a look at the typical components that are usually found on PC audio boards and external-connect sound devices.

Other Key Components

Instead of ADCs and DACs, some PC audio systems utilize a *codec* (coder/decoder) in place of the ADC/DAC. The codec has built-in circuits that perform the ADC and DAC functions, in addition to other required audio processing tasks. Other audio card designs use a digital signal processor (DSP) to handle the recording and playback chores. Since a DSP actually processes the sound information itself, the PC's central processing unit (CPU) doesn't have to concern itself with these chores and is free to perform other tasks.

Regardless of whether the card uses an ADC/DAC, codec or DSP design, it will also usually have these components as well:

- Provisions for inputting sound into the computer, which usually are jacks for a microphone and line-level sources. This process is called *sampling*, since samples of the sound are taken by the sound card's circuits at regular intervals and converted to digital information by the ADC.

- Provisions for outputting the sound—headphone and/or line-output jacks—are usually provided, along with a connector for MIDI input/output, if the board supports MIDI.

- An amplifier to boost the basic signal to an audible level. This can be a one-channel amp for monophonic boards, with two single-channel amps or a dual-channel amplifier for stereo boards.

- A source for generating or synthesizing sounds and music.

Sound Sources

A sound generation source is a prerequisite for any sound board. Most boards use a multitimbral frequency modulated (FM) synthesizer chip or chips for the sound source, although devices that use actual digitized (sampled) sound samples are rapidly gaining favor as the preferred means of generating sound. The process of using actual digitized sounds stored as data for reproduction is called *wavetable sound*. Although more expensive than FM-based sound boards when they were first introduced, sound cards using *wavetable technology* have dropped in price dramatically to a level where they are competitive with the chip-based boards, though still slightly more expensive on the average.

The synthesizer chip or chips in FM-based sound artificially create facsimiles of sounds. These sounds can be simulations of musical instruments, common everyday noises, sonic special effects, synthesized speech, and more by changing the values of the *synthesizer registers* via software. This approach is the most common means of generating sound on an audio board, and it has been the method traditionally used by most manufacturers.

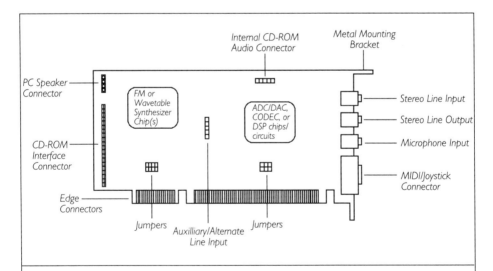

Figure 2.2 *The major components typically found on PC sound cards are illustrated above. Not all cards have all of these features, and the position of these components may vary depending on the card.*

The synthesizer chips most frequently used on sound boards are manufactured by Yamaha and the two leading models are the YM3812 and the YMF262, more commonly referred to as the OPL2 and the OPL3, respectively. As of this writing, the OPL4 chip (which combines wavetable plus FM sounds) has been announced but is not yet available.

The OPL2 is a monophonic synthesizer, while the OPL3 is a stereo chip with some additional capabilities (see Table 2.1 below for the feature comparison of both chips). Some sound board designs use a pair of OPL2s to provide stereo (discrete left and right channel) capability, while many of the newer board designs use the OPL3, which produces cleaner-sounding audio and requires less support circuitry, resulting in a smaller physical board size. This translates to lower manufacturing costs and, ultimately, lower prices for the consumer.

Yamaha FM Synthesizer Chip Comparison

	YM3812 OPL2	YMF262 OPL3
Sound generation	FM	FM
Type	monophonic	stereophonic
Number of operators/modes	2	4
Number of sounds possible	11	20
	(9 sounds or 6 melody sounds with 5 rhythm sounds)	(18 simultaneous melody or 15 melody sounds with 5 rhythm sounds, other sound/operator variations possible; 8 selectable waveforms)
Effects	built-in vibrato oscillator and amplitude modulation oscillator (AM)	LFO for vibrato and tremolo effects

Table 2.1 *Yamaha's OPL2 and OPL3 chips are the most widely used FM synthesizers on PC sound cards. The OPL3 has significantly enhanced capabilities over its predecessor the OPL2. The newly-announced OPL4 combines FM and wavetable sound generation.*

Using digitized sound samples is another way of providing a sound source for the board, and there are advantages as well as drawbacks with this method. The major advantages are that the digitized sample sounds are absolutely pristine renditions of the instruments (or other sources) that created them. They are digital recordings of the actual sounds, and, moreover, sounds can be changed by replacing the EPROMs on the board with a different *library* of samples, or by downloading new sound *patches* to the card's on-board memory. The major disadvantages are that these boards cost more and some software, especially games which make extensive use of synthesized sound effects, may not playback correctly. For satisfactory playback of these programs, each waveform variation of the most commonly-used sounds would have to be recorded, since actual samples of these sounds are required by the wavetable. In a very practical sense, the sonic variations used in game and recreational software products are virtually limitless, so covering all of the bases with a library of sampled sounds would be impossible. To compensate for this, some manufacturers put an FM synthesizer chip and a wavetable chip both on the same board. Other manufacturers offer a wavetable module as an add-on upgrade to their FM-based sound cards.

FM Synthesis versus Wavetable Sound Technology

The principal difference between FM synthesis and wavetable sound is that in FM synthesis, the sound is synthesized (artifically created); in wavetable technology, the data parameters (soundwave characteristics) of the actual sound are stored in internal memory on the sound card.

The sounds that are possible to generate using FM synthesis are limited to the architecture of the synthesizer chip.

Wavetable technology generates sounds by scanning entire waveforms, or portions of them, from sounds produced by a real instrument or other analog sound source such as a human voice. Consequently, there are no limitations to the numbers of types of sounds that can be produced. Different wavetable *patches* load different instrument sounds into memory and make them available for use. Since wavetable technology is RAM based, it offers the ability to load different patch sets that change the instrument selection available. FM synthesis technology is solely limited to the sounds possible from the circuits on the FM chip.

Sound File Formats

As we learned earlier, the sound system's ADC, codec, or DSP converts the analog audio signal into digital format for storage and processing by the computer. The two predominant file formats in use today on IBM-compatible PCs are the VOC and WAV formats.

The VOC format was developed by Creative Labs, and was the native file format of the company's highly-successful Sound Blaster audio card. Due to the popularity and large number of users, the VOC format became one of the *defacto* standard file formats for digital audio files on the PC. VOC files can only support 8-bit audio resolution and are limited to a maximum size of 16 MB. The VOC file format is particularly popular and predominant in the DOS environment, and is supported by the Creative Labs Sound Editor and Sound Editor II software utilities bundled with the company's Sound Blaster cards.

The WAV format was developed by Microsoft Corporation for the multimedia extensions to the Windows environment. Due to the huge installed user base and increasing dominance of the Windows operating environment on PCs, the WAV file format has become the industry-standard format for digital audio. Unlike VOC files, the WAV format does not have a file size limitation. WAV files can be of any size and can represent either 8-bit or 16-bit digital audio. The WAV format is supported by some DOS-based multimedia applications, as well as virtually all Windows-based multimedia applications.

Sampling Rates

Perhaps no other aspect of PC sound is as misunderstood as the terms *sample rates* and *sample sizes*. Because the two terms sound similar, it is understandable why they are confusing to many people. We will eliminate this confusion here by explaining what each is and what its purpose is, in the overall digital audio picture.

The *sampling rate* is the number of times the amplitude of the analog sound wave is sampled for conversion into binary data. On playback, these numbers are again sampled for conversion back into an analog sound we can hear. In short, the more often a sound is sampled, the more accurate the digital representation of the sound is.

Sampling rates are measured in thousands of samples per second, abbreviated *kHz* (for kilohertz). For example, a sampling rate of 22 kHz means that the sound system is collecting 22,000 samples of sound per second for digitization.

Since higher sampling rates collect more sound data than lower sampling rates, they require more memory and disk storage space as well.

The Windows 3.1 operating environment has a sampling limit of 44 kHz, although some audio cards are physically capable of sampling up to 88 kHz. It is also important to note that the *threshhold* of human hearing is about 21 kHz. The benefits of sampling at higher rates than humans can hear is that the higher rates provide much cleaner samples by reducing the amount of alias distortion (unwanted extra noise).

Eight-Bit versus 16-Bit Sampling Sizes

The *sample size* (also referred to as the *sample depth*, *bit resolution*, or *bit length*) determines how closely the digitized sound resembles the original. The more bits per sample, the higher the fidelity and the closer the digitized sound is to the original. Most sampling is done using either 8-bit or 16-bit sample sizes, with 16-bit sampling being the preferred sampling size for any application where higher fidelity and more accurate audio reproduction is required. Some sound cards also support 4-bit sampling, which may be acceptable for some low fidelity speech applications, but unacceptable for music.

Eight-bit sampling offers lower fidelity but requires much less disk space for storing the sound and requires less of the CPU's resources for recording or playback.

Sixteen-bit sampling offers much higher quality sound but taxes the CPU's resources and requires double (or more) the amount of disk space as the same sound using 8-bit sampling.

Sound File Sizes and Data Storage Requirements

As mentioned earlier, higher sampling rates and sampling sizes require more memory and storage space than sounds recorded at lower rates in smaller sampling sizes. Also, stereo files require twice as much space as mono files do. To illustrate this point, Table 2.2 provides examples of the storage requirements for a 10-

second monophonic (single channel) sound file recorded at different sampling rates and sizes.

The sample size and sampling rate directly influences the size of the sound file and the amount of memory and disk space it requires. Four-bit sound, while offering the most economical file sizes, produces low-quality sound and is really only suitable for speech. Eight-bit sound offers better fidelity for speech and may also be acceptable for some music. Sixteen-bit sound provides the best fidelity, but also taxes the PC's memory and storage resources the most.

Sample rate in kHz	Sample size in bits	Size in bytes for 10-second file	KB used per second
11.025	4-bit	56,320	5.5
11.025	8-bit	112,640	11
11.025	16-bit	225,280	22
22.05	4-bit	112,640	11
22.05	8-bit	225,280	22
22.05	16-bit	450,560	44
44.1	4-bit	225,280	22
44.1	8-bit	450,560	44
44.1	16-bit	901,120	88

Table 2.2 *Digital sound file storage requirements. All of the examples shown in this table are for a monophonic sound file. A stereo file requires double the amount of space of a mono file.*

The Redbook Audio Standard

The standard reference specification for digital audio quality is known as the *Redbook Standard* (16-bit stereophonic sound sampled at 44.1 kHz). While this specification unquestionably provides the best sound quality with the highest fidelity, it also makes the highest demands on the PC's memory and storage resources. Requiring 5,406,720 bytes of space for a one-minute monophonic file recorded at this rate, a one-minute stereo file of CD-quality audio requires over 10 MB (10,813,440 bytes) of space. Since compact discs have huge storage capacities of more than 700 MB, which can yield play times in excess of one hour, this high sampling standard doesn't pose a problem for CDs. Computer hard disks, however, store lots of other information in addition to sound files, so economy of storage becomes a primary consideration.

Striking a Happy Medium

Some tradeoffs of sound quality are usually required to find a happy medium to yield acceptable sound quality without taking an enormous amount of storage space on the PC's hard drive. Compromises between sound quality and the space required are usually made by using a lower sample size (8-bit versus 16-bit) and a lower sampling rate (11.025 or 22.05 kHz vs. 44.1 kHz) than the Redbook Standard. These popular sampling rates are usually shown rounded off without their fractional components—44 kHz, 22 kHz, or 11 kHz.

Finding the right combination of sample size and sample rate isn't hard, as there are guidelines to be followed. For example, the playback of most speech and sound effects sound fine when recorded at an 8-bit sample size at a rate of 11 kHz, whereas music recorded at these parameters may have an objectionable amount of alias distortion (static, fuzz, or scratchy sound quality). Generally speaking, a 22 kHz sample rate usually yields acceptable musical quality using an 8-bit data format, whereas a 16-bit format increases the playback quality of the music considerably.

Compression—Putting the Squeeze on Sound Files

Sound files typically contain a lot of redundant data that take up valuable space. For example, periods of silence in a sound file occupy space even though there is no sound during these periods. By compressing these periods of silence it is possible to trim the size of the file considerably. Depending on the amount of compression and the sound file, it is possible to reduce the sound file's size to one-half its original size. Greater compression rates reduce the file size further, but there is also some loss of fidelity.

Pulse code modulation (PCM) is the most popular method for storing uncompressed sound in digital format. The audio information is encoded in the waveform signal by varying the amplitude of pulses. The pulse amplitudes are limited to several predefined values, and the examples represented in Table 2.2 on page 19 are those of uncompressed sound files using PCM.

Adaptive pulse code modulation (ADPCM) is the predominant algorithm method for reducing the amount of memory and disk space required for sound files. The amount of compression is represented in ratio format, as 4:1, 3:1, and so forth. The ratio numbers indicate how much compression has been applied to the sample. For example, a 2:1 ratio means that the compressed sound is only one half the size of the original uncompressed sample, a 3:1 ratio compresses the sound to one third of its original size. The greater the amount of compression, however, the lower the fidelity of the digitized sound.

PC sound devices vary greatly in the methods and algorithms they use to compress audio data, and compatibility between hardware devices is a serious issue that should be considered if sound files are to be shared among several users, as in an office network setting where voice annotation is used.

The Windows operating environment has helped to standardize the audio formats and sound file specification with the WAV file type and subsequently has helped to resolve some of the incompatibility issues that are more prevalent when using sound and audio in the DOS environment.

Glossary

8-bit/16-bit sound   The dynamic range of the sampled sound, with 16-bit having double the amount of sound data of 8-bit sound. Eight-bit sound provides 48 dB of dynamic range, whereas 16-bit sound increases the range to 96 dB, or double that of 8-bit. Since more sound information is involved, 16-bit sound requires more memory and more disk space for storing the sounds than 8-bit sound does, but it provides much better quality.

algorithm A formula or equation that consists of rules or processes for solving a specific problem. Different algorithms are commonly used for compressing sound information in digital files.

alias distortion Audio distortion that occurs when the resolution of the sampling is insufficient to represent the sample accurately. Simply put, aliasing occurs when the sample rate is too low to accurately capture the sound being sampled. For example, severe alias distortion results when music is recorded using a 4-bit sampling rate, taking the form of static, fuzzy sound and background hiss, as well as "clipping" the higher-frequencies.

ADC An abbreviation for *analog-to-digital converter*, which is a special chip and supporting circuits that converts analog information, such as sound, into digital data that can be processed and stored by the computer.

ADPCM An acronym for *adaptive differential pulse code modulation*, an algorithm for compressing audio data so that it requires less memory and disk space. The amount of compression is represented in ratio format, as 4:1, 3:1, and so forth. The ratio numbers indicate how much compression has been applied to the sample. For example, a 2:1 ratio means that the compressed sound is only half the size of the original uncompressed sample, a 3:1 ratio compresses the sound to one-third of its original size.

byte A unit of information used in computer processing and storage consisting of 8 bits that, by their order, represent a single character.

codec An abbreviation for *coder/decoder*, which refers to circuitry on a sound card that converts or codes analog information into digital format and decodes it back again to analog for playback. It can also refer to circuits or software that can compress and expand data.

DAC

An abbreviation for *digital-to-analog converter*, which does the opposite of an ADC. A DAC is a special chip and supporting circuits used to convert digital data from the computer into an analog format (such as sound or music) that can be used by humans or other analog devices (like a stereo system).

digital

Relating to digits or the way they are represented. For all practical purposes here, digital is synonymous with binary because personal computers store and process information coded as combinations of binary digits (bits).

digitize

The act of converting analog data into digital format for processing and storage by a digital computer. ADCs (see entry) are usually used to perform the conversion, while DACs convert digital data back into analog format.

DSP

An abbreviation for *digital signal processor*, a chip-based integrated circuit which is used in place of ADC and DAC circuits.

dynamic range

The span of volume between the loudest and softest sounds, either in an original signal (original dynamic range) or within the span of a sound system's recording capability (recorded dynamic range). Dynamic range is expressed in decibels (dB) and represents the difference between the overload level and the minimum acceptable signal level.

EPROM

Is an acronym (pronounced *ee-prom*) for *erasable programmable read-only memory*. EPROMs are nonvolatile memory chips that are programmed after they are manufactured. They provide a convenient and cost-effective way for hardware manufacturers to update the features and capabilities of their products through software upgrades. In audio cards, EPROMs are frequently used for storing wavetable sound and MIDI instrument patches.

fidelity
Audio quality—the higher the fidelity, the more closely the digitally recorded sound matches the original sound without any added distortion or noise.

FM synthesizer
A chip that contains predefined circuits that can generate sound waves. To synthesize different sounds, one fixed waveform modulates another, thus creating a new waveform with better harmonics (tonal quality) than either of the two waveforms that comprise it would have by themselves. By varying the modulation and adding more waveforms to the mix it is possible to approximate the sounds of musical instruments. The Yamaha YM3812 and YMF262 are currently the two most commonly used FM synthesizer chips.

kilobyte
Abbreviated Kb, K, or Kbyte, one kilobyte is the equivalent of 1,024 bytes. Kilobytes are usually used to express capacities of RAM, floppy diskettes, files, and other measures less than a megabyte (1024x1024=1,048,576 bytes) in size.

line-level
A line-level signal is typically output by audio components that do not require preamplification (CD and cassette players, for example). Line-level signals are based roughly on the standardized signal intensity sent over a telephone line, and it refers to any audio signal having a maximum intensity between .5 and 1.5 volts.

megabyte
Abbreviated MB, megabyte is the measurement term that represents 1,048,576 bytes (1024x1024 bytes). Megabytes express large capacities when referring to total system RAM memory, large disk drives, and CD-ROM data capacities.

multitimbral
A term describing a sound card's ability to play more than one instrument sound simultaneously.

patch
A sound data file that loads desired sound libraries into the sound card's memory. Patch files are usually used with wavetable and MIDI devices.

PCM

An acronym for *pulse code modulation*, PCM is the predominant method for storing uncompressed sound in digital format. The audio information is encoded in the waveform signal by varying the amplitude of pulses. The pulse amplitudes are limited to several predefined values.

RAM

An acronym for *random access memory*. RAM refers to semiconductor-based (silicon chip-based) memory that can be read and written by the microprocessor or other devices in the computer system. RAM is classified as *volatile* (rather than stable) memory, since it loses all of its stored data when power is interrupted or removed (the computer is shut off).

Redbook audio

The standard specification for compact disc audio quality (16-bit stereophonic sound at a 44.1 mHz sampling rate) as detailed and agreed upon by Philips, Sony and other major manufacturers. Since these technical specifications were published in a book with a red cover, this specification for audio became known as the Redbook standard.

sample

The first step required to convert an analog signal into a digital representation. The analog sound is measured at regular intervals called samples. These values are then encoded to provide a digital representation of the analog signal.

sample size

Also frequently referred to as *sample depth* or *bit resolution*, this term indicates the number of bits used per sample to express the dynamic range of the audio frequency; more bits per sample result in higher audio fidelity. Eight-bit and 16-bit sample sizes are used for general and music recording, while 4-bit sample sizes are usually only used for recording low-quality digital speech.

sampling

The process of converting analog signals to digital format for use and processing by computers. An ADC is used to sample analog signals (such as sound) as voltages and convert them to the binary form required by the computer. Sampling is affected by two major characteristics: the sampling rate (usually expressed in samples per second) and the sampling precision (usually expressed in bits—an 8-bit sample contains only half as much information as a 16-bit sample).

sampling rate

The frequency at which samples of a sound are taken. The higher the sampling rate (the more samples taken per unit of time), the closer the digitized samples are to the original sound. The highest sampling rates produce the best quality audio. Measured in kilohertz (kHz), the sampling rate refers to the lowest-possible and highest-possible ranges of sound that can be successfully digitized. According to the *Nyquist Sampling Theorem*, the highest audio frequency that can be reproduced must be sampled at at least twice that frequency. This means that to reproduce a 20 kHz tone it must be sampled at 40 kHz.

waveform audio

Frequently referred to as digitized or sampled sound, waveform audio utilizes an ADC to convert the analog sound files into digital format and requires a DAC for playback.

wavetable sound

An audio technology that generates sounds by scanning either entire waveforms or portions of them from sounds produced by real instrument or other analog sources such as the human voice. These digitized samples are called sound "patches" and are loaded into the sound system's on-board memory to make them available for use. Wavetable technology is RAM based rather than being "hard-wired" as are the sound circuits in an FM synthesizer chip.

LESSON THREE:

Selecting a Sound Device

- What features to look for
- Internal versus external sound devices
- Compatibility issues
- Terms and definitions

While the prices for sound boards have dropped to the point where they can realistically be considered as affordable upgrade peripherals for the average PC user, even the least expensive sound board still costs $100 or more and, as such, isn't a purchase that should be taken lightly. In this lesson we'll cover some of the important features and issues that you should consider in deciding which sound device is right for your computing needs, both for now and for the future.

Playback Only versus Full Functionality

Ultimately, your budget, personal needs, and applications for using sound will be the deciding factors that determine the PC audio device that best suits you. There may be some features that you don't want or need—features that you may never use and, subsequently, will never miss, so you should take stock of what you need before making your purchase. By assessing what you expect to do with sound, you may narrow down your field of choices and save some money by selecting a device that does only what you need without all of the extra "bells and whistles" that some of the higher-end, costlier products offer.

The most economical means of adding sound to your PC is by using the PC's built-in speaker. The principal advantage to using the speaker is that you can add sound very inexpensively, since you'll only need the software driver required to route any sound to the speaker. There are several disadvantages to using the PC's speaker, however:

— The sound will be of very low quality.

— There is no provision for adjusting the volume or mixing sound.

— You can't use any applications that require an FM synthesis chip or a wavetable sound generator.

— You can't play any MIDI files.

— Since there is no recording capability, you can only play back sound.

— You'll have to purchase a software program that includes the required speaker driver, and many sound effects software programs include this driver as a part of the package.

There are also several dedicated playback-only hardware devices available that typically connect to the PC externally (usually through either a serial port or the parallel printer port). These devices usually retail for well under $100 and provide much better sound quality than the PC's built-in speaker. There are still some disadvantages to be considered, however, with the major ones being the lack of a sound generation source (FM or wavetable), there is no MIDI capability, and you won't be able to record with these devices. For users who merely want to play back sounds that come with the software application and don't intend to get into the music, MIDI, or recording aspects of PC sound, these external playback-only sound devices may be a worthwhile option. Typical scenarios where playback-only devices are well suited include using them for presentations with laptop or notebook computers that do not have internal expansion slots, and for PC users who don't want to open up their computer system to install an internal sound card.

The External Connection

Virtually every sound card and audio board requires an internal expansion slot for mounting. However, if you own a laptop or notebook PC you probably won't be able to accommodate an internally-installable card that requires either an 8-bit or a 16-bit expansion slot. Take heart, though—this doesn't exclude you from getting the full benefits of PC audio, it just means that you'll have to select an audio device that can connect externally to your computer. There are several of these devices available.

Most of the external devices connect via the computer's parallel (printer) port and the better ones include the capability to record sound and play music and sound effects. There are also some MIDI-capable devices that connect externally through the PC's serial port, and these, as well as internal sound cards, are covered in depth in Lesson 4.

Sound Blaster Compatibility

The Creative Labs Sound Blaster was one of the first PC audio cards to reach the marketplace several years ago, and it quickly attracted the attention of software developers. With the attachment of an optional breakout cable, the Sound Blaster also supported a joystick and provided MIDI input/output connections, making it an ideal peripheral for use with computer games. The MIDI capabilities of the Sound Blaster also attracted the attention of software developers with musical and MIDI applications software products.

The original Sound Blaster used a Yamaha YM3812 (OPL2) synthesizer chip to provide eleven voices, making decent-sounding music and excellent sound effects possible on the PC for the first time. The Sound Blaster was quickly adopted by software developers as an effective means of adding sound and music to their products and it became the *defacto* standard for sound boards in the industry.

Because of the large library of DOS-based software titles that use sound configured to the Sound Blaster's standards, compatibility with the Sound Blaster is a major feature that is sought by many purchasers of PC sound cards.

If you'll be playing games from DOS and using other DOS-based applications that have sound in them, Sound Blaster compatibility will be an important feature to you.

If you will be using the Windows operating environment exclusively or predominantly, then Sound Blaster compatibility won't be as important a concern since the multimedia extensions of Windows provide a uniform platform for the processing of digital sound and MIDI files.

If you'll be spending time computing in both the DOS and Windows environment, or if you aren't sure what you'll be doing with sound in the future, it's probably safest to select a sound device that the manufacturer claims to be Sound Blaster compatible. (Most of the audio cards reviewed in Lesson 4 are Sound Blaster compatible, but be sure to check the specific details on each product to be certain.)

Desirable Features to Look for

There are several desirable features to look for when shopping for a PC audio device. While reading over this section, it might be a good idea to make a list of the features that are important to you so you'll have some purchasing criteria and a written reference to help you when you go shopping.

— **Sampling.** If you intend to record your own sound, regardless of whether it is your own voice, some sound effects, music, or whatever, the device must have the ability to sample sounds to convert them to digital format. Playback-only units do not have sampling capabilities.

– **Sound synthesis.** Many games and recreational software products use sound effects that are generated by the FM synthesizer on the sound card. If the card does not have a synthesizer chip or other tone generator it will not be possible to create these sounds.

– **DOS functionality.** Most (but not all) audio devices come furnished with drivers and utility software for both DOS and Windows. If you'll be working in DOS, make sure the required DOS software is provided so you'll be able to use the device in that operating environment.

– **Attachment to PC.** If you have a notebook or a laptop computer that doesn't have any expansion slots, you'll want to purchase a sound device that attaches externally through either the serial or parallel port. If you have a desktop PC you can select either an external device or an internal expansion card. The prices, functions, and features vary quite a bit between the external devices, which have some limitations, and the internal cards, which usually have more features and functions and frequently permit upgrading for enhancements.

– **Slot required.** If you are considering a sound card that installs internally in one of the PC's expansion slots, be sure you know what kind of slot (8-bit or 16-bit) you have available in your PC, and select a sound card that matches. Figure 3.1 on the next page illustrates the differences between the two slot types. The three principal slot architectures in use today are industry standard architecture (ISA), which is by far the most popular and most common, extended industry standard architecture (EISA), which provides 32-bit data channels but can also utilize 16-bit cards, and IBM MicroChannel, a proprietary slot type used on IBM PS/2 and PS/1 computers.

Eight-bit slots have only one set of contacts and, subsequently, don't offer as many data paths for the expansion card to communicate with the host PC. Sixteen-bit slots have the same configuration as 8-bit slots, but they also have an additional set of contacts that are slightly separated from the main slot contacts. Sixteen-bit slots offer the best configuration options and data transfer speeds.

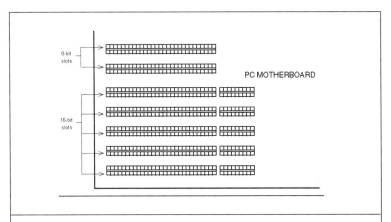

Figure 3.1 *An illustration of a typical PC motherboard showing the expansion slots. ISA slots are shown here.*

– **Microphone input.** Many audio devices have dedicated inputs for a microphone, while others have a single input that must be used for microphone, line, and auxiliary input connections. Individual input jacks are best, since they permit the simultaneous connection of a microphone and other sound sources.

– **Line input.** This is a discrete input connection or connections for accepting sound source input from line-level devices such as a CD player, cassette deck, or radio. While some sound cards use the microphone input for line input functions as well, separate connectors (left and right for stereo devices) offer the best flexibility for installation and use.

– **Audio output jack(s).** A headphone or external speaker connection jack is always provided, although some devices use the same connection for speakers and headphone. The best designs provide both line-level and amplified audio outputs.

– **Manual volume control.** Some audio devices provide either a rotary-type knob or a dial for adjusting the volume of the sound output, while others depend entirely on software for adjusting the loudness of the card. A manual volume control is a handy feature to have, although once set, the volume seldom, if ever, needs further adjustment.

- **Built-in FM synthesizer.** Many game and recreational software products use sound effects and music generated through synthesis. A sound generator, such as an FM synthesizer, is required to reproduce these sounds. Playback-only and external-connect devices frequently do not have FM synthesizers or tone generators.

- **Microphone.** If you wish to record your own voice or other "live" sounds, you'll need a microphone. Microphones vary in quality and price, ranging from about $10 to several hundred for professional-level devices. Most PC sound devices have 1/8 inch mini-phone jacks for the microphone input, so be sure the microphone you select is equipped with a 1/8 inch mini-phone jack or you'll have to purchase an adapter for the jack as well.

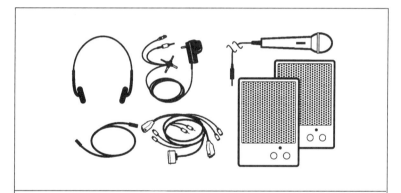

Figure 3.2 *Accessory items that may be required or that make working with PC audio easier include stereo headphones, microphones, Walkman-type extension speakers or amplified extension speakers, AC power adapters, and various audio "patch" connection cables. Since these items aren't usually supplied with the PC sound device, it may be necessary to purchase them separately.*

- **Ear/headphones included.** Many PC sound devices come with either an earphone or a pair of lightweight headphones. These are usually quite serviceable for monitoring audio output and listening to sound files. If the sound device you are considering doesn't include a pair of headphones, you should certainly purchase a pair (usually under $15 for

Walkman-type headphones), since they afford private listening and provide better sound quality than most inexpensive speaker systems.

– **Speakers.** Built-in speakers are usually only found on external PC sound devices, so if you want to hear the output from your sound board you should plan on purchasing a set of speakers. Walkman-type extension speakers are inexpensive and work well when plugged into the headphone jack of the sound device. If additional volume is desired, you may wish to consider purchasing amplified speakers such as the Labtec CS-150 series. Amplified speakers boost the line-out or headphone output signals of the sound device and offer additional treble and bass boosts. Amplified speakers are a must for any type of multimedia presentation applications where extra volume is required.

– **Patch cables.** These are cables used to connect extension speakers or provide line-level connections between an external device (such as a cassette deck or CD player) to the PC's audio device. The most useful configuration for use with sound boards and devices is a cable that has dual-RCA jacks on one end and a single 1/8 inch stereo mini-phone jack at the other end, although several different configurations of patch cables are available. Be sure to purchase cables that have the right jacks for your connection needs.

– **Output power.** Most PC sound devices have audio output power in the .5-watt to 4-watt ranges, with 2 watts per channel being the average. Two watts will provide sufficient volume for headphones or Walkman-type extension speakers in a reasonably quiet room, while 4 watts per channel can drive a larger pair of unamplified speakers. If additional volume is required, however, you can also boost the output by using amplified speakers or routing the audio through a stereo amplifier.

– **Power adapter.** Some of the portable, external sound devices use alkaline batteries, while others depend on getting their operating voltage from an AC power adapter solely and don't support battery operation. All internal audio cards that install in an expansion slot derive their power from the PC's bus, so no batteries or power adapters are needed. When shopping for an external sound device be sure to check its power requirements so you'll know if you'll need to purchase anything additional.

- **Joystick port.** Many sound cards provide a 15-pin port that can accept a single IBM-style analog joystick, or with the proper adapter, a pair of joysticks. This port also frequently does double duty as a connection point for a MIDI breakout cable or breakout box if the card also supports MIDI functions. If you expect to play computer action games that require a joystick, you may wish to select an audio card that has a joystick port.

- **Mono/stereo.** Audio boards and sound devices come in two varieties: monophonic and stereophonic. Generally speaking, the monophonic boards are usually low-cost, entry-level sound cards that are installed internally and only require an 8-bit expansion slot, although some of the external-connect sound devices are monophonic as well. The majority of sound boards in popular use today are stereophonic, however, and many can sample and playback 16-bit sound at 44.1 kHz (CD audio quality). Stereo boards provide better sound quality and offer more features than mono units. They are well worth the additional cost.

- **Number of voices.** The number of voices (different timbres), the sound device can play back simultaneously directly affects the realism of the sound effects and the quality of the music you'll hear from the device. For example, the popular OPL3 synthesizer chip is capable of generating twenty individual sounds (fifteen musical instrument sounds and five rhythm sounds) simultaneously, while the older OPL2 chip could only produce a maximum of eleven (six melody, five rhythm). Some sound boards using wavetable sound generation can produce thirty-two or more voices simultaneously. Generally speaking, twenty voices are sufficient for most users, although if you're interested in seriously pursuing the musical or MIDI aspects of PC sound you may want a more sophisticated sound card that uses wavetable sound as opposed to FM synthesis.

- **CD-ROM interface.** Several audio cards also have a built-in CD-ROM interface as part of their design, which simplifies adding a CD-ROM drive to the PC system. Some sound cards provide a SCSI interface, while others conform to the proprietary Sony bus or Panasonic standards for CD-ROM interfacing. If you intend to add a CD-ROM drive at some time, the SCSI interface provides more options as to the CD-ROM drive make and model you can use with it, while the proprietary interfaces limit your drive selection to those devices which conform to the interfacing standard.

— **MIDI capability.** Musical instrument digital interface (MIDI) software drivers are provided as part of Windows 3.1. All that is required to utilize the basic MIDI playback capabilities of Windows is a compatible sound device. However, to take advantage of the full spectrum of MIDI capabilities, which include controlling external devices (such as MIDI synthesizers or drum machines) you'll require a MIDI interface port. Many of the popular sound cards have MIDI circuitry built-in as part of their overall design and any MIDI software applications that run under Windows should be able to utilize these functions directly. Many sound cards that support MIDI also provide DOS-based software drivers so the MIDI functions can be accessed without running Windows.

— **MIDI connectors.** The 15-pin "D" connector found on many sound cards provides a connecting point for a joystick or for MIDI functions. Usually an optional, extra-cost breakout box or breakout cable is required to take advantage of this 15-pin port's MIDI input/output capabilities. Standard 5-pin MIDI cables are used to connect the external synthesizer, drum machine, or other MIDI device to the ports on the breakout box or cable.

— **Sample sizes.** As discussed earlier, the sample size indicates the number of bits used per sample to express the dynamic range of the audio frequency—more bits per sample result in higher audio fidelity. Eight-bit and 16-bit sample sizes are used for general and music recording, while 4-bit sample sizes are usually only used for recording low-quality digital speech. Some cards also support 12-bit sample sizes. 16-bit sample sizes afford the highest quality, but your needs and budget will dictate what is right for you.

— **Playback sample rates.** This specification is usually found in the manufacturer's advertising and on the packaging of the device. To hear CD-quality audio, the card should be capable of 16-bit stereophonic playback at a 44.1 kHz sample rate.

– **Record sample rates.** The biggest differentiating factor between sound devices is the recording sample rate supported by each. Low-end, inexpensive devices may only be capable of sampling at 11 kHz or 22 kHz, which has much less fidelity and more noise than the pristine audio quality of 16-bit stereo at 44.1 kHz, the standard for CD (Redbook standard) audio.

The Frugal Factor

When shopping for a sound card or external audio device for your PC, it's often tempting to look for a bargain. That's fine, but be sure not to short-change yourself with regard to features and upgradeability. The product that may be quite satisfactory for your present needs may also prove to be woefully inadequate for tomorrow's uses as your demands on it increase.

Many mail-order catalog companies specializing in "close-outs" and "warehouse overstocks" frequently advertise sound cards and other computer peripherals and accessories at very low prices, and these are sometimes excellent bargains. Other times, however, they aren't and the unwary consumer can fall prey to advertising ploys.

Many of the catalog sources often feature reconditioned or discontinued merchandise. If the product is reconditioned, be sure that it is fully warranted and that you'll be able to get it serviced if you ever require repairs. The same holds true for discontinued models.

The best strategy is to do your homework by comparing features and prices between the sound devices you're considering for purchase. When assessing features of brands or models, however, be sure to compare apples to apples—if you're considering the purchase of an inexpensive monophonic sound board that uses an FM synthesizer, compare it to other products that are also mono/FM units as well instead of comparing it to a stereo card using wavetable sound technology.

When shopping for price, it's a good idea to compare the prices of several sources for the same product or products. Computer magazines are an excellent source for doing armchair price comparisons for several mail-order sources, but a trip to some local computer and software stores is also in order to get an accurate barometer of the current street prices for the same goods. And you would also do well to remember that if you have an installation problem or a technical question, the local computer dealer usually provides you with all of the technical support you require at no additional cost. Whereas dealing with the technical support staff of many mail-order houses is often an exercise in frustration (not to mention long-distance phone bills).

If you can possibly afford it, my general recommendation is to go with a model that has more features than you think you'll need, such as a stereo wavetable-based card capable of CD-audio sampling and playback rather than a monophonic FM-based card. You'll be surprised at how quickly you come to regard sound as a standard feature of your computing environment and you'll wonder how you ever got along without it. You'll also want better quality sound as your interest level and expertise in using sound increases. Moreover, sound is an integral component of multimedia, and without a doubt we'll be seeing more and more software that incorporates sound as a standard feature in the coming months and years. It makes sense economically to purchase a sound device today that won't become obsolete or inadequate in the near future. For that reason, sound devices that can be upgraded through new software releases (such as wavetable-based products) or that can have additional feature modules added to them (such as CD-ROM interfaces or wavetable "daughterboards") to increase their functionality are the wisest purchases.

Glossary

breakout box/cable   An assembly (usually an extra-cost optional item) that attaches to the "D" joystick connector on an audio card to provide additional input and output connectors. The breakout box or cable typically provides connections for MIDI input, MIDI output, and MIDI thru for attaching external MIDI devices such as keyboards and drum machines. A connector for attaching a joystick is also usually provided.

bus/expansion bus   A set of hardware lines (wires) used for data transfer among the components of a computer system. Essentially, a bus is a shared highway that connects different parts of the system and provides the pathways for these parts to communicate and work with each other. In addition to data signals, bus connectors also frequently carry electrical voltage to power the installed devices using the bus.

CD-ROM An acronym for *compact disc read-only memory*. CD-ROM is an optical data storage medium for computers that uses laser light to read the binary information imprinted on it.

daughterboard A printed circuit board that attaches to another, which adds additional features or functions to the original device. CD-ROM interfaces and wavetable modules are commonly sold as daughterboard upgrade options for several popular PC sound boards.

DOS An acronym for *disk operating system*, the basic instructions that enable a computer system to accept and process commands and perform useful work (see *MS-DOS*).

DOS-based Any application or utility that operates directly from the MS-DOS operating system rather than through an alternate environment or operating system, such as Microsoft Windows 3.1.

EISA An acronym for *extended industry standard architecture*, a bus standard introduced in 1988. EISA maintains backward compatibility with ISA in addition to adding many of the enhanced features IBM introduced with its Micro Channel Architecture bus standard including a 32-bit data path.

host PC The main personal computer (in a single-user, non-networked system) that controls and utilizes all other connected devices including drives, printers, monitor, keyboard, mouse, joystick, and more. Since the PC provides the logic, input-output, memory storage, computing, and in many cases the actual operational voltage, the PC "hosts" all of the devices as if they were "guests."

ISA An acronym for *industry standard architecture*, the widely accepted (but unofficial) designation for the bus design of the original IBM PC. The ISA specification was expanded to include a 16-bit data path in 1984 from its original 8-bit specification with the introduction of the IBM PC/AT computer.

MCA An acronym for *Micro Channel Architecture*, the design of the bus used in IBM PS/2 computers (except for the Model 25 and Model 30). Micro Channel expansion slots are electrically and physically different from the standard IBM PC/AT (ISA) bus, so accessory or adapter cards for standard IBM-compatible PC's won't work in a Micro Channel machine.

MIDI An acronym for *Musical Instrument Digital Interface*, a specification developed as a cooperative effort among major manufacturers of electronic musical instruments in the 1980s with the objective of permitting musical instruments of different brands to communicate with each other. Additionally, several MIDI-equipped devices can be linked together under the control of a PC and software for creating, storing, editing, and playing back music in precise synchronization.

motherboard The main circuit board containing the primary "system critical" components for a microcomputer system. The components found on the motherboard include the CPU, main memory, controller circuitry required for the expansion bus, and expansion slots, in addition to other components required for the proper operation of these circuits.

mounting bracket A metal bracket found on virtually every expansion card for IBM-compatible PCs that is used for securing the card in its slot with a screw. Sound boards use this bracket for mounting their I/O connectors, such as for a microphone, line in/out, or joystick.

MS-DOS

An acronym for *Microsoft disk operating system* (pronounced *em-ess-doss*). MS-DOS oversees and supervises the basic tasks and services required to run a computer including disk input and output, video support, keyboard control, and other essential functions.

patch cables

A general audio term that refers to any type of audio cable used to connect two or more devices together. The most common patch cables have RCA-type jacks at both ends (like the kind used to connect your home stereo speakers), although some patch cables are outfitted with 1/4 inch phone jacks, 1/8 inch mini-phone jacks, dual RCA-to-1/8 inch stereo mini-phone or other special-purpose connectors.

pin connector

Usually a single or double row of brass contact pins on a sound card used for attaching a flat ribbon cable. Pin connectors are frequently used for attaching a ribbon cable coming from a CD-ROM drive, among other uses.

SCSI

An acronym (pronounced *scuzzy*) that stands for *small computer system interface*. SCSI is a standard high-speed parallel interface as defined by the X3T9.2 committee of the American National Standards Institute that permits devices such as CD-ROM drives, hard disks, and printers to be connected to PCs.

Windows

The popular name for *Microsoft Windows 3.1*, a multitasking graphical user interface environment that runs on MS-DOS-based computers. Drop-down menus, screen windows, and icons that represent entire programs or specific tasks are all features of Windows. Windows makes most computer tasks simply a matter of pointing with a mouse and clicking one of the mouse buttons to activate that application or utility.

LESSON FOUR:

Some Sound Choices

Hands-on reviews of:

- Twenty-seven internal sound cards
- External sound devices for PCs

Table 4.1 lists the PC audio devices that are reviewed in this lesson. These reviews are intended to showcase the important features of each product and aid you in selecting the sound device that best suits your needs, expectations, and budget.

Product Name	Description	Manufacturer
AudioMan	External 8-bit, no SG*	Logitech
Audio Master AMS-8000	Internal 8-bit card	Omni Labs, Ltd.
AudioPort	External 8-bit with FM	Media Vision
Gold 1000	Internal 8-bit	Ad Lib
MicroKey/AudioPort	External 8-bit, no SG*	Video Assoc.
MultiSound	Internal 16-bit	Turtle Beach
Port-Able Sound Plus	External 8-bit	DSP Solutions
Pro Audio 16 Basic	Internal 16-bit	Media Vision
Pro AudioStudio 16	Internal 16-bit	Media Vision
Pro Audio Spectrum Plus	Internal 8-bit	Media Vision
Pro Audio Spectrum 16	Internal 16-bit	Media Vision
Series 3/Z1	Internal 16-bit	Antex Elect.
Speech Thing	External playback only	Covox
Sound Blaster (orig.)	Internal 8-bit	Creative Labs
Sound Blaster Deluxe	Internal 8-bit	Creative Labs
Sound Blaster Pro	Internal 16-bit	Creative Labs
Sound Blaster 16 ASP	Internal 16-bit	Creative Labs
Sound Galaxy NX Pro	Internal 8-bit	Aztech Labs
Sound Master II	Internal 8-bit	Covox
Stereo F/X-CD	Internal 8-bit	ATI Tech.
Thunder & Lightning	Internal 8-bit with SVGA video	Media Vision
ThunderBoard	Internal 8-bit	Media Vision
UltraSound	Internal 8-bit	Advanced Gravis

Voice Master System II	External 8-bit, no SG	Covox
Voice Master Key	Internal 8-bit, no SG	Covox
Windows Sound System	Internal 16-bit	Microsoft
WinStorm	Internal 16-bit with SVGA	Sigma Designs

SG = sound generator

Table 4.1 *Audio devices.*

I've made every attempt to make this listing as complete as possible, but with new sound boards and upgrades being released continuously, it may not reflect the current market selection. For precisely that reason you'll also find a listing of all of the manufacturers' addresses and telephone numbers in Appendix B so you can contact them directly to obtain information on any new models that may have been released after this book has gone to press.

The bundled software included with the hardware is also subject to change as the products are upgraded, so you might want to check with the manufacturer to establish the contents of the current package.

It's also a good idea to do some price-comparison shopping to ensure that you're getting the best deal on the sound card of your choice.

Armed with that knowledge, here then are my personal hands-on reviews of 27 leading sound cards and external audio port sound devices that comprise the most popular and noteworthy products currently on the market.

Product name:	**AudioMan**	*Product type:*	**Audio port**
Manufacturer:	**Logitech**	*Suggested retail:*	**$179.00**
Installation:	**External**	*Can record:*	**Yes**

Logitech's AudioMan is a compact external device for providing audio on any PC (80286 or later CPU) equipped with a parallel printer port. The AudioMan connects to the parallel port and provides a pass-thru connector so the printer can also remain on-line and ready for use, even with the AudioMan installed. The device is transparent, so it doesn't interfere with normal printer operations.

It is important to note that the AudioMan is well suited for voice annotation and sampling/playing back digital audio (.WAV) files, although it does not contain any sound generation source, such as an FM synthesizer chip. However, it is not capable of playing synthesized music or sound effects. Nor does AudioMan have MIDI capabilities. The device is capable of sampling 8-bit sound at a maximum rate of 11 kHz, suitable for voice but not for musical applications.

A two-part device, the AudioMan unit is powered by two AA (penlight) alkaline cells that last about 40 to 50 hours with normal use. The connector portion is a rectangular device that attaches to the computer and connects, via a 6-foot cable, to the main unit of the AudioMan (the batteries are housed in the main unit). The battery-powered device is good for use with laptop and notebook computers, where true mobility free of cumbersome power cords is desirable. You can also power the AudioMan with a standard 9-volt DC adapter (not included), available anywhere.

A unidirectional microphone is built into the unit, as is a speaker. A unique feature of the AudioMan is its indicator light, which flashes whenever a recording is in process. A volume control is located on the unit, along with 1/8 inch stereo miniphone jacks for line-level output to speakers, headphones, or other external sources, and one for accepting input from external devices such as a CD player or an external microphone. The AudioMan also features an automatic gain control (AGC) circuit that adjusts the recording level automatically.

AudioMan is designed and intended to be used from within the Windows environment exclusively, and no software or utilities are provided to access the device from DOS. AudioMan uses OLE, so you can integrate in a single document a variety of data formats from diverse sources. This makes it possible to add voice annotations to your documents and spreadsheets, as well as to add verbal commentaries and narratives to graphic images.

A basic suite of software utilities for recording, editing, and playing back sound are included, along with a rather novel software control panel for the unit. The AudioMan's current battery condition is displayed from this panel, and it also features a facility for adjusting the sound output volume.

Product name:	Audio Master AMS-8000	Product type:	Sound card
Manufacturer:	Omni Labs, Ltd.	Suggested retail:	$299.00
Installation:	Internal	Can record:	Yes

The Omni Labs Audio Master is a modular sound board that accepts accessory modules to enhance its capabilities. This can be a good approach for some users who don't want or don't expect to use the additional features beyond basic recording and playback, such as external MIDI connectivity, since you only pay for what you use and only add what you need.

A single 16-bit expansion slot is required for installation, although having an adjacent slot vacant provides additional room when an optional daughterboard (such as the FM Synthesis Module) is installed on the main Audio Master unit. The board's mounting bracket provides the location for three mini-phone jacks designated as line output, auxiliary input, and microphone input. A standard 15-pin D connector is used for attaching one or two joysticks or the optional MIDI breakout box accessory ($69.95).

A variety of CD-ROM interface modules are available as add-on accessory items ($69.95 to $79.95) that permit adding an internal CD-ROM drive and routing its audio through the Audio Master. Kits are available for generic SCSI CD-ROM drives, for the Sony SLCD drive, for the Sony 531/525 drives, for Mitsumi CD drives, for Matsushita/Panasonic drives, and also an interface module for Philips and LMSI (Philips manufactured) CD-ROM drives. The required driver software, ribbon interface cable, and audio output cable is supplied with each of these kits.

The Audio Master is equipped with its own 32-bit Motorola 68008 CPU complete with an operating system and RAM as integral components of the board. This board uses wavetable look-up synthesizer technology rather than chip-based FM sound and music synthesis. This endows Audio Master with an impressive range of 24 polyphonic channels that are independently controlled via MIDI commands. One-hundred and twenty-eight instrument sounds are available and 24 different voices can be played simultaneously. The excellent voice quality rivals that of expensive keyboard synthesizers. It isn't compatible with software designed to support AdLib or Sound Blaster sound standards, however, unless you add the optional FM Synthesizer Module daughterboard ($69.95). This small board snaps into a connector on the main board and contains a Yamaha 3812 (OPL2) chip that enables the Audio Master to play FM-synthesized sounds and music.

The Audio Master has 384 Kb of on-board memory used to store the 128 instrument sound wavetables; a RAM Expansion Module daughterboard accessory ($99.95) adds another 1,152 Kb of memory, allowing more sophisticated and comprehensive wavetables to be stored and used. A diskette of enhanced instrument files is also supplied with the module that snaps into two connector receptacles on the Audio Master board.

An audio cable, a microphone, 3.5 inch software disks, a user's guide, and a good music-application software manual accompanies the board. The bundled software includes recorder, mixing studio, CD-music player, and MIDI jukebox applications for Windows, plus sound clips, Monologue text-to-speech software, and DOS programs.

Product name:	**AudioPort**	*Product type:*	**Audio port**
Manufacturer:	**Media Vision, Inc.**	*Suggested retail:*	**$199.00**
Installation:	**External**	*Can record:*	**Yes**

Media Vision's AudioPort is a small external unit that plugs into the 25-pin parallel printer port of any PC—desktop, laptop, or notebook. This little device can be powered internally by inserting four AAA batteries in its snap-open compartment, or by the included AC adapter. Batteries usually last about four hours with average use before they're expended.

A Yamaha YM3812 FM synthesizer chip in the unit produces 11 voices, and the AudioPort can sample 8-bit monophonic sound at rates from 2-22.1 kHz with a frequency response of 100 Hz to 12 kHz.

A 1/8 inch mini-microphone jack is provided for audio input, and another 1/8 inch mini-headphone jack is mounted on the side of the unit, next to the input jack, for connecting headphones or amplified speakers. A 1.5 inch diameter internal speaker with surprisingly good sound quality is built into the unit to provide you with audible playback without connecting any other external devices. A volume control is also mounted on the unit.

An assortment of Windows-based software is bundled with the AudioPort. The primary application is Lotus Sound, a recording and playback utility. Pocket

Recorder, also included, permits recording and playing back digital audio in 8-bit sample rates up to 22 kHz. Pocket Recorder also supports extensive editing features including splicing and blending files, as well as adding special effects like echo, reverb, pitch adjustments, and directional reversing of sound files. The user interface for both applications uses the familiar control layout found on home cassette and CD players.

The AudioPort doesn't support DOS-based applications directly from the system prompt, but games and other programs using sound can be run under a DOS window from Windows with the SB2AP utility program, which is a virtual Windows driver that is also part of the supplied software. Windows 3.1 must be running in enhanced mode to use SB2AP.

An animated, talking calendar program, At Your Service, is also supplied with the AudioPort. The program is a personal reminder system that runs as a background task in the Windows environment and features "Jeeves" the talking butler. Based on data entered into the calendar's database, Jeeves reminds you of appointments, phone calls, meetings, and other events that require your action or attention at the appropriate times. This software provides an excellent example of how PC audio can enhance your productivity while providing lots of smiles and diversion in the process. Beyond the novelty value of this application, it is actually a useful tool that provides excellent scheduling capabilities to help you manage your time to best advantage.

MIDI file playback is supported via the Media Player accessory in Windows, although the device doesn't allow MIDI input through it. Since no transparent pass-thru port is provided, you won't be able to use the parallel port for your printer while the AudioPort is attached to the PC.

Product name:	Gold 1000	Product type:	Sound board
Manufacturer:	Ad Lib Multimedia	Suggested retail:	$299.00
Installation:	Internal	Can record:	Yes

Ad Lib is one of the companies that pioneered high-quality music and sound synthesis on personal computers, and the Gold 1000 card is the result of continuing refinement as the basic Ad Lib music card has evolved.

The Gold 1000 card takes a modular approach in its design, permitting you to add optional upgrades when and if you require them. The three-quarter-length card installs into any 8-bit expansion slot easily. The software installation, however, is tedious at best and the most difficult of all the products reviewed in this lesson. The difficult installation is compounded by the fact that the card is severely limited in the DMA channels and IRQ settings it can use, so if your system has lots of peripherals installed in it you may be in for problems here. Since the software does not test which I/O ports, DMAs, and IRQs are available or in use, finding the right combination on some systems may take a bit of doing. The fact that this is an 8-bit card is directly responsible for the lack of options in setting these channels—16-bit boards offer far more flexibility in these areas.

The card features the Yamaha OPL3 chipset for its FM synthesis, and 20 independent stereo voices are supported. The maximum resolution is 12-bit sampling at 44.1 kHz, however, so if you're looking for true CD quality (16-bit at 44.1 KHz), this card falls short of that mark.

Three 1/8 inch miniphone jacks are on the mounting bracket for mike input, line input, and line output. A 15-pin connector is provided for attaching a joystick or a MIDI breakout box.

Good quality MIDI and FM sound are the strong points of the Gold 1000, as is the assortment of software it comes with. The bundled programs include:

- **Voice Pad** is a utility for recording, selecting and playing voice memos as well as for programming voice alarms.
- **Juke Box Gold** is a utility for selecting and playing Ad Lib Gold tunes and it includes a Music Clip Library of songs.
- **Soundtrack Synchronization Editor** is a utility for time-synchronizing images with sounds.
- **Soundtrack Playback Driver** is a memory-resident program for running synced soundtracks with presentation software (such as Harvard Graphics) and other multimedia applications.

Additional bundled software includes an Autodesk Animator Playback Utility, which permits synchronizing animation frames with sound when using Autodesk Animator software. A number of batch file utilities are also provided for playing back music files or voice recordings in batch files from DOS. A TSR mixer panel utility is also provided for controlling the volume, balance, and tone of the card's output. All of the software is provided on 3.5 inch disks, although 5.25 inch diskettes are available upon request.

Additional add-on options for the Gold 1000 board include a SCSI CD-ROM adapter daughterboard that provides SCSI interfacing. The Ad Lib Surround Sound Module is another daughterboard that provides enhancement effects such as echo, reverb, and depth simulation.

Product name:	**MicroKey/AudioPort**	*Product type:*	**Audio port**
Manufacturer:	**Video Associates Labs, Inc.**	*Suggested retail:*	**$295.00**
Installation:	**External**	*Can record:*	**Yes**

This is another external device that connects to the PC's parallel port, and even though a portion of this product's name is similar to the external Media Vision unit reviewed earlier, it is definitely a separate and different product. For starters, it is heavier and comes in a metal case, whereas the Media Vision product uses a plastic case.

The MicroKey/AudioPort does not provide a pass-thru port, so a parallel printer can't be connected simultaneously while the AudioPort is in place. The unit is powered by an included 9V DC adapter and it does not run on batteries, so you'll need an AC outlet anytime you intend to use this unit. This is a point to consider if you are a laptop or notebook PC user who wants to have sound capabilities while traveling.

Two miniphone jacks are located on the MicroKey/AudioPort: one is for input from a microphone or, with the included -40 dB attenuating adapter, from a line source while the other jack is for output. The MicroKey/AudioPort does not have a built-in speaker, but a pair of headphones is supplied to make the output audible. A microphone and mike stand adapter is also provided, along with a stereo miniphone-to-standard phone plug adapter.

The MicroKey/AudioPort supports monophonic 12-bit sampling at eight user-selectable sampling rates—4 kHz, 5.5 kHz, 8 kHz, 11 kHz, 16 kHz, 22 kHz, 32 kHz, and 44.1 kHz. An automatic gain control (AGC) circuit is built into the device to control the strength of the input signal—no manual volume control is provided.

MIDI input and playback is not supported since it doesn't contain an FM synthesizer chip. This is a very important point to consider if you wish to incorporate MIDI music in your computing sessions.

In addition to the necessary Windows drivers, Voyetra's WinDAT digital audio editing software is packed along with the unit. The DAT part in the software's name stands for *digital audio transport*. This is an appropriate moniker since it uses the familiar tape-deck interface featuring mouse-activated push-buttons for play, record, rewind, fast forward, and pause in addition to range selection controls. Drop-down menus further simplify use of the program. The menus allow you to play, record, and edit sound files with the MicroKey/AudioPort.

The documentation consists of a 43-page user manual for the MicroKey/AudioPort itself as well as a 24-page manual for the WinDAT software. Between the two books everything you need or want to know about the device and its use is covered in depth.

This device provides a functional means of inputting and outputting sound from the PC's parallel port without having to open the system unit. Its greatest appeal is to users who are looking for a good device for extensive voice annotation (or even dictation over a network), and who don't want or need the musical/sound effect capabilities of a synthesizer chip and MIDI support.

Product name:	**MultiSound**	*Product type:*	**Sound board**
Manufacturer:	**Turtle Beach Systems,Inc.**	*Suggested retail:*	**$599.00**
Installation:	**Internal**	*Can record:*	**Yes**

If you are primarily interested in music and MIDI applications, the MultiSound board from Turtle Beach Systems is certainly worthy of your serious consideration.

There are several unique features about this full-length board that requires a 16-bit slot for installation, starting with the fact that it is capable of CD-quality (Redbook audio standard) recording and playback with 16-bit sampling at 44.1 KHz. This is above and beyond the MPC Level I specification of 22 kHz for multimedia recording and playback.

Rather than using an FM synthesizer, the MultiSound utilizes wavetable sound generation that is provided by an E-mu Proteus IXR synthesizer that delivers 32 voices simultaneously. Since wavetable sound generation uses actual instrument sounds that are stored in ROM on the board, the realism and clarity is truly breathtaking and unrivaled by any FM-based audio board covered here.

The card's mounting bracket provides a location for the 9-pin MIDI connector (unlike many other sound cards, the MultiSound does not provide a joystick port) and the three 1/8 inch miniphone jacks for line input, auxiliary input, and line output. An additional pin connector is provided on the board itself for connecting CD-ROM output.

It is interesting to note that while the MultiSound is capable of producing music and sound effects paralleling the quality of an audio compact disc, the board does not offer or support compatibility with products designed to the Ad Lib and Sound Blaster audio standards. It is fully compatible for running applications under Windows, however. This incompatibility with the Sound Blaster and Ad Lib standards shouldn't be a major disappointment to most users of the MultiSound, however, since compatibility is usually only an issue for games running under DOS. The high price tag of this board indicates that it is intended for far more serious applications than just playing games. Make no mistake about it—this is a professional-level board that produces uncompromising audio.

The included software includes applications for controlling the various audio input volumes, and a MIDI port patch panel utility for assigning active voices to the "orchestra." A software user-interface program is provided for direct access to the MultiSound's on-board Proteus/1 XR synthesizer, so it isn't necessary to have an externally-connected keyboard controller to access the card's capabilities.

Also included is a limited version of Turtle Beach's Wave for Windows software, reviewed in detail in Lesson 9. This is a powerful audio utility for recording, editing, modifying, and playing-back digitized audio.

While the board is certainly capable of providing voice recording and playback, its superb music quality and MIDI capabilities make it a natural choice for those demanding the top of the line in PC audio cards.

Product name:	**Port-Able Sound Plus**	Product type:	**Audio port**
Manufacturer:	**DSP Solutions, Inc.**	Suggested retail:	**$198.95**
Installation:	**External**	Can record:	**Yes**

The Port-Able Sound Plus from DSP Solutions combines DSP sound generation technology with the convenience and portability of an externally-connected device. The compact Port-Able Sound Plus unit attaches to the PCs parallel port and features a pass-thru connector so the printer can remain attached and on-line even with the device present. Power for the unit is provided by AA alkaline or rechargeable NiCad batteries, or by the included AC/DC power supply.

Since the Port-Able Sound Plus unit interfaces through the parallel port, it can be used on laptop and notebook computers as well as desktop PCs. Unlike all of the internal sound cards reviewed in this lesson that require an ISA expansion slot for installation, the Port-Able Sound Plus can work on IBM PS/1 and PS/2 series computers since it is not slot-dependent.

A high-quality internal speaker is integrated into the unit, and it also features a built-in microphone. A volume control knob and a power on/off switch with LED indicator is provided, as are 1/8-inch miniphone jacks for an external microphone, headphones, audio (line) input, and stereo line output. An audio patch cord outfitted with a stereo miniphone jack at one end and dual RCA jacks at the other is provided for direct recording from a CD or tape player.

The Port-Able Sound Plus uses advanced DSP technology and supports stereo playback of 16-bit digitized audio, 14-bit recording, and SoundBlaster/AdLib compatible music synthesis. The synthesizer is capable of delivering up to nine melodic voices or seven melodic and four percussive voices.

Particularly well-suited for business applications such as voice annotation, the Port-Able Sound Plus is capable of real-time compression and decompression in industry-standard ADPCM sound formats to provide excellent voice audio quality while conserving disk space.

All software drivers and applications are provided on 3.5 inch diskettes, and the installation is simple and straightforward.

The bundled software includes Lotus Sound, a utility that permits creating, editing, and saving sounds as .WAV files. This application also supports OLE technology to add sounds to documents created using your favorite Windows spreadsheet or word processor.

WinReader is a handy text-to-speech utility that reads out loud all or part of any ASCII text file. Show & Tell, DSP's own easy-to-use multimedia authoring program is included, along with DOSTalk and DOSReader, both DOS-based text-to-speech applications for reading selected text from text-mode screens or ASCII files.

Windows 3.1 drivers and DSP's PDIGI Audio and Synthesizer drivers for DOS are included, as well as the BlasterMaster driver, which permits running DOS-based SoundBlaster and AdLib programs with the Port-Able Sound Plus.

Product name:	**Pro Audio 16 Basic**	*Product type:*	**Sound card**
Manufacturer:	**Media Vision**	*Suggested retail:*	**$199.00**
Installation:	**Internal**	*Can record:*	**Yes**

Media Vision has added a new product to its sound card lineup with the Pro Audio 16 Basic, which the company describes as a new entry-level version of its popular Pro Audio Spectrum 16, devoid of some of the more advanced features.

Media Vision's goal was to produce a 16-bit sound card capable of CD-quality audio (Redbook standard) recording and playback for users at a price that's competitive with most other 8-bit boards. To do this, some of the advanced features that would not be missed by entry-level users were eliminated from the design.

Physically, the Pro Audio 16 Basic is the same basic board as the Pro Audio Spectrum 16, except for the absence of some advanced capability components. For example, the Pro Audio 16 Basic has no built-in SCSI interface on it as its higher-priced sibling does, nor does it include the connectors for accepting CD audio as a sound source.

The card uses a Yamaha OPL3 chip to deliver 20-voice FM music synthesis and features a 15-pin D connector on its metal mounting bracket for attaching a joystick or the optional MIDI Mate kit. Three 1/8-inch miniphone jacks are also located on the mounting bracket. Their designated uses are microphone input, line input, and line/headphone output. No manual volume control is provided since all adjustments for playback and recording volume are controlled through software, the customary practice for all Media Vision internal sound cards.

Media Vision products are all easy to install, but the Pro Audio 16 Basic is probably the easiest of all for a novice to install. An intelligent installation program, QuickStart, eliminates the complex installation procedures sometimes required with sound cards and automates the procedure, correctly defining the system settings and automatically configuring the card to comply with them.

The Pro Audio 16 Basic features support for DOS, Windows 3.1, Windows NT, OS2/2.1, and NextStep operating systems, and is 100% compatible with the Pro Audio Spectrum 16. An important feature for gamesters to note, the Pro Audio

Basic 16 is also compatible with the Sound Blaster and Ad Lib sound standards. Any products designed to work with these sound cards should perform as expected with the Pro Audio Basic 16 card as well.

In addition to the standard Media Vision assortment of DOS and Windows drivers, the card is bundled with Media Vision's Pocket Tools application, a handy utility that provides a familiar home-stereo-type graphical user interface (GUI) and permits recording, editing, and mixing PC audio under Windows.

A special bonus included with the Pro Audio 16 Basic is Dinosaur Adventure from Knowledge Adventure. This award-winning interactive title explores the prehistoric era of dinosaurs through the use of full-motion video and stereo sound.

This may be the ideal sound card for users who want CD-quality audio without the high cost usually associated with it, providing they don't feel they'll miss any of the advanced features.

Product name:	**Pro AudioStudio 16**	*Product type:*	**Sound board**
Manufacturer:	**Media Vision**	*Suggested retail:*	**$349.00**
Installation:	**Internal**	*Can record:*	**Yes**

The newest addition to Media Vision's line of sound boards is the Pro AudioStudio 16, an enhanced version of the company's highly popular Pro Audio Spectrum 16 sound card.

In addition to increasing the functionality of the sound card itself, the AudioStudio package adds voice recognition capabilities, easy automated installation, and additional included software applications and utilities.

The card is a 3/4-length unit that requires a 16-bit slot for installation. The mounting bracket houses the familiar 15-pin D connector, which is used for attaching a joystick or a Media Vision MIDI Mate kit ($49.95 additional) to attach external MIDI devices such as keyboards for play through the card.

Three 1/8-inch miniphone jacks are located on the mounting bracket to accommodate microphone input, stereo line input, and stereo line output. No manual volume control is provided, since all volume adjustments are made through software.

The board has a standard 40-pin SCSI interface header for attaching a CD-ROM drive via an internal ribbon cable or using the optional external SCSI cable ($49.95 additional), and a pin connector is provided on the board for routing CD-audio through it. The PC's system beeps can also be channeled through the board by using the 4-pin connector provided for this purpose (appropriate cables for making these connections are available as optional extras). A high-quality, computer-mounted microphone with excellent ergonomic design is included with the sound card.

The card is capable of 16-bit stereo digital audio recording and playback at rates up to 44.1 KHz for CD-quality (Redbook Audio standard) sound. A Yamaha OPL3 synthesizer provides the sound generation with 20 voices and the card features 4-watt speaker audio output and improved sound fidelity over earlier versions.

A voice-recognition software program, ExecuVoice, developed by Dragon Systems, is included with the Pro AudioStudio 16. The application gives users the ability to control the Windows environment by simply speaking commands. The software is capable of recognizing a 300-word vocabulary with what is claimed to be the highest accuracy rate in the industry. I found it to be quite good, although I can't confirm this claim.

Other bundled software includes:

– **Monologue for Windows** text-to-speech software featuring 16-bit samples for higher quality.

– **MIDIsoft's Recording Session**, a Windows-based MIDI sequencer.

– **Sound Impressions**, a professional digital audio editing package from DigiVox.

– **Media Vision's Pocket Tools**, a set of application programs that can be used for everything from recording and editing digital audio to controlling the playback of audio CDs in a CD-ROM drive installed with the PC.

Audio mixer utilities for controlling the volume of the various sound sources are included, as is a Windows-based guided tour application to showcase the card's capabilities.

Product name:	**Pro Audio Spectrum Plus**	*Product type:*	**Sound card**
Manufacturer:	**Media Vision**	*Suggested retail:*	**$199.00**
Installation:	**Internal**	*Can record:*	**Yes**

The Media Vision's ProAudio Spectrum Plus is a high-performance 8-bit stereo sound card that delivers plenty of flexibility and an excellent assortment of standard features.

This 3/4-length card can be installed in any 8-bit or 16-bit slot and it features all of the circuitry needed to support the built-in MIDI interface, a joystick port, and a SCSI interface. The joystick port is ready to use right out of the box, but you'll require the optional MIDI Mate kit to take advantage of the MIDI interface. The MIDI Mate kit is a break-out box that attaches to the card and provides a full duplex (simultaneous play and record) MIDI port. Likewise, to utilize the card's on-board SCSI adapter you'll need the optional SCSI cable kit—internally-mounted SCSI devices (like a CD-ROM drive) can be accommodated via the 40-pin header, which accepts a standard SCSI ribbon cable. External SCSI devices require the external SCSI cable that attaches via the joystick port.

Installing the card in a 16-bit slot enhances its performance while extending the choices for interrupt and DMA settings, something to consider if you have lots of peripherals installed in your system. Jumpers are provided for changing these settings from the defaults, if required.

The mounting bracket carries three miniphone jacks that accommodate microphone input, line input, and audio output, respectively. There is no manual volume control on this card, since it is a function controlled through software. A 15-pin D connector is also located on this bracket for attaching a joystick or the optional MIDI Mate kit.

A Yamaha YMF262 (OPL3) FM synthesizer provides 20 voices for synthesizing music or sound effects. MIDI files can also be channeled through the synthesizer for playback without the need for an external MIDI device. The board also provides a 4-pin connector for sending the audio output of a CD-ROM drive through the board for additional processing and mixing.

A rich assortment of software utilities accompany the Pro Audio Spectrum Plus. The Stereo Studio F/X waveform sound-editor program provides easy recording, playback, and editing functions. Sounds can be recorded directly from a microphone, CD, or another sound source, while effects including echo, reverb, and envelope shaping can be added to alter the original file. Another bundled program, SP Spectrum, is a good MIDI sequencing program that works with the card's on-board synthesizer or with external MIDI devices. A mixer utility is also included for setting the volume levels for CD-audio, digital audio (sampled sound), FM synthesized audio, external line input, microphone input, and PC speaker input (a jumper is provided on the board for routing PC speaker sound through it as well).

Other bundled software includes a four-track music utility, a text-to-speech synthesizer, a DOS-based multimedia application, a rich assortment of MIDI songs, digital sound effects and 4-track music files, and all required drivers and DLLs for Windows.

Product name:	**Pro Audio Spectrum 16**	*Product type:*	**Sound card**
Manufacturer:	**Media Vision, Inc.**	*Suggested retail:*	**$299**
Installation:	**Internal**	*Can record:*	**Yes**

Media Vision's Pro Audio Spectrum 16 is a 3/4-length board that requires a 16-bit expansion slot for mounting. With the ability to record and play back sound at up to 44.1 kHz sampling, this board is capable of CD-quality audio.

Three 1/8-inch miniphone jacks are located on the board's mounting bracket to accommodate microphone input, stereo line input, and stereo line output. A 15-pin D connector is located on the bracket for connecting the optional MIDI Mate kit or external SCSI cable kit.

The board has a standard SCSI interface header for attaching a ribbon cable located on it, as well as a pin connector for routing CD-audio through the board. There's also a 4-pin connector for channeling the PC's system beeps through the board instead of through the computer's speaker (appropriate cables for making these connections are available as optional extras). All volume adjustment is effected via software.

Installing the board involves inserting it in a suitable expansion slot and putting the PC back together again. There are no jumpers or DIP switches to set, making installation a snap.

The software installation is almost as easy as the hardware portion for both DOS and Windows. Default IRQ, DMA, and port settings, subdirectory, and installation options work just fine with the majority of installations, but you're given the opportunity to override the defaults. A nice feature is the automatic IRQ and DMA conflict testing, which alerts you to the possibility of a conflict and even suggests how to resolve it.

The SETUP.EXE program, run from Windows, configures the board, loads the appropriate drivers, creates a program group, and installs the audio applications in that group. There are four applications provided, which are listed on the next page.

- **Pocket Recorder** is a simple recording and playback program with surprisingly good editing and effects features.

- **Pocket Mixer** is a simplified audio mixing console that uses an analog representation of dials to make adjustments.

- **Pocket CD** is a CD-audio player utility that only works if you have a CD-ROM drive installed.

- **Pro Mixer** is a 10-control mixer that uses sliders to increase or decrease recording or playback volumes from all of the audio components. The 10 slider "pots" are labeled SYNTH, REC, AUX, CD, MIC, WAVE, SPKR, BLSTR, Master, and Record, and they control the volumes of these items.

The DOS utilities provided includes:

- **Stereo Studio F/X**, a record, playback, and editing package.

- **SP Spectrum**, a MIDI sequencer program.

- **A DOS** mixer.

- **TrakBlaster Pro**, a four-track music studio.

- **Audiomate**, a DOS-based multimedia presentation package.

- **Monologue**, a text-to-speech synthesizer.

A virtual device driver is included for Windows that permits Windows and DOS software applications to share the PAS 16 hardware without conflicts. This feature allows you to run DOS applications (such as games) through DOS Windows and still have full access to the sound card from DOS or Windows.

Product name:	**Series 3/Z1 Sound Board**	*Product type:*	**Sound board**
Manufacturer:	**Antex Electronics**	*Suggested retail:*	**$595.00**
Installation:	**Internal**	*Can record:*	**Yes**

The Z1 Sound Board is a professional-level product with an impressive list of technical specifications that are sure to satisfy the most discriminating user with industrial-strength requirements.

The full-length board requires a 16-bit expansion slot for installation and uses a modular design that accommodates an optional expansion upgrade. A Yamaha

OPL3 FM synthesizer chip is the standard sound generation source that provides 20 voices. An optional Z-Wave upgrade daughterboard ($395 additional) is available to significantly increase the musical capacity. The Z-Wave uses an Ensoniq synthesizer that incorporates wavetable sound generation to produce 32 simultaneously active voices. Since wavetable sound is actual samples of real instrument sounds stored in ROM on the card, the realism, clarity, and vibrance of the resulting musical instrument sounds is astonishing. No FM synthesis-based sound even comes close to wavetable sound quality.

The mounting bracket of the Z1 provides a 15-pin connector for attaching a MIDI breakout box, and four 1/8 inch stereo miniphone jacks are also provided to accommodate microphone input, line input, auxiliary input, and line output. Additional pin connectors are located on the board itself for microphone and CD-audio input as well as output. Additional pin header connectors are provided for attaching the Z-Wave daughterboard.

A 50-pin SCSI interface connector is another standard component of the Z1, and the required drivers and CD-ROM extension software is provided with the board. Antex can also provide optional connector cables for installing internal or external SCSI drives using the Z1's on-board interface, if required.

The Z1 utilizes a Texas Instruments digital signal processor (DSP) chip, which is programmable. Several special effects including delay, reverb, phase shifting, and more is made possible through the DSP's programmability. It offers a high level of immunity to obsolescence since its capabilities can be enhanced through software upgrades.

The Z1's MIDI interfacing is highly superior to that found on other sound boards because it features added data buffers for both receiving and transmitting MIDI information. This means that uninterrupted recording and playback of MIDI files is guaranteed since the MIDI functions require less time from the PC's CPU.

The Z1 was formally introduced shortly before this review was written, and the software that accompanies the board is somewhat sparse at this early point in the board's life. The bundled software consists of DOS drivers, CD-ROM drivers and extensions, a demonstration program, Windows drivers, a Mixer utility, and record and play utilities. The board is also capable of several compression formats in ratios up to 4:1 to reduce the size of sound files and conserve hard disk space. This is a superb, professional-level product for those who want the best.

Product name:	Speech Thing	Product type:	Audio port
Manufacturer:	Covox Inc.	Suggested retail:	$99.00
Installation:	External	Can record:	No

The smallest and least expensive of the external audio hardware devices covered here, Covox's Speech Thing is one of the first products released for sound on the PC. While the device has remained basically unchanged over the last few years, Covox's driver and utility software has undergone constant improvement and finessing, with the latest release providing support for the playback of .WAV files through Speech Thing in Windows.

Measuring only about 2-1/8 inch square and weighing well under an ounce, Speech Thing plugs directly into the PC's parallel port. Unlike some of the other parallel devices covered here that monopolize this port, Speech Thing is a transparent device that fits between the printer cable and the port itself. Since it doesn't interfere with normal printer operations, Speech Thing can be left permanently installed at the port, which adds to its convenience of use and overall appeal. It should be noted, however, that there is no FM sound synthesizer in Speech Thing, so MIDI playback and encoding is not possible.

Speech Thing uses FIFO (first-in, first-out) data streaming instead of the DMA (direct memory access) schemes used with other external-connected devices. While this doesn't affect sound quality, it does cause other operations to come to a standstill while sound is being output through it. FIFO streaming literally takes over all of the I/O operations while sound is being accessed, whereas using DMA permits other events (like video refreshing, mouse control, and keyboard input) to continue unabashed while sound is playing.

Covox provides an amplified speaker with Speech Thing, which mates with the miniphone jack on Speech Thing's cable. A second cable fitted with a subminijack is used to deliver an additional +5 V of power to the speaker by picking up this additional voltage directly from the parallel port.

> **Note:** Covox's documentation states that on some computers Speech Thing sounds better without the +5 V plugged in—this is true with some computers that generate static sounds anytime the floppy or hard drive was being accessed. Unplugging the +5 V connector silences these noises without compromising sound quality at all.

Covox provides a 9 V DC power adapter with the unit, and the speaker can be powered via a 9 V battery that fits into a snap-off compartment in the enclosure.

Speech Thing is a DAC playback-only device—you cannot sample sounds or digitally record your own voice with it. For these capabilities, you'll require one of Covox's other products—SoundMaster II or VoiceMaster Key Systems in either the internal or external configuration.

Covox provides plenty of software with Speech Thing, including a playback utility for CD-ROM and IBM talking programs, SmoothTalker text-to-speech software, a music synthesizer utility that modulates sampled sound, utility software for playback of digitized speech and sounds, and speech and sound editing software. Also included is a Windows driver for .WAV file playback.

Product name:	**Sound Blaster (original)**	*Product type:*	**Sound board**
Manufacturer:	**Creative Labs**	*Street price:*	**$79-$129**
Installation:	**Internal**	*Can record:*	**Yes**

Sound Blaster established itself years ago as the *defacto* standard for PC audio in the DOS environment, and it was the only sound card directly supported by the Multimedia Extensions 1.0 for Windows 3.0. The Sound Blaster is unquestionably the most-supported audio card, as evidenced by the hundreds of applications and recreational titles that are compatible with it. Though no longer being manufactured in its original form—the Sound Blaster Deluxe, Sound Blaster Pro, and the Sound Blaster Pro 16/ASP have succeeded it—there are still quite a few of these cards in various versions (Sound Blaster 1.0, 1.5, and 2.0) around, and coverage is being included here for the sake of completeness.

The Sound Blaster is a 3/4-length 8-bit audio board that mounts in an 8-bit or 16-bit slot. The heart of the board is the Yamaha 3812 synthesizer chip, which delivers 11-voice FM sound. Some of the older versions of the Sound Blaster—its design has undergone continual changes over the years—are about 2 inches longer than some of the newer models, and characteristically they only have one audio input jack that is shared for both microphone and line input tasks. One reason for the larger board size of these older units is that they used lots of individual electronic components rather than integrated components that require less space. Overall sound quality also improved as the design matured.

Jumpers are used for selecting the port address and the IRQ settings, although the default settings of I/O port 220 and IRQ 7 should prove satisfactory for most installations.

The mounting bracket of the card provides access to a thumbwheel volume control, the miniphone audio output jack, and a 15-pin D connector used for attaching an analog joystick or the optional MIDI connector box.

Sound Blasters come with an assortment of software that almost has a cult following. The included FM Intelligent Organ program is easy to use and permits composing and playing compositions directly from the PC keyboard or from an attached MIDI device. A Talking Parrot program, included as a novelty, displays a gaudily-colored parrot on the video screen that mimics your speech, talks back, and makes wisecracks to passersby. An AT-class or higher machine is required for this program to run properly. The digitized voice of the parrot has a markedly "pidgin English" accent with some erroneous pronunciations and misplaced inflections, good for evoking a laugh.

Voxkit is a well-rounded assortment of sound and voice development tools that permits recording, compressing, editing, and playback of digitized sounds. Since Sound Blaster supports DMA transfer, sound files of any length up to the hard or floppy disk's available capacity can be accommodated.

The required Windows drivers and DLLs are also provided with Sound Blaster, so you can take advantage of its sonic capabilities from either the DOS prompt or from Windows 3.1. Sound Blaster is definitely an oldie but a goody.

Product name:	**Sound Blaster Deluxe**	*Product type:*	**Sound board**
Manufacturer:	**Creative Labs, Inc.**	*Suggested retail:*	**$129.95**
Installation:	**Internal**	*Can record:*	**Yes**

An oldie but a goodie, the original Sound Blaster from Creative Labs was one of the first audio cards on the scene for PCs, setting the industry standard for sound. The card has continued to evolve, and this deluxe model is its latest incarnation. Smaller than earlier models, the SB Deluxe is a half-length card that installs in any available 8-bit slot.

Three 1/8-inch miniphone jacks on the mounting bracket are provided for line input, microphone input, and line output. There's also a thumb-wheel manual volume control and a 15-pin D connector for attaching a joystick. The joystick port doubles as an attachment point for adding an optional MIDI Connector Box to use a MIDI keyboard or instrument with the board. No CD-ROM interface is provided, however.

Sound Blaster Deluxe comes preconfigured to use I/O address #220, IRQ #7, and DMA channel #1. These default settings work with most systems, although there are some instances when IRQ #5 may be more desirable (LPT1 is usually assigned to IRQ #7 and this might be troublesome in some systems). Changing any of these default values is done by relocating the jumpers over the desired pair of pins to correspond with your choice.

Once the physical installation is completed, all that remains is to run the automated installation application provided on the two high-density 3.5 inch diskettes supplied. One contains the DOS programs and the other contains Windows drivers and programs. An Optional Disk Format Request card is supplied in the package if you need low-density 3.5 inch diskettes or either low- or high-density 5.25 inch media. The only cost for the optional-size media is the price of a stamp to mail the card back to Creative Labs.

The automated installation and configuration program is very simple to use and it works without a hitch, correctly locating the card, identifying the IRQ, I/O, and DMA settings.

A rich assortment of software is bundled with the card, and it includes applications for both DOS and Windows environments. Creative Labs "favorite" programs such as the Talking Parrot, FM Organ, and other applications are provided along with a complete suite of drivers and utilities for using the card in the Windows graphical environment.

The card's on-board synthesizer provides good sound for most applications and for playing MIDI files, although if you're interested in taking full advantage of the MIDI interfacing capabilities of the card you should consider purchasing the optional MIDI connector box.

The Sound Blaster Deluxe is an economical 8-bit sound card that provides lots of good features at an affordable price. An important factor to consider is that, since it is a genuine Creative Labs Sound Blaster product, it is completely compatible with all software applications designed to work with the Sound Blaster.

Product name:	**Sound Blaster Pro**	*Product type:*	**Sound board**
Manufacturer:	**Creative Labs**	*Suggested retail:*	**$299.95**
Installation:	**Internal**	*Can record:*	**Yes**

Using the original Sound Blaster as the starting point, the Sound Blaster Pro improves on a good thing by expanding the capabilities of the board and adding some additional features.

Like the original monophonic version that only used a single chip, the Sound Blaster Pro uses a pair of Yamaha 3812 FM synthesizer chips to produce 22 voices of synthesized sound (11 voices per channel).

A 3/4-length card that requires a 16-bit slot, the Sound Blaster Pro has several additional features that aren't found on the monophonic models of the Sound Blaster. A 40-pin CD-ROM interface header is located on the board for attaching an internal or external CD-ROM drive from Creative Labs, Panasonic, Matsushita, or others that are compatible (note that this is *not* a standard SCSI interface).

A 4-pin connector is provided for routing the CD-ROM audio output through the card, and a pin header is provided for connecting the PC's speaker signals to the SB Pro as well. The mounting bracket features dual submini phone jacks for mike and line input, a thumbwheel volume control, and a stereo submini jack for audio output. A 15-pin D connector is provided for attaching single or dual joysticks as well as the included MIDI cable kit. With the exception of the Covox SoundMaster II, the Sound Blaster Pro is the only other product reviewed here that includes all required MIDI cabling and software as part of the basic package. MIDI kits are extra-cost optional accessories with the other MIDI-supporting products reviewed here.

All of the standard configuration features are selectable by changing jumper positions on their respective headers, although the default settings should work fine for most installations.

The included software assortment is good and includes the FM Intelligent Organ program included with the original Sound Blaster. Additional software that comes with the Pro includes:

— **SB Voice Editor II**, an advanced recording, editing, processing, and playback utility.

— **SB Talker**, a memory-resident program that converts text to speech. (It isn't as good as the Monologue text-to-speech software provided with the Media Vision products, however.)

- A **CD Music Player utility** that brings all of the features of your home audio CD player to your computer so you can play audio CDs from your CD-ROM drive.

- A **complement of Windows drivers**, DLLs, and utilities including a Mixer accessory that permits mixing all attached audio sources—stereo DAC, stereo FM synthesis, microphone input, stereo line input, stereo CD audio, and the PC speaker signal.

- **Voyetra's Sequencer Plus Pro MIDI sequencer** lets you use the 22-voice capability of the on-board synthesizers. This "bundled" software product is comprehensive enough to satisfy the demands of even the more-than-casual computer musician and it is easy to use and well documented.

- A **multimedia presentation** utility is also included.

Product name:	**Sound Blaster 16 ASP**	*Product type:*	**Sound board**
Manufacturer:	**Creative Labs, Inc.**	*Suggested retail:*	**$349.95**
Installation:	**Internal**	*Can record:*	**Yes**

Creative Labs has updated its Sound Blaster Pro audio card by endowing it with ASP (advanced signal processing) technology to produce true 16-bit stereophonic recording and playback while maintaining full compatibility with software designed to run on the original Sound Blaster and Ad Lib sound boards.

A 20-voice Yamaha YMF262-M (OPL3) chip provides the FM synthesis for this 3/4-length card that requires a 16-bit expansion slot for installation. A thumbwheel manual volume control is mounted on the mounting bracket along with miniphone jacks for microphone input, line-level input, and speaker or headphone output. A 15-pin D connector for attaching joysticks or the optional MIDI breakout box is also located on the bracket.

Several connectors for channeling various sound elements through the board for recording, playback, mixing, or integrating are included. Connector pins are provided for routing the sound of the PC's internal speaker and CD-audio through the card. A CD-ROM interface that supports internal CD-ROM drives from Creative Labs or Panasonic drive models CR521 and CR523 is located on the board, as well as a pin-connector for attaching the Wave Blaster Upgrade option daughterboard.

The Wave Blaster option board attaches directly to the Sound Blaster 16 ASP and gives it 32-voice multi-timbral stereo sound using E-mu System's sampled wavetable synthesis technology. If you're interested in exploiting the musical and MIDI capabilities of this board, the Wave Blaster Upgrade option should also be considered for purchase.

The 16 ASP comes with plenty of software packed along with it. The assortment includes:

- **Creative Wavestudio**, a Windows-based wave editor that supports editing multiple sound files simultaneously.
- **Creative Soundo'le**, an object-linking recording and playback utility.
- **Creative Mosaic**, a tile-matching game with bit-mapped graphics and, of course, sound effects.
- **Creative Talking Scheduler** is an appointment calendar and scheduling application that gives you voice-annotated reminders.
- **HSC's Interactive**, a multimedia presentation-authoring, icon-animating, and image-enhancement package.
- **PC Animate Plus**, an animation creation program.
- **Monologue for Windows**, a text-to-speech utility.

Several of the Creative Labs "standard" software offerings are also packed along with the Sound Blaster 16 ASP, and they include SBTalker with Dr. Sbaitso, FM Intelligent Organ, SBMIDI (MIDI file driver), SBSIM (Sound Blaster Standard Interface Module), MMPLAY (multimedia presenter), and DOS and Windows 3.1 software drivers. All software is provided on 3.5 inch media, although a card for requesting 5.25 inch media at no charge is also included in the package.

A high-quality dynamic microphone and a miniphone-to-RCA patch cable are also supplied with the 16 ASP.

Product name:	SoundMaster II	*Product type:*	Sound card
Manufacturer:	Covox, Inc.	*Suggested retail:*	$229.95
Installation:	Internal	*Can record:*	Yes

Covox's SoundMaster II is a 3/4-length 8-bit sound card that installs in any available 8-bit or 16-bit slot. This board has all of the recording, playback, and voice-recognition capabilities of the Voice Master Key board, reviewed later. It also provides FM sound synthesis and MIDI capabilities.

The SoundMaster II is a monophonic sound card, although all of the board's functions have alternate addresses so that two SoundMasters can be installed in a PC at the same time for stereo output or extended instrument voicing using FM synthesis. Three banks of jumpers are provided on the board for avoiding any device conflicts with other installed peripherals.

The metal mounting bracket of the card houses the dual miniphone microphone jacks, designated M1 and M2 for high- and low-impedance mikes, respectively, a rotary volume control, an earphone/external speaker jack, and a 9-pin D connector for attaching the included combination MIDI in/out cable. A jumper wire is also included for routing the PC's speaker sounds through the SoundMaster II for enhanced audio.

A Covox headset/microphone comes as part of the standard complement of accessories. The headset is outfitted with dual 1/8 inch miniplugs, one from the high-impedance hands-free microphone and the other from the earphone built into the headset. The headset/microphone is useful for recording sound or using the voice-recognition features in noisy environments, and the headset's padded earphone affords private listening.

A Yamaha YM3812 FM synthesizer chip is the sound generator for creating music and sound effects, with a one-watt audio amplifier to provide gain for the signal. A pair of stereo Walkman-type speakers is provided, along with a stereo-to-mono miniphone adapter. Since the SoundMaster's output is monophonic, this adapter routes the signal to both speakers to give you mono output from both.

The SoundMaster II user's manual tells you everything you could want to know about the device and the software provided with it, as well as how to program for it. In addition to the Voice Master Key software supplied with the Voice Master systems, the SoundMaster also comes with Covox's DSP-FX digital signal processing software. This utility facilitates real-time pitch changing, harmonizing, flanging, chorusing, echoes, reverb, distortion, and numerous other special effects. The Covox graphic waveform editor program is included, along with dozens of MIDI song files, sound samples, and other interesting tidbits.

A real bonus is the inclusion of an external MIDI in/out cable set and PC-Lyra, a graphics-based music-composition program that facilitates musical input using a mouse or the computer keyboard, or directly from a MIDI instrument connected to the PC via the included SoundMaster's cables. The PC-Lyra software is very easy to use, provides many of the features and capabilities normally found in expensive, stand-alone sequencer programs, and serves as an excellent medium for getting started in MIDI.

Product name:	**Sound Galaxy NX Pro**	*Product type:*	**Sound board**
Manufacturer:	**Aztech Labs**	*Suggested retail:*	**$179.00**
Installation:	**Internal**	*Can record:*	**Yes**

The Sound Galaxy NX Stereo Pro sound card provides many desirable features, as well as plenty of enhancement options for those who want more than the standard configuration delivers.

A 3/4-length card that requires a 16-bit expansion slot for installation, this card uses only Aztech proprietary chips for sound generation instead of the familiar Yamaha OPL2 or OPL3 synthesizers that are so popular. The board has a connector for routing CD-ROM audio through it, and another connector permits channeling the PC's speaker audio as well.

Two CD-ROM interfaces are built into the Sound Galaxy NX board. Both are 40-pin interfaces, and they can accommodate either a Panasonic CR-521/522 or a Mitsumi LU005S CD-ROM drive. A Future Domain SCSI upgrade kit (a FD SCSI controller chip and device driver software) is available as a $30 option that adds SCSI capability to the sound board.

The card's mounting bracket holds three miniphone jacks used for microphone input, line input, and speaker/headphone output. A thumb-wheel volume control is nestled between the speaker and the mic input jacks, as is a 15-pin D connector used for attaching a joystick or the optional MIDI cable.

Installation is simple and consists of inserting the board into any available 16-bit slot. All supplied software is provided on 3.5 inch media only.

In addition to the Sound Galaxy NX sound card and the installation software, an RCA patch cable and a pair of mini Walkman-style speakers is also provided, along with a cable for routing the PC speaker's output through the board.

A software bonanza is bundled with this card:

— **First Byte's Monologue** text-to-speech synthesizer.

- Voyetra's **WinDAT** waveform editor for Windows.
- **SoundScript**, a multimedia authoring program.
- **Galaxy Master**, a digitized recording and playback program.
- **Jukebox** permits you to create playlists and play sound files.
- **CD Player** is a CD audio control panel.
- **Sound Tracks** is a collection of song files, and another disk contains Windows 3.1 drivers.

The Sound Galaxy NX Stereo Pro's strongest suit is its compatibility, which supports four sound standards, thus making it the most-compatible sound card of any covered in this lesson: AdLib, Sound Blaster Pro II, Covox Speech Thing, and Disney Sound Source standards are all supported, as well as offering full compatibility with the Windows environment and .WAV files.

An all-around sound card at a good price, the Sound Galaxy NX Stereo Pro provides stereo sound, exceptional compatibility, a nice selection of features, and good upgrade and expansion possibilities for the future.

Product name:	Stereo F/X-CD	*Product type:*	Sound board
Manufacturer:	ATI Technologies, Inc.	*Suggested retail:*	$199.00
Installation:	Internal	*Can record:*	Yes

ATI's Stereo F/X-CD is a 3/4-length card completely devoid of jumpers or DIP switches. All configuration is done through the software, making the installation simply a matter of inserting the card into any available 8-bit or 16-bit slot and running the installation software. Interrupts 2, 5, or 7 are available for audio use, and addresses of either 220 or 240 can be selected. A 16-bit slot is recommended to take full advantage of the card's capabilities.

Pin connectors are provided on the board, as well as a cable for routing the PC's speaker sounds through the Stereo F/X-CD. Another connector is provided for channeling a CD-ROM drive's audio output through the board, and a 40-pin interface for Mitsumi and compatible CD-ROM drives is also on the board.

The card's mounting bracket houses a 15-pin D connector for attaching joysticks or the optional MIDI connector box. Three miniphone jacks are used for the microphone and line-level input and speaker/headphone output chores. A rotary-knob manual volume control is located at the top of the mounting bracket.

Twenty stereo voices with 8-bit sampling rates up to 44 kHz in mono and 22 kHz in stereo are supported. The Yamaha YMF262-M (OPL3) synthesizer chip provides the FM synthesis sound.

Ad Lib and Sound Blaster compatibility is featured and all software designed to run under these standards under DOS and Windows should perform without a problem.

All of the bundled software is provided on two 5.25 inch high-density diskettes, with no mention of the availability of 3.5 inch media. Universal DOS and Windows drivers are provided, as well as several utilities and sound applications, including WinDAT and DOSDAT, two programs developed by Voyetra Technologies that provide an interface similar to the controls found on a home stereo system or cassette deck. The DAT portion of these program names stands for *digital audio transport*, and they run from Windows and DOS respectively.

The Stereo F/X-CD also has the ability of adding a stereo effect for full, rich sound on applications written for mono FM synthesis. This capability is truly impressive and it adds a noticeable difference—a fuller dimensional sound—to any sound file with which it is used.

A set of mixer programs for DOS and Windows that permit actively mixing and blending the signals of six different sound sources (FM, Wave, CD-audio, PC speaker, line input, and microphone) are also provided. In addition to controlling the individual volume of each, the left-to-right balance and overall master volume can be regulated from these mixers.

Since the F/X-CD has such good sound quality, it isn't at all surprising that a generous selection of MIDI song files and a DOS MIDI player utility are included in the bundled software assortment so you can start enjoying the card immediately.

Overall, the ATI Stereo F/X-CD is a good product that provides stereo FM-sound synthesis and audio capabilities at an affordable price.

Product name:	Thunder & Lightning	*Product type:*	Sound and video
Manufacturer:	Media Vision	*Suggested retail:*	$349.00
Installation:	Internal	*Can record:*	Yes

Media Vision's Thunder & Lightning board combines audio and video both on a single card for use under Windows 3.1. This multifunctional card combines super

VGA graphics with high-quality audio. The board is capable of displaying 24-bit color up to 640x480 resolution from a palette of up to 16.8 million colors. Additional standard and enhanced VGA modes up to 1024x768 in 256 colors are also supported as well as 15-bit and 16-bit color (800x600 is the maximum resolution for 15-bit and 16-bit color, but the 16.8-million-color palette is active in these modes). A comprehensive set of drivers for Windows and other popular applications are included with the hardware.

Thunder & Lightning is a 3/4-length board that requires a 16-bit slot for installation. It features a Yamaha 3812 (OPL2) 11-voice FM synthesizer as its sound center, and it can sample and play back 8-bit sampled sound. The mounting bracket holds a thumbwheel volume control, miniphone jacks for audio input and output, and a 15-pin video connector. A 10-position DIP switch is utilized for enabling/disabling various audio features as well as selecting the I/O addresses. A four-pin header is also located on the board for routing the PC's speaker audio. There's also a 15-pin header on the board used for mating to an included ribbon cable, which terminates with a standard IBM joystick port on a second mounting bracket. This port also serves double duty as the MIDI connector for attaching Media Vision's optional ($69.95) MIDI Mate breakout box. If slots are at a premium in your machine and you don't intend to use a joystick or an external MIDI device, then the ribbon connector and second mounting bracket need not be installed. Jumpers are provided for selecting IRQ, DMA, and MIDI settings.

The audio section of this board, its features, and functions are virtually identical to the ThunderBoard for Windows reviewed elsewhere in this Lesson, and the Thunder & Lightning card is guaranteed to be fully Sound Blaster, ThunderBoard, and AdLib compatible.

The included software bundle consists of Lotus Sound, Sound Forge for Windows, At Your Service, Pocket Recorder, and Monologue for Windows (see the ThunderBoard review for more details on this software). As a special bonus, a working sample demo of Passport Designs Master Tracks Pro MIDI sequencer for Windows is included, as well as a generous assortment of MIDI song samples.

This board provides a great single-slot solution for providing high-resolution video along with good 8-bit sound. If you're looking for a single product that provides audio and video enhancement, the Thunder & Lightning board is a good choice.

Product name:	Thunder Board	Product type:	Sound board
Manufacturer:	Media Vision, Inc.	Suggested retail:	$179.00
Installation:	Internal	Can record:	Yes

Media Vision's Thunder Board is an inexpensive way to get into the world of sound and audio for both DOS and Windows.

A compact half-length card that installs easily into any available 8-bit expansion slot, the Thunder Board uses a six-position DIP switch to select address lines, activate/deactivate the joystick port, enable or disable FM synthesis and other functions, along with a bank of four jumpers that are used to change the default IRQ setting, if required. For the majority of installations, however, the default settings should work just fine.

A thumb-wheel manual volume control, a pair of 1/8-inch miniphone jacks (one each for input and output), and a 15-pin D connector for attaching a joystick are all located on the mounting bracket. External MIDI functions are not supported by the Thunderboard, nor does it have a CD-ROM interface.

The card makes use of the trusty Yamaha 3812 (OPL2) synthesizer chip to produce 11-voice FM music synthesis, and it is capable of recording and playing-back 8-bit sounds up to 22 kHz. The Thunder Board's microphone input circuit also has AGC (automatic gain control) to provide smooth recording at the proper volume level with minimal distortion.

Installing the software is done from DOS using an automated installation program that creates a subdirectory on the hard drive and copies over a series of files. The software is supplied both on 3.5 inch and 5.25 inch diskettes.

During installation, the card is tested to determine the address and IRQ settings, and a test tone is played to aid the user in adjusting the volume. The entire process takes only a few minutes and is efficient and straightforward.

A series of DOS-based utilities are included with the card and copied to the Thunder subdirectory during the installation process:

- **RECFILE.EXE** records sound files.
- **PLAYFILE. EXE** plays them back again.
- **SETVOL.EXE** produces an audible tone so you can manually adjust the volume (using the thumb-wheel on the board's mounting bracket) to a suitable level.

– TBTEST.EXE is a diagnostic that determines the board's hardware settings and optionally plays the test tone for checking volume.

The Thunder Board comes with plenty of software samplers in the package. A full working copy of MicroProse's F-15 Strike Eagle II is supplied along with a complete 96-page user manual for the game. In addition, sampler editions of the following games are also provided: Nova 9 (the sequel to Stellar 7), Lemmings, Lexi-Cross, Rex Nebular, and Gobliiins. If you're into games, the software included justifies the purchase price of the board alone.

Aimed primarily at the recreational and non-business computer user, the Thunder Board makes a good entry-level sound card that provides basic sound capabilities at a good price.

Product name:	**Ultrasound**	*Product type:*	**Sound board**
Manufacturer:	**Advanced Gravis**	*Suggested retail:*	**$249.00**
Installation:	**Internal**	*Can record:*	**Yes**

The Advanced Gravis Ultrasound is a full-length board that installs in any 8-bit or 16-bit expansion slot and uses jumpers to alter the board's default settings if required, although they should work for the majority of installations just as they are. If changing the jumpers is necessary, the design of the UltraSound's jumper caps makes the task considerably easier than with other sound cards. This card's jumper caps have little extended "handles," which make them easier to remove and reinsert using the fingers alone, as opposed to standard jumper caps that usually require using tweezers, needle-nosed pliers, or similar implements to get a grip on the tiny components.

A 15-pin D connector is located in the middle of the mounting bracket for attaching joysticks or the optional MIDI breakout box. Four miniphone jacks, two on either side of the D connector, provide audio input and output. The two uppermost jacks provide amplified output and line-level output, while the lower two jacks accommodate microphone input and line-level audio input.

The UltraSound uses a proprietary audio signal processor and wavetable synthesis to produce sounds. It does not contain an FM synthesizer chip. This board is capable of 16-bit, 44.1 kHz audio playback and is capable of recording 8-bit sound from 2 kHz to 44.1 kHz in either mono or stereo. Sixteen-bit recording capability is only supported when the optional daughterboard is installed. Another daughterboard is also available as an optional accessory item for implementing the CD-ROM interface capabilities.

Music and sound on the UltraSound is impressive: Its on-board 16-bit synthesizer is capable of generating 32 independent voices. Since wavetable synthesis utilizes software "patches" of sounds that can be loaded as desired, the ability to play 32 of these sound patches gives you the flexibility to create any type of orchestral arrangement you want. This capability is sure to find favor with serious computer musicians and MIDI users.

While installing this board is somewhat more involved than with some of the other boards, it is highly automated, so novice users should be able to complete it without a problem. A series of function tests permit checking the board's operation and detecting any conflicts that may require resetting the board's jumpers. This is a great aid for troubleshooting and correcting any problems that might arise with other installed peripherals.

The standard configuration of the board is 512 Kb of RAM, which can be upgraded to 1 MB by adding 128 K DRAM chips. Adding additional RAM to the board increases its capacity for storing wavetable patches and thus increases the number of sounds that are available for use.

Software is supplied on 3.5 inch media and includes an application for recording, playing, mixing, and customizing digital sound files, along with Windows and DOS drivers. A MIDI play utility and samples of music, sequences, and sounds are also included, as are 192 MIDI instrument patches.

Product name:	Voice Master System II	*Product type:*	Audio port
Manufacturer:	Covox, Inc.	*Suggested retail:*	$239.95
Installation:	External	*Can record:*	Yes

The Voice Master System II is the external version of Covox's internal PC-card Voice Master Key System, also reviewed in this lesson. Aside from the fact that it is an external unit, it shares all of the same capabilities as the internal version, but it has the advantage of connecting to the parallel port rather than requiring an internal expansion slot. This feature makes it compatible for use with laptops and notebooks as well as desktop PCs—even IBM Micro Channel machines. Since it attaches via the parallel port, there are no I/O address, IRQ, or DMA settings to contend with.

Other features of the external model include separate tone and volume controls located on the front of the unit along with 1/8 inch miniphone jacks for MIC in and speaker out. The front panel of the unit also houses a built-in speaker and a high/low microphone impedance selector switch. Also located on the front is a red LED to signify power-on status, while a green LED next to it denotes that the Voice Master recognition mode is active. A pass-thru printer port is located on the rear of the cabinet, along with a parallel-input port (a 3 foot cable is provided for connecting to the PC). This pass-thru port permits keeping the System II and the printer connected simultaneously, and a three-position preference switch is provided on the front of the unit. This switch establishes priority for the System II, the printer, or an automatic selection of either. The power jack is located at the rear of the cabinet, along with dual miniphone jacks for external input and output, respectively. A DC power adapter is also supplied with the unit, along with a Covox microphone/headset that facilitates hands-free recording, playback, and speech recognition.

The Voice Master System II doesn't contain an FM synthesizer, so it is not capable of playing back digital sound files or MIDI files. It can record and play back digital speech and sampled sounds in either the native Covox .VOX format or (under Windows) .WAV filetypes.

Aside from providing an excellent monophonic means of digitally recording and playing back sampled sounds, the Voice Master System II's strongest feature is its ability to provide speech recognition for voice control of the PC and application software. Covox's Voice Master Key software utility lets you add voice commands to existing programs. These commands activate a predefined series of macros that perform tedious tasks, repetitive keystrokes, or multiple mouse movements by uttering a spoken command. The voice-recognition software features a pull-down menu, context-sensitive help, and mouse support.

Covox's user manual provides lots of basic information, as well as references for writing your own programs in BASIC or C that utilize the Voice Master Key System. The manual, along with the additional software and utilities provided with the System II is identical to that supplied with the internal model, and it is covered in more detail in that review.

Product name:	**Voice Master Key**	*Product type:*	**Sound card**
Manufacturer:	**Covox, Inc.**	*Suggested retail:*	**$199.95**
Installation:	**Internal**	*Can record:*	**Yes**

As the internal counterpart to the Covox Voice Master System II reviewed earlier, the Voice Master Key is a half-length card that fits into any 8-bit or 16-bit expansion slot. This internal version has DMA circuitry built in, so you can record and play back single audio files up to the maximum capacity of your available hard disk space. A side benefit of DMA access is that audio files can be playing in the background while you are simultaneously accessing other software applications in the foreground.

It is important to note that this card is not capable of playing back digital sound (music and sound effects) files or MIDI files since it doesn't have a sound generator (such as an FM synthesizer chip). It can record and play back digital speech and sampled sounds, however, in either the native Covox .VOX format or (under Windows) .WAV file types.

Jumpers are used to alter the card's port address if it conflicts with any other installed peripherals, although the default setting should work fine in most installations. A cable is provided with the card for bypassing the PC's own internal chassis-mounted speaker and routing the sound through the Voice Master Key card for enhanced audio. Eight-bit sound recording and playback are both under software control, although the volume can be controlled either through software or via the bracket-mounted knob. Two miniphone microphone jacks (high and low impedance) are also mounted on the card's mounting bracket, as is a miniphone jack for connecting an earphone or extension speaker.

A Covox microphone/headset is also included in the package, and this useful accessory is outfitted with a 6 foot cable to provide adequate length for virtually any installation. The sensitive microphone and comfortable padded earphone are ideal for voice recognition in noisy situations or for private listening.

In addition to recording and playing sampled sounds, the Voice Master Key system is capable of voice recognition. Two recording and editing programs are provided as part of the standard software complement. The first is a very sophisticated graphics-based editing program that displays sound waveforms and supports cut and paste, raising/lowering sound levels, high- and low-pass filtering, inversions, duplications, and more. The sampling rate is user selectable and variable between 1,000 to 25,000 bytes per second, and an included data compression utility can compress the sound file to save disk space. The second utility is much easier to use and, though barebones in its capabilities, is enough for the needs of most users.

Another included program is CONVERT, which facilitates converting custom-made sound files created with the graphics-based editor to the SAY executable format. In addition, Covox provides several sound samples, a talking blackjack game, and an oscilloscope program, so there's plenty of value and utility packed along with the hardware itself.

Product name:	**Windows Sound System**	*Product type:*	**Sound board**
Manufacturer:	**Microsoft Corp.**	*Suggested retail:*	**$289.00**
Installation:	**Internal**	*Can record:*	**Yes**

Microsoft's Windows Sound System, as its name strongly implies, is designed for Windows only and it is targeted for the business—rather than recreational—computer user.

The half-length board takes a unique design approach by incorporating both FM sound and digital signal processing all on the same product to give it additional compatibility and flexibility. A Yamaha YMF262-M FM synthesizer and an Analog Devices CODEC digital sound processor are both provided as sound generation sources.

Three miniphone jacks to accommodate line input, microphone input and headphone/speaker output are located on the metal mounting bracket along with two RCA jacks for routing the board's line output to another device using standard audio cables.

Along with 5.25 inch and 3.5 inch high-density software diskettes, a decent pair of lightweight stereo headphones and a microphone are included as part of the Windows Sound System package. You are ready to record, play back, and use sounds as soon as the installation is completed, and that doesn't take too long.

Installing the WSS consists of inserting the sound board into any available 8-bit or 16-bit expansion slot. A 16-bit slot is highly recommended, however, since it provides the best flexibility for the hardware configuration. Jumpers are provided on the card for changing the default address of 530 if required, although this I/O address should work without a problem in most systems.

Software installation can be performed either from DOS or Windows. The setup program installs Volume Control, Recording Control, SoundScapes, and Sound Control Panel in the Windows Control Panel, since these are required components. The setup program also creates a Windows Sound System program group and installs the system sound software icons and other applications in this group as well. The ProofReader application is installed as a Proof menu in Microsoft Excel and Lotus 1-2-3 for Windows, if selected as options during the installation process.

In addition to creating annotated voice files that can be imbedded and linked into word processing documents, spreadsheets, and other Windows applications, the most innovative feature of the Windows Sound System is its voice-recognition capabilities. The supplied voice-recognition application, Voice Pilot, enables users to execute commands by voice using the microphone that comes with the Windows Sound System. With Voice Pilot it is possible to navigate through the Windows operating system and 15 popular Windows-based applications via limited voice recognition. (See Lesson 6 for additional information.)

The voice recognition is quite accurate and provides a training mode to adapt it to different accents or dialects.

The ProofReader application is handy for checking the data input of spreadsheets created using either Microsoft Excel or Lotus 1-2-3 for Windows.

Product name:	WinStorm	Product type:	Sound and video
Manufacturer:	Sigma Designs	Suggested retail:	$429.00
Installation:	Internal	Can record:	Yes

The WinStorm Multimedia Display Adapter provides a way to add full 16-bit audio and 24-bit TrueColor SVGA video along with joystick, MIDI, and SCSI interfacing capabilities all on a single card that installs in a single 16-bit expansion slot.

The WinStorm is a 3/4-length board that features a 15-pin D connector for attaching a color monitor, along with three miniphone jacks for microphone input, line input, and headphone/speaker output on its mounting bracket. No manual volume control is provided, since this is handled through software.

A second expansion slot in the PC's case is required for the auxiliary mounting bracket that holds the 15-pin D connector for attaching a joystick. This port also doubles as the MIDI I/O connector and attaches via a ribbon cable to the board.

The WinStorm's video is excellent, providing 24-bit True Color (16.8 million colors) and SVGA modes up to 1024x768/256-color with fast vertical refresh rates and VESA bios compatibility. A MultiMode Control Panel application utility is provided that allows resolution switching via software under Windows instantly, a very novel and handy capability. Numerous DOS video drivers are also provided for popular applications, such as AutoCad.

The WinStorm uses a Yamaha YMF262 (OPL3) 20-voice stereo synthesizer chip as its sound source, and this chip also gives the board full AdLib and Sound Blaster compatibility. Since the audio chipset used on the WinStorm is from Media Vision, the board is also fully compatible with the Thunder Board and Media Vision Pro Audio Spectrum 16 sound standards.

Jumpers are used to enable or disable functions (such as VGA on/off), altering default settings (such as IRQ) and other variables, although the defaults will prove satisfactory for most installations. Several pin connectors are also found on the board, used for attaching various cables. One is provided for routing the PC's sound through the board, and another for channeling the CD-ROM drive's audio through it. Another 4-pin block is provided for attaching external audio sources, and a 50-pin SCSI interface connection is also mounted on the board in addition to the connector for attaching the joystick/MIDI ribbon.

The WinStorm software is supplied on high-density (1.44 MB) 3.5 inch media, and quite a selection is provided spanning a total of nine disks in all. Three of the disks contain Windows drivers, OS/2 2.0 drivers, DOS drivers, and utilities.

Additional software is provided to exploit the sound and multimedia capabilities of the WinStorm card. Animotion's MCS MusicRack is a Windows-based utility that allows controlling multimedia hardware like a home stereo system is included, and so is Midisoft's Multimedia Music Library, a collection of MIDI music and sounds. Multimedia Make Your Point, a Windows-based presentation program from Asymetrix, completes the assortment.

The Winstorm is a good way to add high quality sound and video all on one card.

Glossary

DMA An abbreviation for *direct memory access*, it refers to memory access that does not involve the microprocessor, frequently employed for data transfer directly between memory and an "intelligent" peripheral device, such as a sound card. Numeric designations refer to the particular channel that is set up for communication with the device.

MPC
An abbreviation for *multimedia personal computer*, it refers to a set of specifications drafted by Microsoft and other major manufacturers and developers that defines the minimum hardware and software requirements for acceptable multimedia production and presentation on personal computers.

IRQ or Interrupt Request
An electronic signal that is sent when a hardware device (such as a sound card) or software needs to use the microprocessor. This signal is a special instruction that switches control of the microprocessor to the operating system for the task to be completed.

Redbook audio standard
The standard specification for CD Audio as detailed and agreed upon by Philips, Sony, and other major manufacturers. Since these technical specifications were published in a book with a red cover, this specification for audio became known as the *Redbook* standard.

TSR
An abbreviation for terminate-and-stay-resident, a type of program that runs under DOS and remains loaded in memory even when it is not running so that it can be quickly invoked for a specific task performed while any other application program is operating.

LESSON FIVE:

Overview of Basic Recording, Playback, and Editing

- Microphone recording
- Line and aux recording
- Basic audio editing
- Mixing and playback
- Some basic terminology

Most sound boards and externally-connected PC audio devices permit you to record your own sounds and save them on disk for playback. Depending on the sound device you're using, you may have several input options for recording the desired sounds, or you may only have a single recording port that serves as the input channel for all sound to be digitized. The basic recording techniques you use and what you'll require in the way of input hardware depend on the card's features as well as the source of the sound. In this lesson we'll examine the hardware requirements and some basic tips and techniques for recording, editing, and playing back sound on your PC.

Microphone Varieties

The microphone is the most commonly-used device for sampling and recording live sounds with a sound card. It is important to understand that all microphones are not created equal, and they vary greatly not only in their prices but also in their capabilities and intended uses.

The pickup pattern of the microphone is a major factor to consider when contemplating a purchase. The two major types of pickup patterns for microphone are *unidirectional* and *omnidirectional*.

Unidirectional microphones can pick up sounds primarily from one direction, usually from directly in front of the mike. Conversely, omnidirectional microphones can pick up sound from all directions—the front, sides, and back.

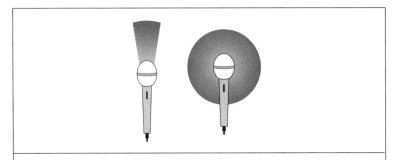

Figure 5.1   *The difference in sound pickup patterns between microphones is illustrated here. The unidirectional microphone at the left has a narrow reception band for sound, while the omnidirectional mike at the right can receive sound from all directions.*

Unidirectional microphones are best suited for situations where lots of ambient noise is present. A unidirectional mike can be aimed directly at the source of the sound, such as the speaker's mouth, and the mike's narrow reception band will pickup the voice while the other ambient sounds are greatly subdued. Unidirectional microphones work best when the source of the sound consistently comes from the same direction, as when you are seated at your PC.

Omnidirectional microphones have a greatly increased pickup range, with some microphone models capable of full 360° pickup patterns. Omnidirectional mikes are good for situations where sound is coming from several directions, as when several speakers are seated around a desk.

Radio Shack carries a good assortment of microphones in both unidirectional and omnidirectional pickup patterns at prices ranging from about $12 to over $50, depending on the model. For better sound quality, purchase a decent microphone rather than using one you've liberated from an old cassette recorder, since these rarely provide optimal recording quality.

Virtually all internal and external PC sound devices that accept microphone input are equipped with 1/8 inch monophonic or stereophonic jacks. Many microphones are outfitted with 1/8 inch jacks, although many also come with 1/4 inch (standard) phone jacks. Adapters are available from Radio Shack and in the audio accessory sections of department and record stores that convert 1/4 inch phone plugs to the 1/8 inch jack size you'll require for PC audio use.

The cord attached to the microphone should be at least six feet in length so you'll have sufficient slack to locate the mike conveniently. Most microphones have a six foot or longer cord, but it may be necessary to purchase a microphone extension cord for special installations, such as a tower-cased PC that sits on the floor.

It is very important to make sure the microphone is the correct impedance level, measured in ohms, to match the acceptable range of the sound device with which you're using. The impedence level for microphones will be listed on the sound device's packaging or in the technical specifications section of the owner's manual.

Attenuating adapters, available in various varieties at Radio Shack and other electronics supply stores, can sometimes be used to adjust the signal load level of an incompatible microphone to within the acceptable range of the sound board, but it's always best to use a microphone that is correctly matched to the input levels accepted by the sound system.

Some sound cards and audio port products use a single port for both microphone and line-level input, and for these devices an attenuating adapter may prove to be an invaluable accessory for conforming the incoming audio signal to the optimal recording levels of the sound device. These adapters usually cost less than $5 and are very worthwhile for some PC audio configurations, particularly those with sound devices sharing a single input port.

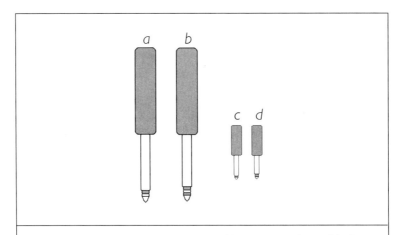

Figure 5.2 *The 1/4 inch monophonic (a) and stereophonic (b) phone plugs frequently found on microphones are larger than the 1/8 inch mono (c) and stereo (d) miniphone plugs that are the standard on PC sound devices. Adapters are readily available at Radio Shack stores and in audio/record shops which reduce 1/4 inch plugs to 1/8 inch size.*

Line-Level Inputs

You'll probably want to record music, sound effects, or bits of dialogue from sources such as tapes, compact discs, or videocassettes. While it is possible to record these sounds with a microphone placed close to the speakers of your stereo or TV set, you'll get much better sound quality by using the line-level inputs of the sound card or audio port device.

Line-level inputs, also called auxilliary (*aux*) inputs on some sound cards, are specifically designed and attenuated to accept sound from the line-output jacks of other audio/video products such as home stereos, cassette decks, CD players, and so forth.

The line-ouput jacks of most consumer products (stereos, cassette decks, etc.) are RCA-type jacks, whereas most PC audio devices use a 1/8 inch stereo miniphone plug for input. A special cable commonly called a "Y" cable is required to mate the two different jack types successfully, and they come in various varieties with different types of plug combinations. The particular type of "Y" cable that you'll want for a PC sound card or audio port device has RCA-type plugs on the forked end of the "Y" (one plug each for the left and right channels) and a single 1/8 inch stereo miniphone plug at the stem end of the cable. These cables are usually 3-4 feet in length, although some can be as long as 6 feet; as with microphones, make sure the cable is sufficiently long to accommodate the hook-ups you'll need or purchase an extension cable as well. These "Y" cables are extremely handy but, unfortunately, are not always supplied with the PC sound device and may have to be purchased separately. They're a good investment, however, since they can do double-duty by also routing the sound from the PC to an external device such as a cassette recorder or a stereo amplifier during playback as well.

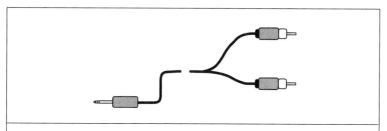

Figure 5.3 *A typical "Y" cable is illustrated above. The split ends of the Y are terminated in RCA-type plugs, while the stem end is outfitted with a single stereophonic 1/8 inch miniphone plug. Not all sound cards come equipped with this handy cable, so a separate purchase may be required.*

Recording Sound Under Windows

The Sound Recorder accessory is a basic component of the Windows 3.1 operating environment, and it is the standard way of recording and storing sound in

Windows. It provides the tools required for recording and some limited editing of sound files. There are even some provisions for altering the sound file with special effects and mixing multiple sound files together.

While virtually every sound card and audio port device that supports recording functions comes with its own recording software and editing utilities, the Sound Recorder accessory is the simplest and fastest to use for most routine sound recording tasks. Even though Sound Recorder's editing and effects menus are somewhat limited, the software still provides an enormous amount of functionality for most uses. For more advanced sound projects, either the sound device's supplied software or a dedicated stand-alone sound editing software package, like those reviewed in Lesson 9, may be required. The inherent capabilities of Sound Recorder, however, shouldn't be discounted or glossed-over since it is a solid Windows resource that you'll find yourself using frequently for "down-and-dirty" editing and recording chores.

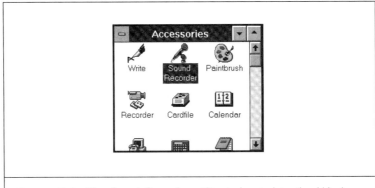

Figure 5.4 *The Sound Recorder utility is located in the Windows Accessories group.*

Sound Recorder provides useful information about the sound card, its configuration under Windows, and the resources available. By opening the Help menu and selecting **About Sound Recorder**, the information screen becomes visible, as shown in Figure 5.5. Of particular interest is the fourth line down (right below the copyright line), which shows you the current configuration for recording. Sound Recorder uses the default sample rate of 22 kHz, with the sample size (8-bit or 16-

bit) determined by the configuration of the installed sound device. It should also be noted that Sound Recorder is only capable of monophonic recording, even though your hardware may support stereo and 44 kHz sampling.

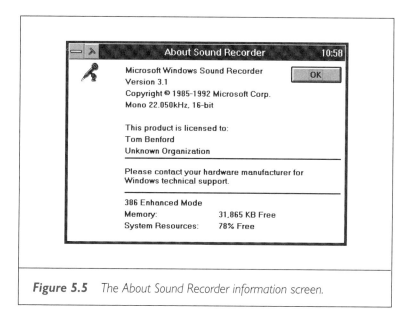

Figure 5.5   *The About Sound Recorder information screen.*

The amount of memory and system resources currently available is also shown at the bottom of this screen.

Sound Recorder provides a user interface that closely resembles a standard cassette player transport, which makes it very easy to understand and use. While a sound is being recorded or played-back via the Sound Recorder, a graphic representation of the sound file is displayed as it would look if viewed on an oscilloscope in the wave box section of the screen. Figure 5.6 on the next page shows the various components of the Sound Recorder application screen.

Before we actually go through the basic recording procedures, it's a good idea to go over the controls of the Sound Recorder and how they're used to move around in a sound file.

You can use the mouse to move to any point in a sound file by either clicking on a scroll arrow at either side of the scroll bar or on the scroll bar itself. Clicking on an arrow moves the sound back or forward one-tenth of a second (.1), while clicking on the scroll bar moves the sound forward or back a full second. You can also click on and move the scroll indicator button itself to any desired point in the sound file, using the position indicator window to the left for your relative position within the file.

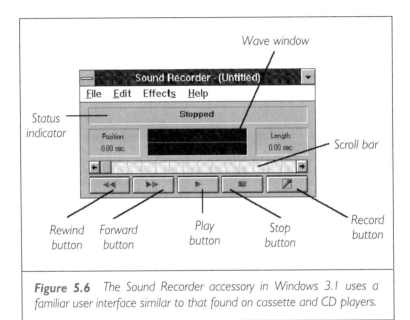

Figure 5.6 *The Sound Recorder accessory in Windows 3.1 uses a familiar user interface similar to that found on cassette and CD players.*

The keyboard can be used for controlling the scroll bar, although the mouse is the most efficient control medium. When using the keyboard, The **Tab** key is used to select the desired button or the scroll bar, and the **Left Arrow** and **Right Arrow** keys move the sound file back or forward .1 second each time you press either key.

To quickly move to the beginning of a sound file from any point, simply click on the **Rewind** button with the mouse or press the **Home** key on the keyboard.

Similarly, to move to the end of a sound file expeditiously click on the **Forward** button or press the **End** key on the keyboard.

Basic Sound Recording

To record sound, you'll need these three components:

- an installed and configured sound card or audio port that supports recording
- a microphone or line-input cable
- a sound source

To record your voice or other live sound, connect the microphone to the correct input of the sound device and make sure the mike's on/off switch is turned on, if it is so equipped. To record music or sound from a line-level source, such as a stereo, connect the proper cable to the line-out jacks of the source and the line-input jack(s) of the PC's sound device. As noted earlier, an attenuating adapter may be required with some sound devices to adjust the incoming audio signal to an acceptable level.

Click on the Sound Recorder icon in the Accessory group of the Windows Program Manager, and then select **New** from the Sound Recorder's File menu.

Click on the **Record** button and speak into the microphone. If you're using a line-input source such as a cassette player, first click on the **Record** button and press **Play** on the source device, in that order.

The Sound Recorder accessory permits a maximum recording length of one minute, although you can join and link several files to extend the overall length (this is covered in more detail a bit later). When you are finished recording your segment, click on the **Stop** button. The recording also automatically ends at one minute if you don't click on stop prior to that.

At this point you can now save your file by selecting **Save As** from the File menu and giving the sound file a name. The file name can be up to eight characters and you should give it a .WAV file type extension to make it recognizeable as a Windows sound file to other applications that can process it.

You may also listen to your recorded segment prior to saving it by clicking on the **Play** button, and you may perform editing at this point if desired. It's always a good idea to save the original file as it was first recorded in the event you need to revert back to it in its unedited form.

Insertion Recording

In addition to recording original sound files, the Sound Recorder accessory also makes it possible to insert some additional sound into existing sound files. This capability varies between sound cards, and not all PC audio products support this feature. Insertion recording is one of the ways you can extend a sound file beyond the 60-second file length limitation imposed by Sound Recorder for new files.

For those devices that are capable of insertion recording, the procedure is almost as simple as that used for basic sound recording:

1. First open the existing sound file to which you wish to add material. Select **Open** from the Sound Recorder's File menu, and select or type in the name of the desired file.

2. By using the **Play** and **Stop** buttons or the scroll bar, locate the place you want to add the new material.

3. Click on the **Record** button and speak into the microphone or play the appropriate segment from a connected line-level device. Click on the **Stop** button when you're finished. The amount of available memory on your system will determine how long the recorded segment can be.

As with initial sound recordings, you can review the result, perform some editing, or save the file at this point.

Basic Editing and Mixing

The Sound Recorder accessory provides the tools required for inserting one sound file into another, for mixing sound files together, and for increasing or decreasing the volume of a sound. It also gives you some creative tools for producing special effects like slowing-down or speeding-up the sound, reversing the sound so it plays backwards, adding echo effects, and deleting portions of a sound file.

One of the most basic and frequently performed editing tasks is the removal of unwanted portions of the sound file that aren't needed, such as ambient noise or silent periods at the beginning or end of a sound file. This process is called *trimming*. Trimming these unwanted segments helps to conserve system memory and disk space, while improving the overall quality of the sound file at the same time.

It's important to note that Sound Recorder does not support true cut-and-paste functions, such as those found in a word processor. While you can cut portions of a file, the cuts are restricted to all sound either before or after the current cursor position. There is no provision for pasting cut portions back into the file, so these delete functions should be used very carefully.

To delete unwanted sound from the beginning of a loaded file or newly-recorded segment, use the scroll bar or Arrow keys to locate the actual beginning of the sound you wish to keep. Once located, click on the Edit menu and select **Delete Before Current Position**. A confirmation dialogue box is displayed telling you how much of the file will be deleted and presenting you with the options to continue or cancel the action. Clicking on **OK** completes the cutting process, and the adjusted file size, minus the segment just cut, is displayed in the file length window at the right side.

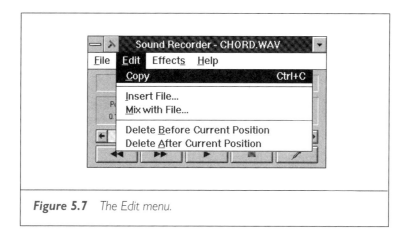

Figure 5.7   *The Edit menu.*

The procedure is basically the same for trimming unwanted portions from the end of a sound file. After locating the end of the desired portion of sound, click on the Edit menu and select **Delete After Current Position**. A confirmation dialogue box is displayed that informs you how much of the file will be deleted and gives you the option to continue or cancel the action. Clicking on **OK** completes the cutting process, and the adjusted file size, minus the segment just cut, is displayed in the file length window at the right side.

A copy function is also provided on the Edit menu that permits making a copy of the current sound file. This is useful for making the original sound file longer by inserting copies into the original file. To try the copy function and hear its effect, try the following exercise:

1. Record your own sound file or use an existing sound file as the source, such as the CHORD.WAV file that comes with Windows.

2. Either click on the copy selection or use the **Ctrl-C** keyboard combination (hold the **Control** key down and press the **C** key). This makes a copy of the CHORD.WAV file.

3. From the File menu select **Save As** and name the copy COPY.WAV.

4. You can now use the COPY.WAV file for modifications or adding special effects while leaving the original CHORD.WAV file intact and untouched.

5. To add your copy to the original sound file, select **Insert File** from the Edit menu and select **COPY.WAV** from the file list menu that is presented. The copy is inserted as soon as you click **OK**.

6. Click on the **Rewind** button to get to the beginning of the file, and then click on the **Play** button to hear the results of the inserted file combined with the original file (you should hear the chord sound twice).

7. You'll notice that the Length window also reflects that additional material has been added to the original file, which is now 2.26 seconds in length (up from the original size of 1.13 seconds).

The Mix function on the Edit menu permits mixing different files together, one on top of the other, so that the sound is combined. This technique gives the effect of *sound-on-sound* recording, which was developed by Les Paul, who is interviewed in Lesson 8. Mixing is a most useful function that can be used to add a spoken narrative on top of a musical background file, among other uses.

You can hear the effect of Mix for yourself by trying the following exercise:

1. Load the TADA.WAV file into the Sound Recorder, then choose **MIX file** from the Edit menu.

2. Select **CHORD.WAV** and click on **OK**. Use the **Rewind** button to get to the beginning of the file and click on the **Play** button.

Your should hear the TADA.WAV and CHORD.WAV files play combined with both sounds intermingled.

Special Effects

Sound Recorder gives you the tools required to add some interesting special effects to your sound files. These are quite easy to use. All of these effects can be *layered*, meaning that you can apply several layers of the desired effect (or combinations of them) to alter the sound file to your liking.

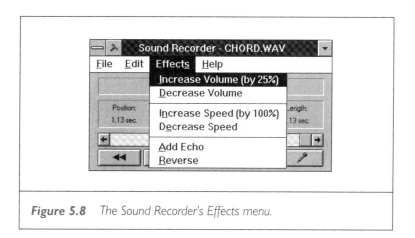

Figure 5.8 *The Sound Recorder's Effects menu.*

No provision for working on a partial segment of a sound file is included, since all of the selections from the Effects menu affect the entire sound file currently in memory.

For example, to increase the overall volume of the sound file by one quarter, simply click the **Increase Volume (by 25%)** selection. You can increase the volume further by clicking it additional times, since each time you click, the volume increases by an additional 25%. You can also decrease the volume, also by 25% per application, by clicking on **Decrease Volume**. This menu selection choice can also be used more than once to augment its effect. As an example, if you wish to decrease the volume of a sound file by 50%, click twice on **Decrease Volume**.

The **Increase Speed (by 100%)** and the **Decrease Speed** controls also work on the entire file, and they too can have multiple applications to achieve the desired effect on the sound file. Increase Speed has an effect similar to playing a 45RPM record at 78RPM (actually it would be 90RPM)—both the playback speed and the pitch of the sound are doubled making the sound faster and higher than the original, since the increase factor is 100% each time this function is applied. Conversely, each time the **Decrease Speed** selection is used the speed and pitch is halved, resulting in a slower, lower sounding file.

The **Increase Speed** function is useful for creating novelty effects such as making spoken words or singing sound like *The Chipmunks* did the recording, and **Decrease Speed** gives the impression of slow-motion audio playback.

The **Add Echo** effect is useful for adding a slight reverberation effect to the original sound or, by applying multiple applications, creating a repeating echo effect. Unlike the increase/decrease volume and speed effects, there is no way of reversing or undoing the **Add Echo** effect once it is applied.

The **Reverse** menu selection does precisely what its name implies: it reverses the playback order of the sound file so that the sound is heard backwards. This is an interesting novelty effect, although it doesn't have have too many practical applications aside from recording sections of some heavy metal albums and reversing them to hear any "Satanic messages" that might have been implanted on them.

Sound Playback

Windows provides two means of playing sound files. The Sound Recorder accessory can be used, as well as another accessory, Media Player (shown in Figure 5.9), that is also an integral component of Windows. It resides in the Accessory group of the Program Manager, and is capable of playing .WAV audio files as well as several other file types.

The File menu of the Sound Recorder, shown in Figure 5.10, permits loading sound files for playback and editing as well as other options for saving the file. It also provides a function, **Revert**, that cancels all unsaved current changes to the file and reinstates the last saved version to the work area.

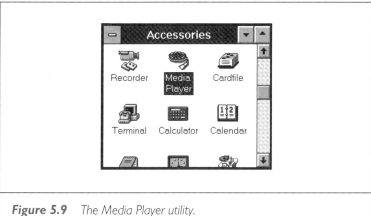

Figure 5.9   *The Media Player utility.*

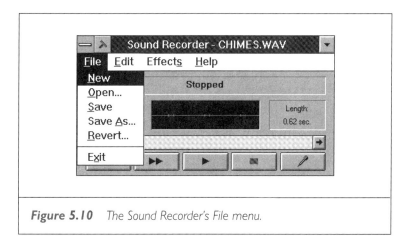

Figure 5.10   *The Sound Recorder's File menu.*

The principal difference between the two utilities is that Media Player is a playback-only accessory, whereas Sound Recorder can record, modify, and play back audio files. Media player has other capabilities that Sound Recorder doesn't have, however. It can play back MIDI, CD-AUDIO, animation, video, and other types of files (provided the correct hardware and drivers are installed) in addition to WAV sound files.

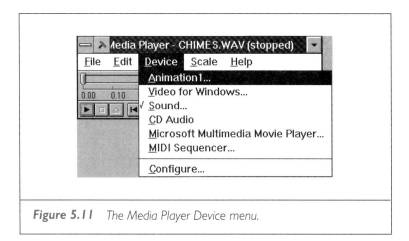

Figure 5.11 *The Media Player Device menu.*

Media Player uses the same button scheme as Sound Recorder for the transport and playback control of files, so using it is also very simple and straightforward.

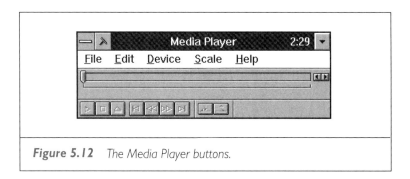

Figure 5.12 *The Media Player buttons.*

Media Player provides some additional editing features including the ability to mark a segment of the file and to link a file to another application or embed it within a document using the *object linking and embedding* (OLE) facilities of Windows 3.1.

Additional Sound Tools

Both the Sound Recorder and Media Player accessories are useful and worthwhile utilities that permit working with sound files, although their respective capabilities are somewhat limited.

For more extensive sound editing and manipulation capabilities, Microsoft's WaveEdit utility, which comes as part of the Windows *Software Developer Kit,* is an excellent tool. It permits fading the volume up or down, changing the characteristics of a file (such as from 16-bit stereo to 8-bit mono), true cut-and-paste, mix-paste, and other functions.

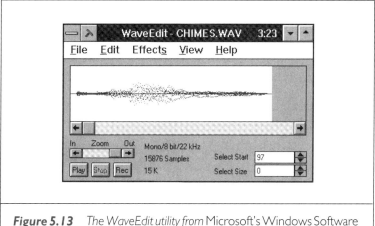

Figure 5.13 *The WaveEdit utility from* Microsoft's Windows Software Development Kit.

There are many other outstanding commercially-available sound packages that provide extensive editing and sound manipulation capabilities. Many of them eclipse and exceed those found in the WaveEdit utility, and all of them are far superior to the basic capabilities of the Sound Recorder accessory. These software products are covered in depth with individual reviews in Lesson 9.

Glossary

acoustic   Also *acoustical.* Pertaining to sound or the science of sound. In musical usage, it refers to non-amplified instruments as opposed to electronic or amplified instrumentation, such as an acoustic guitar versus an electric guitar.

ambient noise   Acoustic noise in a room or other location, also sometimes referred to as *room noise*. Any unwanted background
noise picked up by a microphone and any acoustic
coloration that influences sounds, brought about by the
acoustic properties of a room in which a recording is
being made or replayed, is described as ambient noise.

attenuating   Electronic devices that reduce the amplitude of a signal
adapters   during its transmission from one point to another. Audio
attenuating adapters reduce the signal strength of loud
sounds to conform them to the acceptable range of sound
cards and other recording devices that require a lower
signal level.

container document   A document file that has objects that are still connected
to the original application that created them. The objects
residing in a container document may be text, charts,
spreadsheets, bitmap pictures, vector drawings, sounds,
video clips, and anything else that can be displayed or
controlled by a Windows application.

impedance   A term that refers to resistance in the flow of an electrical
current. Resistance impedes the current flow by convert-
ing electrical energy to heat, and it is measured in units
called *ohms*. For proper sound recording, a microphone's
impedence level must be in the acceptable range of the
recording device and for proper playback the speakers or
headphones must be in the proper impedance range of
the playback device.

insertion recording   The process of inserting additional sound material into an
existing sound file without disturbing or erasing the
current material. Insertion recording is a useful technique
for extending the length of sound files created with the
Sound Recorder accessory beyond the 60-second maximum file length permitted by the utility.

layering   The process of repeatedly applying a special effect such
as echo or increase/decrease speed to augment the effect.

For example, layering the echo effect three times produces a triple-echo effect.

ohms
The unit of measure for electrical resistance. A resistance of one ohm passes one ampere of current when a voltage of one volt is applied.

OLE
An acronym for *object linking and embedding*, which is a set of application protocols in Windows 3.1 that enables one application to use seamlessly the services of another application. Applications that conform to the OLE protocols enable you to create documents that contain linked or embedded information from documents created by other applications, and such an application is referred to as a container document. Unlike normal cutting and pasting, the data in an OLE object can be linked (where the data resides in another, separate document), or embedded (where the data resides in the container document). In either case, the object can be edited only by the application that created it, not the application in whose document it currently resides.

omnidirectional microphone
Also called a nondirectional microphone, this type of microphone responds to sound waves reaching it from virtually any angle or direction.

oscilloscope
An electronic instrument that displays waveforms in graphical format. The display typically shows the horizontal and vertical deflection of the electron beam of a cathode-ray tube. These deflections are, respectively, proportional to a pair of applied voltages.

sound-on-sound recording
A method by which material previously recorded on one track of a tape may be recorded on another track while simultaneously adding new material to it. The technique is often employed with music to give the effect of one musician playing several different instruments or parts simultaneously. This technique was pioneered by Les Paul in the late 1940's.

trimming

The process of removing unwanted portions of the sound file that aren't needed, such as ambient noise or silent periods at the beginning or end of a sound file. Trimming helps sound quality and also reduces the amount of memory and disk space required by the sound.

unidirectional microphone

A microphone that is most sensitive to sounds arriving at it from one direction, usually from the front.

LESSON SIX:
Voice and Speech Recognition

- What it is
- Hardware and software requirements
- Proprietary and universal approaches
- Some additional terminology

The Power of the Spoken Word

Just a few short years ago the notion of giving a computer spoken commands was the subject matter of science fiction writers and future visionaries, and yet today it is an affordable reality. Voice recognition and voice command of computers and the software they are running will continue to become an increasingly important aspect of technology development. As computers become faster and more powerful they can process the additional instruction "overhead" required to process voice commands more easily, and the spoken word is probably the ultimate in user interfaces.

Two terms come into play regarding this technology: *voice recognition* and *speech recognition*. While they are both related, they are indeed separate and distinct applications that we should understand before going any further.

Computer voice recognition is, as the term implies, the ability of a computer to recognize a user's voice and respond to it in some fashion, such as executing a spoken command or entering spoken words as text or numbers in a software application. The particular feature of voice recognition that distinguishes it from speech recognition is that voice recognition can also be used as a means of providing computer security by preventing anyone but an authorized user from gaining access to the system. This is done by storing the authorized user's voice pattern in a *recognition template file*, which is compared to the user's voice when he or she logs on the system. If the pattern of the spoken password matches that of the recognition template, access to the computer is granted. If the pattern doesn't match, access is denied. This type of a system is called *speaker dependent*, since whether it works or not is determined by whether or not it recognizes the person speaking into the microphone.

Speech recognition also refers to the ability of a computer to understand the spoken word for the purpose of receiving commands and data input from the speaker. Some speech recognition systems have been developed that can recognize limited vocabularies as spoken by numerous individuals, although changes in the inflection, pronunciation, and the dialect of their speech affect the accuracy of the speech recognition to a large degree. This type of system is said to be *speaker independent*, since it recognizes any user whose speech falls within its *recognition threshhold*.

Different Approaches

There are currently three different approaches to voice and speech recognition, and all have their good points as well as their drawbacks.

The first approach enables computers to recognize and react to a small number of words when spoken by a broad range of people. The principal advantage of this approach is that many different users can access the computer through the spoken word without any specific "training" of the system to understand their individual voices or speech patterns. While this method has proven to be fairly accurate, it depends on *acoustic models* of words that are stored as patterns for menus, commands, and actions. These acoustic models are based on the averaged sound patterns of multiple speakers all saying the same words. The drawbacks are that it is impossible to cover all possible variations in pronunciation, accent, inflection, or dialect so it won't always work as expected with all speakers, and some custom adjustment or training may be required. Since this approach is designed to accept spoken input from the widest possible range of speakers, it is also subject to "hearing" and, subsequently, acting upon speech coming from other people in the room that is not intended to control the computer's actions.

The second approach to making computers respond to spoken words involves "training" the computer to recognize a larger number of words spoken by one specific individual. The trained words are stored in recognition template files. The chief advantage is that this approach provides a highly accurate means of achieving voice control, provided the speaker's speech patterns are consistent. It can also be used as a security measure for the computer system by only permitting access to an authorized user whose voice pattern is recognized. Multiple authorized users can be accommodated by storing each individual's recognition patterns as separate templates and specifying who the current user is for voice verification. The drawback is that training takes a small investment in time and effort, although once the templates are created they shouldn't require any more attention. Additional training is required anytime the user wishes to add more words to the vocabulary, since additonal templates must be created.

The third approach takes the direction of the computer learning the user's speech patterns and applying these patterns over a broad range of words. The advantage of this approach is that, if or when it works correctly, it provides the best potential for complete speech-to-text conversion, since dedicated vocabularies of trained recognition templates won't be required. The disadvantage is that, at least for the present time, it is the least accurate of the three, although there is much research and development currently going on in this area.

Humans have remarkably varied and inconsistent ways of speaking, and this presents the major problem in creating recognition systems that work accurately for the masses. If you take a moment to consider the ways that speech can vary in different locales, you'll start to appreciate the hard time computers have of recognizing human speech. For example, a Bostonian's accent is quite different from a Brooklynite, which is also quite different from a Californian's. And, since most computer hardware and software products aren't restricted to the United States alone, there are also British, Australian, and East Indian accents and pronunciations that recognition systems also have to deal with on an international level. Combine the accent and dialect factors with the number of variations in which a request or a statement can be made, and you can appreciate the difficulties involved in creating recognition systems that work accurately.

Hardware and Software Requirements

Humans don't have any problem recognizing different voices, pronunciations, and dialects among speakers in comparison to computers. Human hearing and intellect instantaneously set about the task of identifying and understanding speech as soon as it is heard. Computers have much more work to do before a user's speech can be acted upon.

Since speech and voice recognition both depend on the user's spoken words for input, a microphone is a required hardware element. The microphone is the input instrument that converts the user's spoken words into electrical signals that are converted by the *analog-to-digital converter* (ADC).

As we learned earlier, before a computer can process any type of analog audio information (such as human speech), it must first be converted into digital format. This is done by the ADC circuitry of the sound device. The analog-to-digital converter is an essential element, therefore, in recognition and must be a component of the sound card or audio port device. Playback-only units are not capable of providing speech and voice recognition since they don't have ADCs.

The digitized sound is then analyzed and compared by the voice recognition software against a previously-defined template. This template may be the voice pattern of a particular user, or it can be a general acoustic model of the word to accommodate a large number of users. The recognition software provides the routines required to create and store templates, as well as those required to compare the spoken samples with those contained in the templates to establish a match.

Once a match has been established between the spoken word and the recognition template, the corresponding action or data entry can be invoked or accepted. The actions performed are determined by the software application and the recognition list. For example, with the recognition program loaded while working from the Windows Program Manager, the spoken command "File" has the same effect as using the mouse to open the File menu or using the Alt-F keystroke combination. In a data-entry situation, such as when you're working in a word processing application, speaking the word *file* while dictating a letter could produce the letters *f-i-l-e* to be entered in the document as if they were typed directly on the keyboard.

Proprietary Versus Universal Recognition Systems

Since the inception of the personal computer itself, the quest for a machine that could be either entirely or largely controlled through speech has endured. In recent years we've seen this become a reality with such stunning examples of voice control as in the cockpits of today's high-tech fighter aircraft and, most recently, in a wireless VCR controller that can be programmed simply by speaking to it.

Several hardware manufacturers have produced expansion boards and even some totally dedicated computer systems that, to one extent or another, make voice control possible. "Talking" typewriters have been marketed in different designs over the years, although they have always been slow, have varying degrees of recognition accuracy, and all cost several thousand dollars.

Voice control systems have been in use in industrial and manufacturing situations for several years where verbal commands such as *stop* or *shut down* could be used for emergency situations away from the main control panel of the machinery. You may have even been in an elevator that politely asks you *What floor would you like, please?* when you enter and it waits for your spoken reply before moving.

All of these uses for voice control are examples of proprietary recognition systems that are specifically designed and manufactured to perform their own distinct functions in response to spoken words. The military jet cockpit is another example of proprietary recognition, as are several high-end recognition boards available for IBM-compatible computers.

The Microsoft Windows Sound System is another example of a proprietary recognition system, since it requires the Windows Sound System board to be installed in the PC for it to function. Since the Windows Sound System has a large installed user base and uses the acoustic model approach to recognition, we use it to illustrate the differences of a proprietary approach to a universal approach such as the one provided by the Covox Voice Blaster system that can be used with numerous different sound cards.

Microsoft's Voice Pilot

The Voice Pilot application, part of the Windows Sound System, is invoked by double-clicking on the icon in the Windows Sound System application group in Program Manager.

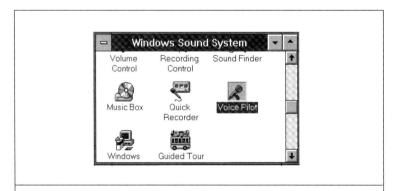

Figure 6.1   *The Voice Pilot application is an integral part of the Windows Sound System from Microsoft.*

The Voice Pilot application is used to control your computer with its built-in vocabulary of voice commands. Many of the most-used commands are already provided for numerous Windows-based applications, and you can also add your own commands or modify those included to customize Voice Pilot to your own needs and preferences.

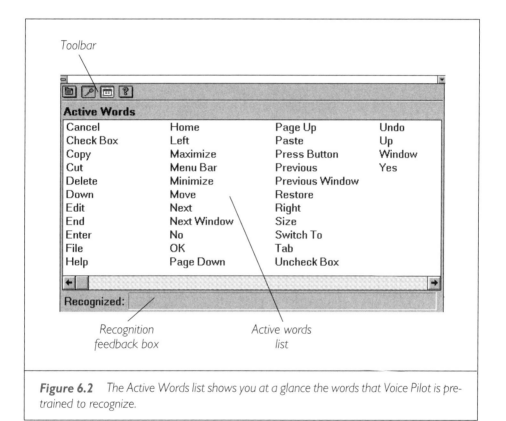

Figure 6.2 *The Active Words list shows you at a glance the words that Voice Pilot is pre-trained to recognize.*

Once Voice Pilot is started, it can be run in minimized mode that only displays an icon, as a toolbar containing four function icons, or as a window that displays the active words list and provides a recognition feedback box.

In the window view, as you speak Voice Pilot displays the word it recognized in the Recognized box—a handy feature for confirming how well the current training suits your speech style. If Voice Pilot doesn't understand what you said, it instead displays question marks in the feedback box.

The toolbar provides four icons that make available additional features and functions. The left-most icon provides commands for customizing the vocabulary, setting the active user, customizing a list of users, and the fonts.

The microphone can be turned on or off using the next icon in the toolbar. For Voice Pilot to acknowledge and execute your verbal instructions, the microphone must be plugged into the Windows Sound System card and turned on via the toolbar.

> **Note:** By default the microphone input is always off when Voice Pilot starts. You must turn it on before anything will happen.

The third icon from the left displays or hides the active words window, and the question mark icon at the right opens the Voice Pilot on-line help and provides access to the About Voice Pilot dialog box.

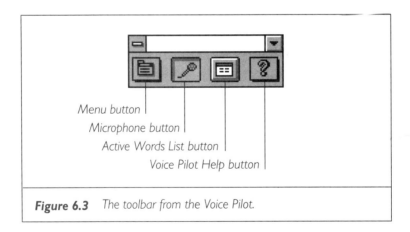

Menu button
Microphone button
Active Words List button
Voice Pilot Help button

Figure 6.3   *The toolbar from the Voice Pilot.*

The icon to the far left is a menu button, which displays the commands to customize the vocabulary, set the active user, and more. The next icon turns the microphone on or off. The third icon displays or hides the active words list (the view show in this illustration has the words list hidden). The question mark icon invokes Voice Pilot help and provides the About Voice Pilot dialog box.

Voice Pilot "stays on top" of all other applications currently running when you are in either the active words or toolbar view. This means that as you use the **Alt-Tab** keystroke sequence to switch applications, Voice Pilot keeps either the toolbar or active words list windows on top of the application to which you switch. Using Voice Pilot merely requires switching to the application and speaking any of the commands listed in the Voice Pilot window.

The application also supports *dynamic updating* of the active word list as you work, so any new commands you add or modify immediately become a permanent part of the Voice Pilot environment.

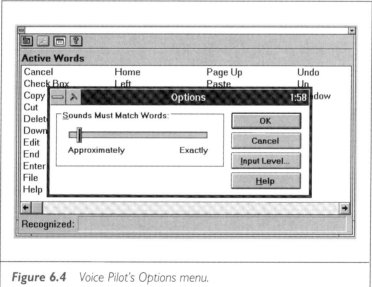

Figure 6.4   *Voice Pilot's Options menu.*

Voice Pilot provides a means of adjusting the recognition threshhold to better suit the speech patterns of individual users. This is done via the Options menu, which is produced by clicking on the menu button on the toolbar. The adjustments are made by moving a slider arcoss the setting bar, which goes from wider threshhold patterns (approximately) to very precise recognition patterns (exactly), and it affords a great deal of latitude between the two extremes. Some users, the author included, find that keeping the setting more in the "approximately" zone affords more recognition accuracy than keeping it set closer to the "exactly" end of the scale using the predefined acoustic models shippped with the system. Individual training of each word in the vocabulary, however, greatly increases the recognition accuracy in most cases.

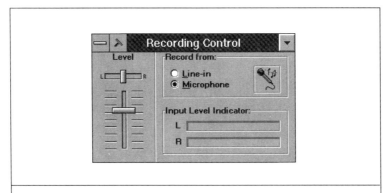

Figure 6.5 *Clicking on the Input Level button on the Options screen produces the display shown above.*

Clicking on the **Input Level** button on the Options screen invokes the *applet* for adjusting the volume. Adjustments are easily made to the volume and the balance by moving the sliders with the mouse. This recording control applet also permits selecting either the microphone or line-input as the recording source.

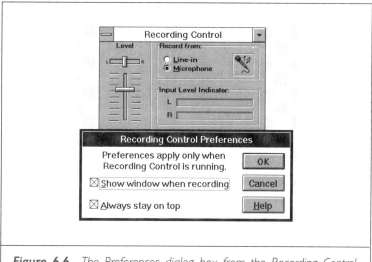

Figure 6.6 *The Preferences dialog box from the Recording Control applet.*

The Windows Sound System does an excellent job of recogizing a wide variety of commands from a wide range of users, and it also permits you to custom-train the vocabularies to increase the recognition accuracy. The system comes with pre-defined built-in vocabularies for the following applications:

- Aldus PageMaker, version 4.0
- Lotus 1-2-3 for Windows, version 1.0
- Micrografx Designer, version 3.1
- Microsoft Excel, version 4.0
- Microsoft Mail, version 1.0
- Microsoft Money, version 1.0
- Microsoft PowerPoint, version 3.0
- Microsoft Project for Windows, version 3.0
- Microsoft Publisher, version 1.0
- Microsoft Windows Program Manager, version 3.1
- Microsoft Word for Windows, version 2.0 and later

- Microsoft Works for Windows, version 2.0
- Microsoft Write, version 3.1
- Norton Desktop for Windows, version 2.0
- WordPerfect for Windows, version 5.1

All of the included vocabularies match the menu structures for the versions of these applications as specified above, although the commands may also work with older versions of these products. In any case, you can change, delete, or retain any of the items in these vocabularies and, of course, you can create your own custom vocabularies based on your needs and preferences.

Voice Pilot automatically shifts the command levels of the current application to reflect valid choices for that segment of the program. For example, if you say a top-level command, the active words list changes to second-level commands defined as follow-up choices for the top level command. You can then say one of these second-level commands to complete the desired task or operation.

An example of this would be the file command, which many vocabularies have on their top levels. If you say "file" at the top command level, you are then presented with the second level of choices which may include *new, open, close, save, save as,* and so forth.

You can return to the top command level from any other level by simply saying "cancel," clicking twice on the microphone button, or pressing twice the **Ctrl-Alt** key combination.

All command functions can also be edited, have new commands added, and unwanted commands deleted. Different user voice models can be created and saved for optimal recognition in situations where more than one person may use the same PC.

The Windows Sound System provides a number of other sound and audio features, covered in more detail in Lessons 4 and 10.

Covox Voice Blaster

Covox is one of the oldest developers and manufacturers of audio enhancement products for personal computers, and a pioneer in the field of voice and speech recognition. The company released its first version of the Voice Master for Commodore 64 users in 1983, followed by versions for the Apple II and Atari family of home computers. The IBM-PC version of the Voice Master made its debut in 1987, and the company has added several other products to its line including the Speech Thing, the Sound Master and the MIDI Maestro, in addition to updated versions of the Voice Master and the Sound Master II products. (These other Covox audio products for IBM-compatible computers are reviewed and covered in Lesson 4 and other appropriate sections).

Covox released the Voice Blaster in 1992 to make voice commands possible with virtually any Sound Blaster-compatible sound card, regardless of the manufacturer. In so doing, Covox opened the world of voice recognition to many users who would otherwise be unable to harness and use this technology.

An important distinction of the Covox Voice Blaster is that, unlike the Microsoft Sound System that can only be used under the Windows operating environment, the Voice Blaster can be used from DOS as well as from Windows. This makes it possible to add and use voice control to existing DOS applications, as well as for games and recreational software packages. Covox includes the package drivers and utilities for both DOS and Windows environments.

Voice Blaster uses the concepts of speaker dependency, voice macros, and isolated word recognition. Designed to work with either gender in any language, each user must train the Voice Blaster in advance to recognize his or her voice. It is important to note that the Voice Blaster has not been designed for *voice imprinting* and is not a recommended tool for determining the identity of a speaker.

Since the system uses isolated word recognition, you must pause briefly between each voice command so that the system can determine the beginning and end of your command to compare it with the trained templates.

Using voice macros, the system associates each vocal command with a series of keystrokes to be entered into the computer, which is how the system is able to perform actions in response to spoken words. The sequence of keystrokes, called a *macro*, usually takes the place of something you type frequently, thus enhancing your productivity.

The Voice Blaster voice recognition system is a combination of software plus a small hardware module. The module plugs into the PC's parallel printer port. It is a *transparent device* that permits the printer cable to be attached to its opposite end so that it is sandwiched between the printer cable and the PC itself. This unit is called an *E/Q module* and it is used for converting the microphone input signal to a level required by the Voice Blaster system.

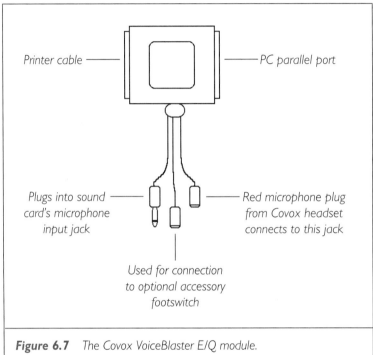

Printer cable ———— *PC parallel port*

Plugs into sound card's microphone input jack ———— *Red microphone plug from Covox headset connects to this jack*

Used for connection to optional accessory footswitch

Figure 6.7   *The Covox VoiceBlaster E/Q module.*

A combination headset and microphone is provided to accommodate voice input and to monitor the output of the sound card or audio port device through the earphone if you don't wish to use loudspeakers.

Installing the software is a highly automated process that runs from the Windows Program Manager. The installation program automatically creates a program group and installs the icons representing the included applications in the package.

Although the Voice Blaster can operate from DOS, for the sake of clarity and for comparison purposes with the Microsoft Windows Sound System, only the operation of the recognition functions of the Voice Blaster under Windows is covered here. The other features of the product are covered in Lessons 4 and 10.

With the E/Q module and software installed, the system is ready for use as soon as a microphone is plugged in and the software is loaded. Since the Voice Blaster system is speaker dependent and has to "learn" your speech patterns, the first requirement is to train the system to your voice.

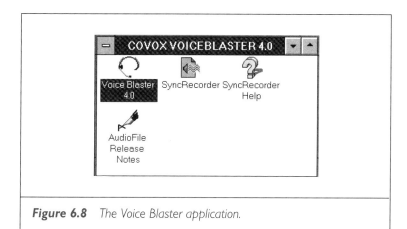

Figure 6.8   *The Voice Blaster application.*

Double-click on the Voice Blaster 4.0 icon in the Covox group of Program Manager to display the main work screen of the application. Like the Voice Pilot, a toolbar is provided at the uppermost portion of the application screen that provides controls and drop-down menus for additional functions and preferences. Status windows are provided to let you know if the command was recognized and what the current active application is. At the top of the display is a blinking square area to signify when the recognition system is active and receiving sound through the microphone headset.

When the Voice Blaster is run for the first time, you are presented with a Logon dialog box. You must enter your name in the text field of this box, up to eight characters. Voice Blaster creates a user file using the name you entered, assigning the extension .USR to the file. This user file contains the command templates that Voice Blaster depends on to match your spoken commands to a sequence of predetermined actions.

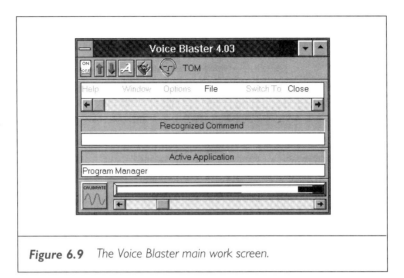

Figure 6.9 *The Voice Blaster main work screen.*

The lower-left corner of the Voice Blaster window contains a button that calibrates the unit. Calibration sets the background noise threshhold level to an acceptable level. Calibration takes only a second and should be performed anytime a new voice command session is started, or anytime the sound level of the operating environment changes significantly.

The toolbar provides an on/off switch for voice recognition. It is necessary to set the switch to the **off** position for recording or playing back .WAV sound files, since working with files isn't possible while the recognition features are active. Up and down arrow buttons on the toolbar simplify navigating through the active command list directly below them.

Clicking on the toolbar button with the capital *A* displays the Language menu. This menu provides options for tailoring the user and command lists, as well as for accessing the training window. The three selections available from this menu are Edit commands, Train commands, and Edit user.

The Edit User screen handles all of the administrative functions for users including the ability to switch active users, rename a user file, create new user files, or delete those no longer required.

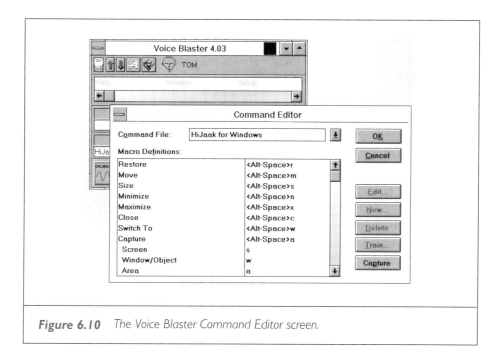

Figure 6.10   *The Voice Blaster Command Editor screen.*

Voice Blaster can capture the top-level commands for all applications, but due to the variation in software applications, it can't always detect the commands that are deeply imbedded in a program. The Command Editor adds the additional commands that aren't automatically captured by the Voice Blaster software. It also edits the commands for maximum flexibility with the way you work. To use the **Edit**, **New**, **Delete**, and **Train** buttons in the Command Editor window, a command must first be selected by highlighting it with a mouse click.

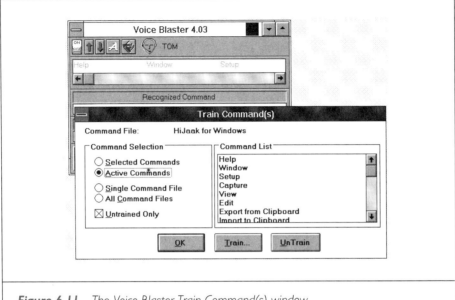

Figure 6.11 *The Voice Blaster Train Command(s) window.*

The Train Command(s) menu selection enables you to work with individual commands or groups of commands by providing you with command selection options. The choices include:

— **Selected commands**—Those highlighted in the command list.

— **Active commands**—Only the commands shown in the active command list of the main window.

— **Single command file**—A vocabulary file for an application.

— **All command files**—This includes all of the commands from all of the known applications.

When you have made your command selection(s), simply click on the **Train** button to begin the training process.

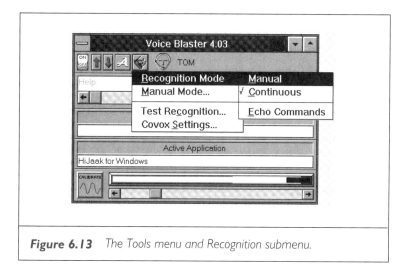

Figure 6.12   *The Train Command screen of the Voice Blaster.*

Depending on your command selections, Voice Blaster will present you with command words that you will train. Training consists of clicking on the **Start** button and speaking the target word into the microphone according to the screen prompts. When the word is successfully trained, the software presents you with the next word to train, which is again instituted by clicking on the **Start** button. When the training session is completed the screen returns to the main Voice Blaster display. Once the vocabularies are trained, they should not require any further attention.

Figure 6.13   *The Tools menu and Recognition submenu.*

The Configuration and Fine Tuning Menu is accessed by clicking on a button in the toolbar that looks like a Swiss Army knife. From this menu, you can tell the Voice Blaster how the sound should be monitored (either continuously or on demand) and when to look for commands in the Manual Mode. Testing for commands that have been trained can also be accessed from this menu, as well as tailoring the settings for sound input to customize them for your voice and environment.

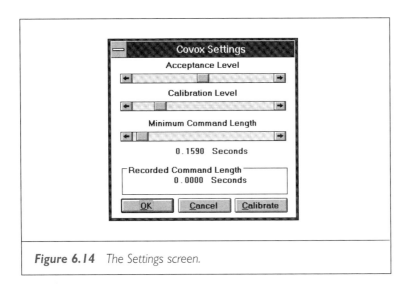

Figure 6.14   *The Settings screen.*

The Configuration and Fine Tuning Menu also provides a selection for adjusting the Voice Blaster's settings through the use of sliders that are moved with the mouse.

The Acceptance Level slider adjusts the accuracy level for command recognition. When the slider control is positioned at the left of the scale, your pronunciation of each repetition during the training session must be very exact for the iteration to be accepted. You will also have to be very close to these original pronunciations when issuing a verbal command for it to be recognized and accepted. Moving the slider to the right permits more latitude in pronunciation variations—it is also even possible for more than one user to issue commands that can be recognized with the slider all the way to the right. The optimal setting for you depends on how consistent your pronunciations were during training, as well as when you issue the spoken commands during work sessions. The test recognition function is a great aid in adjusting the acceptance level for optimum recognition with your voice.

A slider is provided for adjusting the calibration level manually, although the calibration can be set automatically for your environment by clicking on the **Calibration** button at the lower-left corner of the main Voice Blaster window. The adjustment slider changes the setting to something other than the one set automatically by the software, which may be useful in extremely noisy situations or those where the sound levels are subject to abrupt changes.

A third slider is provided to adjust the minimum command length, which is the shortest length a word can be for recognition as a command by the system. Move the slider to the right to increase the minimum length, move it to the left to decrease it. The default setting should work best for most applications and situations.

The Covox Voice Blaster works very well with all of the Sound Blaster-compatible sound cards I have used it with, and Covox's ongoing development efforts are geared toward continually refining the recognition capabilities of the product. The company provides its latest driver and utility software versions on its BBS, which can be downloaded by users. The Covox BBS line is (503) 342-4135.

Glossary

acceptance level   A tolerance level outside of which a voice template will not be considered for recognition purposes. (See *recognition threshhold*.)

acoustic model   A pattern or template of the sound pattern of a word or phrase that is the average of spoken samples taken from a broad range of speakers. Acoustic models are usually used for broad-based recognition systems that use limited vocabularies and do not normally require training by individual speakers.

action button	An area of the screen in a graphical environment that usually looks like a button or pad. Clicking on the button with the mouse causes an action (such as continue, quit, retry, etceteras) to start, hence its name.
applet	An informal term used to describe a small application or utility program, usually a component of a larger application or utility, running under the Windows graphical environment.
background noise level	Also called the *ambient noise level*, it refers to any noise extraneous to the spoken command in a voice control system.
dialog box	A special window displayed by the system or application to solicit a response from the user in a graphical environment. Dialog boxes are commonly used to provide a user with the opportunity to cancel an action or continue with it.
dynamic updating	A means of immediately implementing any changes to the current environment that are made by the user or as a result of a process initiated by the user. Examples of dynamic updating include the immediate addition of a newly-added command to the active words list in an for recognition, or an update of the current disk directory automatically as soon as a file is added or deleted.
isolated word	A voice command that has a silent pause before and after it that aids the recognition system in determining the beginning and end of the command for comparison to its internal recognition templates.
recognition template file	A file that contains the voice pattern of an individual. The template is used for comparing current spoken words with those stored in the template for purposes of validating the user's access or for purposes of recognition. Templates of specific spoken commands used for recognition are called *recognition training templates*.

recognition threshhold	The limits of a recognition template to recognize a spoken word. Some voice command systems permit adjusting the threshhold to widen it for a broader range of recognition among multiple users, or tighten it to recognize the precise speech patterns of a specific user.
Sound Blaster-compatible	Any internal sound card or external audio device that is functionally compatible with software applications designed for the Creative Labs Sound Blaster series of sound cards.
speaker dependent	Any voice-recognition system that depends on matching speech patterns of the speaker against voice templates stored in the system. Speaker dependent systems are trained to recognize and respond only to the voices of specific users rather than the general populace. (See *speech recognition* and *voice recognition*.)
speaker independent	Any speech-recognition system that uses averaged acoustic models and responds to any speaker whose voice falls in its preset recognition threshhold. (See *speech recognition* and *voice recognition*.)
speech recognition	The ability of a computer to understand the spoken word for the purpose of receiving commands or data input from the speaker. The term *speech recognition* is generally used to describe systems capable of understanding limited vocabularies from a broad range of people, as opposed to voice recognition, which is trained to recognize and respond only to the voices of specific individuals. (See *voice recognition*.)
training	The process of recording the speech pattern of a command, or template, for use in recognition by a voice command system.
transparent device	A device that performs its own tasks, usually while sharing a resource such as a system port, without affecting or impeding the operation of any other component in

the system. During use, a transparent device is said to be "invisible" to the user, since the usage is occurring without the user's knowledge or intervention.

user interface
The point at which the user and the elements in a computer system connect and communicate. Different types of hardware user interfaces include the keyboard, the mouse, and the joystick. Software user interfaces include drop-down menus, point-and-click operation, action buttons, and dialog boxes. Voice and speech recognition are also user interfaces that permit the spoken word to cause the computer to execute commands or accept data input.

voice macro
A series of keystrokes that are entered when a voice control system "hears" and recognizes a spoken command.

voice control
A blanket term to generally describe any product, application, or situation that can be controlled through spoken utterances and can apply to speech or voice recognition technologies.

voice recognition
The ability of a computer to identify the voice of a speaker as an authorized individual. Voice recognition has several applications in addition to receiving commands and data input. It can also be used as a security medium that only allows access to the system for authorized individuals whose voice patterns, stored in templates, match those of the current speaker. (See *speech recognition*.)

LESSON SEVEN:

Let the Games Begin

- How games started the aural revolution for PCs
- An interview with George 'The Fat Man' Sanger, the "godfather" of music for PC games
- Capsule reviews of twelve outstanding games with sound

From Beeps to the Big Time

Using an IBM PC or a clone was a silent activity aside from the audible clicks of the keyboard and the occasional beep of the puny internal speaker when Big Blue introduced the first IBM Personal Computer. Since the machine was intended to do serious, business-oriented tasks, it wasn't given any sound capabilities to speak of.

Before very long, however, some enterprising folks with vision and time on their hands devised games for the PC that were similar in appearance and principal to such coin-operated favorites as *Pong*, *Space Invaders*, and *PacMan*. Clearly, the PC was capable of doing more than number crunching and processing words, but it still came up short in the audio department. While software was indeed capable of producing oscillated signals and sending them to the machine's speaker to the point that simple melodies could be played, the PC was basically impotent when it came to sound.

Covox, Ad Lib, and Creative Labs were among the first companies to realize the vast potential for adding audio capabilities that the PC platform presented, and each of these companies set out to achieve different ends.

Covox concentrated primarily on digital sampling and playback (as well as voice recognition). Ad Lib focused its attention on musical applications. Creative Labs combined digital sampling and playback with FM-based music and sound synthesis and, in so doing, established what was to become the *de facto* standard for PC audio in the DOS environment.

The Creative Labs SoundBlaster card provided a rich aural palette for software developers and end users alike. The SoundBlaster's digital sampling capabilities and Yamaha YM3812 (OPL2) 11-voice synthesizer chip attracted the attention of game programmers. The fact that the card was also equipped with a combination joystick/MIDI port made it an instant hit with the growing PC user base interested in playing computer games and the fringe MIDI users.

The SoundBlaster broke new ground and achieved a dominant market position. Having undergone continual refinement, the card's current ultimate form is the SoundBlaster 16 ASP, reviewed (with other SoundBlaster models) in Lesson 4. The SoundBlaster started the sound revolution for PCs, and the rest is history.

Game soundtracks that consisted of beeps and boops only a few years ago have progressed to elaborate sonic tapestries that very often combine sampled real-world sounds and voices with FM-based sound effects and MIDI music and/or CD audio. And just as the SoundBlaster and its successors have improved the sound of games, the VGA and SVGA monitors have made the imagery better, too, with outstanding animation, fast action, and complex scenarios. The combination of sight and sound possible on a modern PC equipped with a sound card goes a long way in creating the illusion of an alternate reality, as millions of computer gamesters will attest.

Best-selling computer games are the result of many talented people working to make their respective elements the best they can be. Producing the music that plays such a major role in games often requires the extraordinary skills of a particularly talented—and somewhat unusual—individual known as "The Fat Man."

The Long, Tall Texan

If this were still the old Wild West, you might come upon a poster nailed up in a conspicuous place that reads:

WANTED: GEORGE A. SANGER alias THE FAT MAN

Wanted for creating compelling musical soundtracks for games, for organizing a band of fellow game music composers known as *Team Fat*, and for marauding the PC game market, leaving their "brand" on over 80 leading games.

I had the opportunity to chat with The Fat Man at length and interview him over the phone, and among the first items I wanted to clear up was this Fat Man moniker, especially since George stands a shade over six feet tall and only weighs about 175 lbs. soaking wet—hardly what you'd call fat.

Within minutes I realized The Fat Man was certainly not going to be at a loss for words, nor can he be accused of being shy, low-key or modest. "Colorful" is an excellent term to describe this guru of game music, right down to the custom-made Nudie "cowboy" suit he wears at public appearances (Nudie is best-known for creating the gold lame' suits worn by Elvis as well as other country and western performers).

Figure 7.1 *George Alistair Sanger, alias The Fat Man, is a colorful figure, especially when wearing his country and western duds.*

During our conversation it became evident in subtle ways that "fat" could be used to describe a number of things associated with George Alistair Sanger—his music often has a "fat" sound thanks to multiple layering and selected voicing. "Fat" can also refer to the size of a bankroll or it can also accurately describe the current position George's music holds in the computer game world, as well as several other meanings. Having cleared the air on that issue, we moved on to other topics, and here's what was said:

Tom: Let's start with your musical background, George. Evidently you're a musician of some skill.

Fat Man: Well, I wasn't always. I had a lot of trouble getting my degree in music because I don't really play an *instrument*—I play guitar. They had a very strict, pretty competitive academic music department at Occidental College in Los Angeles, and I did not play classical style guitar. I played what was sneeringly referred to as "pop"—you know, amplified music. Getting a music degree was one of the most difficult things that I've ever done since I have absolutely no skill at playing the keyboard.

Around that time I saw one of the early digital synthesizers—actually I don't even know if it was digital—and I saw that it had sequencing on it. When I saw it I said wow—if I could get my hands on one of these things I might actually be able to compose, I might actually be able to write some music. But anyway, a lot of time went by between then and now, and at one point not long ago I got my hands on some good sequencing software and found that I really could write. But I was not a musician of recognizable skill before I found my medium, which is a MIDI sequencer.

Tom: What do you use as a MIDI controller for entering your music?

Fat Man: The keyboard works real well for me, and what I do is enter my music in very small amounts at a time—I step-enter it. Then I'll go back and find the parts that, you know—if I'm writing a piece for an elephant—sound the least like an elephant and remove them. So I really sculpt the music without having to depend on executing it in real time. I'm entirely comfortable and it turns out that I am skilled. Creating the music as much as I can in my ear first, before I actually start hitting keys, also gives me an advantage of freshness over people who have a lot of riffs under their fingers.

And because I was a musician for many years without a medium in which to play, I'm driven extremely hard to want to excel and make every note really count, not waste any of my notes. I strive to write pieces that really touch people's hearts, and hopefully ensure my place in the field, because I don't ever want to go back to a position of being one of many guitar players, where there's a huge supply but not much demand.

Tom: You're responsible for producing the music on over 80 games, and you're latest triumph is *The 7th Guest*. The fact that *The 7th Guest* comes on two CD-ROMs is a bit unique, isn't it?

Fat Man: That's right, and it's coming at a time when most other games that are on CD are probably taking up just a little fraction of the available space. I mean, here's a game that was made for the CD medium right from the start—the people at Trilobyte [the game's developers] really tried to pack as much quality into the game as they possibly could.

Tom: Did you create the musical score and the sound effects?

Fat Man: I didn't do the sound effects on that game, I did the musical score.

Tom: Tell me a little more about *The 7th Guest*. How would you describe it?

Fat Man: I think they're calling it a Gothic-horror adventure, it's not very conventional. They're getting a really good response from people who have never played games before as well as from people who are good at *Ultima* and other games. There's a lot of puzzle solving in it, there's a lot of creeping around through a mysterious old house, there's a lot of exploring, that kind of thing.

Tom: The audio that you created for it—how is that stored on the CD-ROM, is that Redbook audio or...

Fat Man: The way that the music is on *The 7th Guest* is really kind of interesting. It was originally meant to be half MIDI and half Redbook, but it turned out that the technological limitations just couldn't *quite* be overcome, so it's all MIDI. But it's General MIDI, and I created a patch set so that I could play the MIDI files through all of the different types of sound cards, in fact I suggested that they do General MIDI in the first place.

We really made a lot of significant advances on *The 7th Guest*, including the creation of a patch bank for AdLib and OPL-compatible cards that we licensed to Yamaha. It's now being distributed with their new Windows drivers for their card, so evidently they consider it the best sound patches they've heard, and they probably are.

There's also about 30 minutes of music on Disc 2 that can be played through your audio CD player. They [Virgin Games] also included a lot of album notes in the instructions, so they treated music with a lot of respect on that project. There are notes on 'what I was thinking when I wrote piece number 6 for *The 7th Guest*'...I'm all over... it's fantastic...

Tom: How did you get involved in programming music for computer games? It's not the ordinary path that most guitarists take...

Fat Man: It goes back to the [Mattel Electronics'] Intellivision and Atari 800. I was pretty convinced around 1978-79—you know, the *Donkey Kong* days—that my mental prime directive was figuring out what made the Beatles so cool. And, trying to be that cool, I realized that one of the things they were doing was blazing trails. And it occurred to me that a rock band could never be the next Beatles, because there are no trails to blaze, all the trees are cut down—there's nothing to hit with your machete. But computer games provided a rich new forest to work on—and in.

A friend by the name of Dave Warhol came by one day and I found out that he was writing games for Intellivision. I asked if there was any way I could get involved, and knowing I wrote music, he asked, "Can you write music for penguins ice skating?" and I said "sure, sure, sure!" I pounded my head a lot, and came up with a 10-second tune, sold it to him, and shortly thereafter Mattel Electronics went out of business—but I got a thousand bucks for a 10-second tune!

Then I got together with a friend of mine's brother-in-law, Paul Edelstein, the guy who wrote *Wayout* for the Atari 800, who had me write a piece for his follow-up for which was basically a better version called *Capture the Flag*. But Sirius software (the game's publisher) went out of business shortly after that. I did that piece but got paid for it much later, in parts. That was it from about 1982 or whenever until about 1989. I took a sabbatical from writing game music and went to work at Rising Star designing a paint program called *Valpaint*—then they went under, too.

Then I ran into Dave Warhol, my old acquaintance from the computer game business again at my brother Rick's wedding, and he said "What are you up to?" I said, "Well, I write custom music for $79.95 per tune. It started out at $49.95 and when I get busy enough so that I can't do anything else, I'll raise my price. This year's goal is a four-figure income!"

So he said, "Well that's great," and he hired me to do a bunch of work since he was a very busy Nintendo game producer. His company, Realtime Associates, put me to work on *Dick Tracy* for Nintendo, and *Total Recall*, and some other things.

What really kicked it off into high gear was doing the music on *Loom* for Lucasfilm games, then *Wing Commander* for Origin.

Tom: Which projects were responsible for putting you on the map, so to speak?

Fat Man: Lightning has struck three times with *Loom* and *Wing Commander* and *The 7th Guest*, and I guess *Star Trek: 25th Anniversary* is a big monster and *Ultima Underworld* was big, so we've had a lot of real hits, and for a while we had five games on *Computer Gaming World's* top ten best selling games, so things have come a good long way.

I did a lot of other things along the way: I went to USC film school, had a band, designed some software, wrote a cartoon book about sheep, and a series of articles about producing bands. I got some brand-name gigs doing audio engineering in L.A., and scored some films and TV shows. But now when someone comes to me with a film score offer, no matter how tempting it is, it doesn't make sense for me to consider taking the job. Everything I do with the game business keeps me at the cutting edge, puts me in a position where I'm in the future of entertainment rather than dwelling on the past. Everything that I do in computer games is actually my career. I'm not using this as a stepping stone, and none of the guys in Team Fat are using it as a stepping stone to get somewhere else.

Tom: So this is where it's at? This is where you want to be?

Fat Man: Yeah, yeah this is what we do.

Tom: What do you think the accessibility of MIDI is going to do to the music market in general and, what do you think it's going to do to the musical-scores-for-games market that you are finding to be so lucrative yourself right now?

Fat Man: I think that the supply of musicians compared to the demand is absolutely ridiculous already, and it'll just get a little more ridiculous. I think its major effect, though, is that people will have a chance to express themselves artistically, which is great. People will be making music, dealing with notes and rests and MIDI and enjoying themselves. And I really hope that there will be a realization that you don't have to make money on music for music to be a good thing.

I think that there's less of a supply and demand problem in my field right now than there is in the rest of the music industry. But, still, if there's anything else you can do besides music for money, you should do it. And if you can do music, you definitely ought to do music, but not for money—you ought to do it for your friends, for people who want to hear it—find a place where your music is needed and wanted and enjoyed. Our artistic philosophy for Team Fat is to touch people's hearts, pull their heart strings, and make music that is appropriate to the game.

Figure 7.2   *The Fat Man logo, shown above, is being widely used on packages of games that utilize his music to make them more readily identifiable. Could this be the start of FatMan-ia?*

Twelve Outstanding PC Game Titles—A Quick Look (and Listen)

With so many excellent recreational products on the market for PCs and more being released every day, it is virtually impossible to review or even list them all here, but here are capsule reviews of a dozen noteworthy games with sound that really stand out in the crowd.

Title:	**The 7th Guest**	*Suggested retail:*	**$99.99**
Publisher:	**Virgin Games**	*Media:*	**Two CD-ROMs**

Without a doubt, *The 7th Guest* is the most ambitious recreational title yet released for IBM compatible PCs, and has been called the first PC game to tap the true potential of CD-ROM-based gaming. The fact that *The 7th Guest* comes on two CD-ROMs gives credence to these statements.

The graphics and full-motion video of the live actors, specially cast for the game, take full advantage of SVGA resolution and a 256-color palette making it a treat for the eyes as well as for the ears.

The scenario is a 22-room haunted house the user must explore. Along the way you'll encounter six guests each of whom speaks to you. Outstanding sound effects and digital speech make you feel as though you're actually trekking through this old mansion. The owner of the house speaks to you throughout the game, particularly when you encounter one of his many puzzles that must be solved to advance in the game.

George "The Fat Man" Sanger and his Team Fat crew members produced the musical soundtrack, which is written to take full advantage of the General MIDI capabilities of sound cards that support this standard. The second CD contains about a half-hour of excellent original songs composed for the game and these can be played on a home CD player—a nice touch, since the music is really good!

Title:	**Alone in the Dark**	*Suggested retail:*	**$59.95**
Publisher:	**I-Motion**	*Media:*	**Floppy disk**

Thrills and chills await you inside a house filled with eerie sounds and creepy creatures in this virtual adventure inspired by the works of H.P. Lovecraft that provides the player with a third-person point of view.

The game utilizes a sound card's FM synthesizer for the music, and it is used effectively in most places throughout the game. Sound effects are also quite prevalent throughout the story line, with all on-screen objects and actions having the actual sounds they would have in real life. For example, you hear the sound of your own footsteps on the creaking floor as you "walk" across the room, there are painful cries when being hit by one of the monsters, the sounds glass breaking, gunshots, and so forth impart the feeling of realism and give the game additional dimension. The music and sound effects can also be muted for silent play if desired, and the game's graphics, animation, and story line are all top notch.

Spontaneous, unexpected occurrences keep the suspense high since there's no telling what's waiting around the next corner or behind the next door. If you enjoy games that put you on the edge of your seat, then *Alone in the Dark* is definitely going to be your cup of tea.

Title: **Monopoly Deluxe for Windows** *Suggested retail:* **$49.99**
Publisher: **Virgin Games** *Media:* **Floppy disk**

This perennial favorite board game has successfully made the transition to the PC for both the DOS and Windows environments, and the Windows version takes full advantage of an installed sound card.

In addition to excellent graphics and superb animation on everything from each player's place marker to the rolls of the dice, sound is what makes *Monopoly Deluxe* a refreshing and most enjoyable recreational software product.

All of the original rules and board layout have been preserved in the computer version, but there are added enhancements as well. For example, the "man with the mustache" rolls the dice for each player and a small text window keeps a log of the gameplay for reference.

The audio quality is excellent, and although there isn't any music there is still plenty of sound. Some of the audio "gems" of this title include the fast-talking voice of an auctioneer when a piece of property is up for sale, a locomotive's whistle-toot whenever a railroad is landed upon, a splash whenever you land on the Water Works and much, much more.

Monopoly Deluxe for Windows elevates an old-time favorite board game to a new multimedia level that's sure to make it a classic in the electronic format as well.

Title:	**Populous II**	*Suggested retail:*	**$49.95**
Publisher:	**Electronic Arts**	*Media:*	**Floppy disk**

Truly a game for those who enjoy power trips, *Populous II* has the player create a "deity" endowed with supreme power over the lives and landscapes of the citizens inhabiting this fantasy universe. The player's deity must compete with Olympian gods with the overall objective of conquering the hundreds of worlds that comprise the game.

The graphics are excellent, especially when viewed and played on an SVGA system, and some of the animated sequences, though sparsely sprinkled throughout the game, are quite eye-catching.

Though *Populous II* doesn't have any musical score, it does supply a good amount of digital sound, some of which may bring about a chuckle or two with its humorous twists. For example, the plague option (one of the deity's powers) causes vultures to hover over the infected citizenry of your opponent's land, squawking loudly while awaiting their death.

Title:	**Eight Ball Deluxe**	*Suggested retail:*	**$59.95**
Publisher:	**Amtex Software Corp.**	*Media:*	**Floppy disk**

If pinball is your penchant, you'll love *Eight Ball Deluxe*. Amtex, a leading developer and publisher of pinball games for IBM and Macintosh PCs, has outdone itself with *Eight Ball Deluxe*, and if you have a sound card installed in your system you're in for a real treat.

Looking as good or better than the original coin-operated classic, *Eight Ball Deluxe* makes full use of the 256-color VGA palette and provides changeable options including the inclination of the playfield and the bumper voltage (which changes the rebound action of the balls).

Though there's no music in *Eight Ball Deluxe*, there is plenty of superb-quality digital sound for everything from the ball rolling through the wooden channel after being released, to a man's voice telling you to "shoot the eight ball, corner pocket" once you've "sunken" all the rest.

Eight Ball Deluxe is just what you need to keep those "crazy flipper fingers" busy.

| *Title:* | **Chess Maniac 5,000,000,001** | *Suggested retail:* | **$59.95** |
| *Publisher:* | **Spectrum Holobyte** | *Media:* | **CD-ROM** |

I could start this off by telling you that Chess Maniac 5,000,000,001 is a most unusual computer chess simulation, but that would be like calling the Space Shuttle just another kind of glider. So I'll get right to the more accurate descriptors for this game: it's lewd, crude, bawdy, ribald, uproarious, and hilarious. It is a safe bet that you've never played chess like this before.

The influence of National Lampoon's twisted humor is felt throughout Chess Maniac starting with the fact that the pieces fight when capturing one another. A capture can result in something as simple as a pie in the face or as harsh as being bloodily impaled by a broadsword.

While the animation, graphics, and on-screen antics alone more than justify the purchase of Chess Maniac, the real treat is the game's soundtrack, and sound is everywhere in this game. From the opening credit displays which have a "Chess Maniac Rap" accompaniment to the voice of Hal (the computer from 2001) that narrates the game's movements, to the "Nyah, nyah, nyah" taunts after you lose a piece, this game is an assault on the eardrums that will evoke guffaws from even the most jaded computer gamer.

Oh, yes—I should mention, on a more serious note, that it is also an outstanding chess program that provides plenty of play options and levels. It's a real treasure that you'll enjoy for a long time to come.

| *Title:* | **Might and Magic: Clouds of Xeen** | *Suggested retail:* | **$69.95** |
| *Publisher:* | **New World Computing** | *Media:* | **Floppy disk** |

The Might and Magic series is a long-standing favorite among computer gamers and the latest additions to the series continue on in the tradition and theme of the original storylines, which date all the way back to the early days of the Apple II!

Might and Magic takes an inter-connected approach to adventure game sequels, building on the experiences and knowledge from having played earlier installments to aid in playing and solving the current adventures. If you elect to install the sequel programs on the same hard drive, you're given the option to create the World of Xeen, which melds the two games (*Clouds of Xeen* and *Darkside of Xeen*) together to produce a third storyline.

Speech and digitized sound is used generously throughout the game, and the graphics and animation are first-rate throughout. If you're looking for an adventure game that you can sink your teeth into, *Clouds of Xeen* is a good one to start with. And as your skills and familiarity with Xeen builds, you'll undoubtedly want to get the *Darkside of Xeen*, reviewed next.

Title: **Might and Magic: Darkside of Xeen**   *Suggested retail:* **$69.95**
Publisher: **New World Computing**   *Media:*   **Floppy disk**

Darkside of Xeen is the other sequel for the Might and Magic series, and it makes the perfect companion product for *Clouds of Xeen*. As mentioned in the *Clouds* review, you can join these two latest sequels together to form the *World of Xeen*, which requires the player to travel between both games to solve the final quest. This third adventure even has its own end-of-game sequence, and the games can also be played individually as well if so desired.

Like *Clouds*, *Darkside of Xeen* has excellent graphics and wonderful digital sound. All of the audio takes its toll on the amount of hard drive space required, however. Thirty-five megabytes of free disk space is required to load the game.

Aside from the hefty hard disk space requirements, the *Darkside of Xeen* and its sister title, *Clouds of Xeen*, are a real treat for PC users who enjoy the adventure game genre.

Title: **Prince of Persia II**   *Suggested retail:* **$69.95**
Publisher: **Broderbund**   *Media:*   **Floppy disk**

Another long-time favorite of gamers from the olden days of Apple II computing, *Prince of Persia* made a very successful transition to the IBM platform in the recent past and this sequel to the original adds lots of additional new scenery and great sound to this timed adventure game.

You're given approximately 70 minutes to complete all 15 of the game's levels, which are fraught with hazards, villains, and puzzles throughout. The realistic animation and colorful high-resolution graphics make it easy to forget that you're playing a game, and the count-down timer adds to the urgency of your quest.

The metallic ring of sword blades clashing together, and anguished "aughh" when a character is struck, the dull "thud" a body makes as it falls lifelessly to the floor—all of these sounds and many more are provided with chilling realism that appeal on a visceral level to the blood-lust of virtually anyone who plays it.

Title:	**Betrayal at Krondor**	*Suggested retail:*	**$69.99**
Publisher:	**Dynamix**	*Media:*	**Floppy disk**

A third-person perspective gives you a commanding view of the action and storyline of *Betrayal At Krondor*, a role-playing adventure that can provide over 100 hours of wandering through the terrain of the game.

Using standard VGA resolution (320 x 200 x 256), the graphics are better than you'd expect in this video mode and the game has above-average playability. The sonic portions of the game are truly noteworthy, however, with music setting the moods and accentuating game sequences like battles.

For example, you'll hear subtle passages of "traveling" music while you wander the countryside, which might surprisingly be interrupted with a shout of "Halt there!" voiced by a nonplaying character who demands a conversation with you. Elements like this give *Betrayal At Krondor* a persona all its own and an appeal that's hard to resist.

The voicing selections for the music are excellent, making use of low-pitched horns, organs, and flutes to carry the melodies—even into battle. The music gives the game an earthy, mortal feel that synthesized sounds wouldn't work well for.

This game provides uncountable hours of enjoyment for the role-playing game novice as well as for the most experienced of computer adventurers.

Title:	**Amazon Guardians of Eden**	*Suggested retail:*	**$69.95**
Publisher:	**Access Software**	*Media:*	**Floppy disk**

Access Software's Realsound technology makes it possible for gamers who don't have sound cards installed in their PCs to hear the audio contained in *Amazon* by routing the digitized sound through the PC's speaker. While that's better than no sound at all, it's nothing compared to the treat you're in for if you do have a sound card in your machine. *Amazon* literally comes alive when heard through a SoundBlaster or similar device.

If it is gore you seek, then you'll find opportunities for it frequently in the Amazon. Some of the scenes are gory to the point of being brutal (such as a shot of your character's face completely stripped of its skin as the result of a piranha attack after falling into a lake). However, a red flashing "Shock Warning!" message is displayed before each gory scene, so there's ample warning and time to avert your eyes if you don't want to view such explicit scenes.

The digital speech is synchronized to the movements of the on-screen characters, and the game has some interesting music that ranges from "thriller" scores to jazzy passages. Currently available only on magnetic media, *Amazon* may become available on CD-ROM by the time you read this.

Title: **X-Wing**   *Suggested retail:* **$69.95**
Publisher: **LucasArts**   *Media:*   **Floppy disk**

A sound smorgasbord is what you'll get with *X-Wing* from LucasArts, a direct result of the innovative company's I-Muse (interactive music) system. Spectacular sound coupled with fast-paced action makes this game a natural both for thrill seekers and for those who demand a strong and continued challenge level.

The I-Muse system is quite unique and it pioneers a new area in computer gaming sound tracks. The I-Muse system plays music that fits the current "mood" of the game's scenario, and your actions have a direct influence on the music you'll hear. For example, when things are calm at the start of a mission the music is low-key and sedate as well. The music picks up immediately when the first laser blast comes your way and builds to complement the activity of the ensuing battle. A triumphant fanfare is played when you take out an enemy fighter, and messages at the bottom of the screen keep you posted on what's happening in the battle—although you can get a pretty good handle on it all just by the music!

There's more to *X-Wing* than music, however. There's an incredible store of voices and sounds digitized from all three of the *Star Wars* movies, and all of the characters from the films are here as well—with speaking parts, no less!

If you enjoy *Star Wars* films, you're a natural to enjoy X-Wing as well. It's great family fun on the PC.

LESSON EIGHT:
MIDI—The Musical Instrument Digital Interface

An introduction to MIDI:

- What it is and what it can do

- The General MIDI standard

- Some noteworthy MIDI devices

MIDI Here, MIDI There, MIDI Everywhere

If you've ever attended a live rock, pop, new age, fusion, or even jazz music concert you've most likely experienced MIDI output first-hand, perhaps without even realizing it. Moreover, it is virtually impossible to listen to any contemporary musical recording that uses electronic or amplified instruments without MIDI playing some role in the production. MIDI is all around us in the musical world, and that's no exaggeration.

MIDI, which is an acronym for *musical instrument digital interface*, has been in existence almost as long as personal computers themselves. The MIDI specification was developed as a cooperative effort among major manufacturers of electronic musical instruments in the early 1980s, with the objective of permitting musical instruments of different brands to communicate with each other.

Some additional benefits that MIDI delivers is the ability to synchronize music precisely with film and video, cueing tape decks, digital mixers, and other recording studio gear to start and stop together and, most importantly, permitting complete control of numerous "tracks" and several MIDI-compatible instruments via a single personal computer. There are lots of other benefits as well, like letting a "hunt-and-peck" musician assemble complete musical scores of complex arrangements on a note-by-note basis, performing automatic tempo corrections, and more. But before we get into the advanced features and capabilities of MIDI, let's examine in more detail just what MIDI is and how it is able to do all that it does.

MIDI: A Control Medium

It is important that we dispel any misconceptions you may have that MIDI signals carry audio data—they do not. MIDI signals transmit control information only—no sound! Since MIDI is, by definition, a digital interface, this control information is in binary data format consisting of ones and zeros that can be processed by the host computer or any other digital MIDI devices that are connected.

MIDI control data is sent in *words* (or bytes) that, collectively, can be called *messages*. MIDI messages typically consist of one or more words that include a status byte and one or two data bytes. For example, a status byte might be a "note on" message (such as *play this note now*); the first data byte could be the pitch register

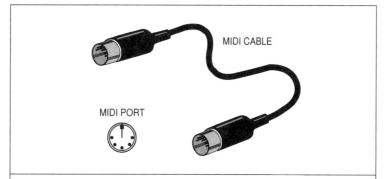

Figure 8.1 *MIDI uses cables outfitted with 5-pin DIN connectors at each end that fit into the MIDI ports on various devices. The information transmitted through these cables and ports is control data only—no audio signals are carried by MIDI.*

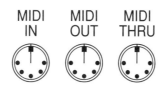

Figure 8.2 *The port layout commonly found on MIDI interfaces and MIDI devices is shown above. MIDI IN receives information from other devices, MIDI OUT sends information to other equipment, and MIDI THRU duplicates the MIDI IN information for pass-along use by any other connected MIDI devices. MIDI THRU is an optional port not found on all MIDI devices.*

(such as Middle C); the second data byte could be the volume register (such as play it loudly); and additional data bytes could provide more information regarding this particular note including *vibrato, velocity, timbre, pitch-bending* and other details.

These MIDI messages can be categorized as either *channel* messages or *systems* messages. MIDI instruments provide 16 channels for data transmission. Each channel can carry its own separate and distinct messages over the same cable, thus making it possible to play different musical parts on the same instrument or control different MIDI instruments simultaneously. A transmit channel carries the messages sent from the MIDI instrument, while a receive channel carries messages from the host PC to the MIDI instrument.

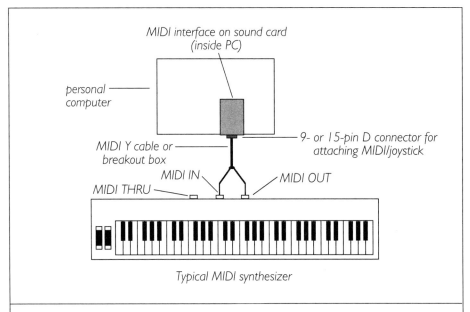

Figure 8.3 *A basic MIDI setup is illustrated above. Most sound cards supporting MIDI utilize either a MIDI breakout box or a "Y" cable for connecting external devices such as synthesizer keyboards.*

System messages are "broadcast" to all components connected to a MIDI system, rather than being restricted to any specific channel or channels. This provides an efficient way of issuing system control information to several instruments simultaneously.

In MIDI jargon, virtually all messages are called *events*, and they include playing a note, sending a program change, changing the panning or volume, or virtually any other type of action.

MIDI also makes it possible for several devices to be interconnected (called *daisychaining*) and all controlled by one computer. In such setups, the computer is referred to as the *master device* and all MIDI devices connected are called *slaves*.

MIDI devices can also be daisychained without using a computer as the control device. In such arrangements, the principal device (the first one in the daisychain) is the master and all others are slaves. Control messages are sent via the master device.

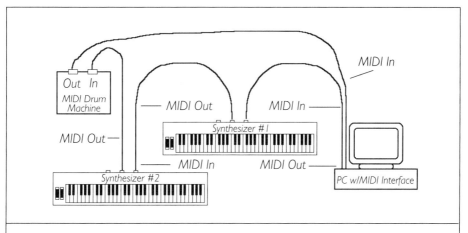

Figure 8.4   *This illustration shows two synthesizers and a drum machine daisychained to the PC's MIDI interface. Note that the MIDI thru ports on the two synthesizers are bypassed in this arrangement and only the MIDI in and out ports are utilized. The overall effect is a big loop that starts and finishes with the master device, the PC.*

MIDI Interface Types

To control and communicate with MIDI instruments and special-effects devices from a PC, it's necessary to have a hardware interface to handle the data communication chores between devices. Two major MIDI interface types are currently available for handling these tasks. Other proprietary interfaces have also appeared on the market from time to time, but we'll just cover with the two major standards in popular use: the Roland MPU-401-compatible interfaces and the UART-compatible interfaces.

The Roland MPU-401 Standard

The original MPU-401 MIDI interface was developed by Roland (a major developer and manufacturer of music synthesizers and sound processors) for use with PC-compatible and Apple II series computers. Although it also has a "dumb" (UART) mode, the 401 can process MIDI data by virtue of its own on-board CPU.

This processor permits the 401 interface to do time-stamping and some of the other general housekeeping chores necessary for keeping track of data, rather than relying on the host computer to handle these routines. MPU-401 had been the accepted standard for MIDI interfacing in the early days when PCs with only 256K or 512K of RAM and slow 8086 and 80286 microprocessors were common. The popularity of MPU-401-compatible interfaces has fallen off substantially since the advent of 80386- and 80486-based machines. Two reasons for its decline in popularity are that it costs more to manufacture (because of its more elaborate circuitry and CPU chip) than the UART interface, and today's high-speed, muscular CPUs can easily handle the housekeeping overhead of MIDI management, aided by megabytes of RAM as the standard PC configuration has continued to evolve.

The UART Standard

Consisting of a basic serial communications chip, a timer chip, and a few other circuit components, the UART (which stands for *universal asynchronous receive and transmit*) interface functions like a "dumb" terminal by merely passing MIDI information in and out of the respective ports without performing any time-stamping or other processing. All of these functions are handled by the host computer and the software it is running, rather than by the interface itself.

Basically acting as an intermediary between the computer and the MIDI devices attached to it, the UART interface doesn't need it's own CPU and, therefore, results in a less complicated, less costly board. UART interfaces have soared in popularity and are now the predominant PC-to-MIDI interface type because of their reduced manufacturing cost. It is also popular because writing software that supports them is simplified: The program only has to deal with one CPU—the computer's—instead of two with the MPU-401 standard (the one in the computer and the one on the 401 MIDI interface board).

Points in Common

Despite their differences, both the 401 and UART interfaces found on sound cards as well as the internal, stand-alone versions have several points in common. Both require installation in an expansion slot inside the PC; both have jumpers that determine the port address and interrupts for the card's functions; both provide means of connecting the control cables (usually a 15-pin or a 9-pin D-type connector); and both require some sort of software program to make them respond to the host PC's commands.

The Cable Connection

MIDI cables are used to complete the connection between the host PC and the external MIDI device(s). Some MIDI interfaces come with a Y-connector for attaching the required cables, while others utilize a breakout box to accommodate the cable connections. Few sound cards provide either, and a separate purchase is generally required to get these items.

A Y-connector cable has one end fitted with either a 9-pin or a 15-pin connector that mates with a matching jack on the interface or sound card. The two remaining ends of the Y have five-pin DIN jacks on them. One jack is assigned to MIDI IN functions and connects to the musical instrument's MIDI OUT port. The DIN jack on the other side of the Y handles the MIDI OUT functions and connects to the instrument's MIDI IN port. By successive coupling (*daisychaining*) of the OUT to IN ports, several instruments can be connected to the host computer (remember, there are 16 available MIDI channels, so there's lots of control flexibility and power on tap here).

A MIDI breakout box is generally a small plastic case that has a cable leading from it that attaches to the interface or sound card connector. Ports designated as MIDI IN and MIDI OUT (and also often MIDI THRU) are provided on the breakout box for plugging standard 5-conductor MIDI cables into it for attaching external devices.

External MIDI interfaces are rapidly growing in popularity, spurred on by the acceptance and wide-spread use of laptop and notebook PCs. These external interfaces are available from several manufacturers and connect to either the parallel or serial ports of any PC. They are very convenient to install and use. Some are even self-powered, which makes them truly portable—a big plus for the on-the-road musician who uses MIDI as part of his live performance equipment.

Installing and Configuring An Internal MIDI Interface

If the MIDI interface is integrated into your sound card, it will probably work with the factory default settings without any problem. However, if your PC already has lots of other peripherals installed (such as a hand scanner, a fax board, a CD-ROM interface), there may be a conflict between devices that requires resetting the communication addresses the interface uses. Changing these settings is usually accomplished by changing the position of the jumper caps on the circuit board.

Changing a board's jumpers is a simple matter, easily accomplished with needle-nose pliers, tweezers, or a surgical hemostat if you have one (if you're really dexterous, your fingers will do.) Most MIDI cards and sound cards that support MIDI interfacing use IRQ2 and address port 330. These are usually the default jumper settings made at the factory, and, as noted earlier, work fine in most cases but may conflict with some other device installed in your system. If everything doesn't check out and work as it should using default settings, refer to the installation instructions for your particular MIDI interface or sound card for information on resetting the interrupt and port addresses to resolve any conflicts.

Installing a dedicated internal MIDI interface card is very similar to the procedures for installing a sound card and the process shouldn't take more than a few minutes at most to accomplish. As with any peripheral or add-on card installation, the first step is to unplug the power cord from the PC or wall outlet and disconnect and remove the monitor, keyboard, and any other cables or devices that might impede removing the system cover retaining screws so you can lift off the cover and gain access to your PC's expansion slots.

Once you're inside the PC, select an available expansion slot that permits easy and clear access to the rear panel of the system unit, and remove the screw that retains the chrome blocking plate used to cover the slot opening you've chosen. Being careful to handle the MIDI interface card by only its edges and avoiding contact with any components mounted on it, plug the card into the expansion slot with firm, even pressure until you feel it "seat."

You can now secure the card's mounting bracket with the same screw you removed from the blocking plate. Reinstall the system unit cover, connect your keyboard, monitor, printer, and anything else you removed prior to installation.

Plug the Y cable for your MIDI interface into the D connector on the card at the back of the computer. If you are using a breakout box instead, attach the breakout box's cable to the connector on the card.

Connect the two remaining ends of this Y cable to your MIDI keyboard, drum machine, or other MIDI device using standard 5-pin MIDI hookup cables, or plug the cables into the breakout box.

The proper cable orientation is essential for all MIDI hookups. The cable end labeled MIDI OUT coming from the interface plugs into the instrument's MIDI IN jack and vice-versa. If the correct orientation isn't observed, communication between the PC and the instrument isn't possible.

The General MIDI Standard

Early in MIDI development there was no standard assignment for instrument sounds, so MIDI files created with one type of synthesizer would sound quite different from the original score if played back on another brand of synthesizer. For example, what might be assigned as a violin sound on a Roland MT-32 synthesizer could possibly be a muted trumpet sound when played-back on a Korg or Casio synthesizer. To solve these instrument-assignment inconsistencies, a standard was needed and the General MIDI standard is the result.

General MIDI is an industry-wide system of agreed-upon features that are found on any instrument bearing the General MIDI logo. In simple terms, the General MIDI specification provides guidelines for how the instrument should be set-up.

The great advantage of General MIDI is that if you record a sequence it should sound the same (or at least very similar) no matter what General MIDI module or instrument you play it back through. The Windows operating environment uses the General MIDI instrument assignments for its MIDI mapping.

The General MIDI specifications for devices are as follows:

- A minimum of 24-voice polyphony.
- All voices should respond to velocity.
- Middle C is MIDI note 60.
- General MIDI devices should be capable of responding on all 16 MIDI channels, with each channel capable of playing a changing number of voices (polyphony) using its own program.
- Percussion voices are always located on Channel 10.
- Specific drum sounds are assigned to specific MIDI note numbers.
- The 128 sound programs are stored in a specific order according to the General MIDI sound set (see Table 8.1 on the next page).

- Each channel should respond to continuous controllers 1 (mod wheel), 7 (volume), 10 (pan), 11 (expression), and 123 (all notes off).

- The registered parameter numbers (part of the MIDI continuous controller set) can be used for setting pitch-bend sensitivity and for coarse and fine tuning.

The *General MIDI System, Level 1 Specification* document is published by and available from the International MIDI Association (5316 West 57th Street, Los Angeles, CA 90056) for anyone who wants more information on the General MIDI standard.

Virtually all of the sound boards and audio port products covered in this book that support MIDI are compliant with the General MIDI standard, as shown in Table 8.1.

1. Acoustic Grand Piano	44. Contrabass	87. Lead 7 (fifths)
2. Bright Acoustic Piano	45. Tremolo Strings	88. Lead 8 (bass + lead)
3. Electric Grand Piano	46. Pizzicato Strings	89. Pad 1 (new age)
4. Honky-Tonk Piano	47. Orchestral Harp	90. Pad 2 (warm)
5. Electric Piano 1	48. Timpani	91. Pad 3 (polysynth)
6. Electric Piano 2	49. String Ensemble 1	92. Pad 4 (choir)
7. Harpsichord	50. String Ensemble 2	93. Pad 5 (bowed)
8. Clavi	51. Synth Strings 1	94. Pad 6 (metallic)
9. Celesta	52. Synth Strings 2	95. Pad 7 (halo)
10. Glockenspiel	53. Choir Aahs	96. Pad 8 (sweep)
11. Music Box	54. Voice Oohs	97. FX 1 (rain)
12. Vibraphone	55. Synth Voice	98. FX 2 (soundtrack)
13. Marimba	56. Orchestra Hit	99. FX 3 (crystal)
14. Xylophone	57. Trumpet	100. FX 4 (atmosphere)
15. Tubular Bells	58. Trombone	101. FX 5 (brightness)
16. Dulcimer	59. Tuba	102. FX 6 (goblins)
17. Drawbar Organ	60. Muted Trumpet	103. FX 7 (echoes)
18. Percussive Organ	61. French Horn	104. FX 8 (sci-fi)
19. Rock Organ	62. Brass Section	105. Sitar
20. Church Organ	63. Synth Brass 1	106. Banjo
21. Reed Organ	64. Synth Brass 2	107. Shamisen
22. Accordion	65. Soprano Sax	108. Koto
23. Harmonica	66. Alto Sax	109. Kalimba
24. Tango Accordion	67. Tenor Sax	110. Bagpipe
25. Acoustic Guitar (nylon)	68. Baritone Sax	111. Fiddle
26. Acoustic guitar (steel)	69. Oboe	112. Shanai

27. Electric Guitar (jazz)	70. English Horn	113. Tinkle Bell
28. Electric Guitar (clean)	71. Bassoon	114. Agogo
29. Electric Guitar (muted)	72. Clarinet	115. Steel Drums
30. Overdriven Guitar	73. Piccolo	116. Woodblock
31. Distortion Guitar	74. Flute	117. Taiko Drum
32. Guitar Harmonics	75. Recorder	118. Melodic Tom
33. Acoustic Bass	76. Pan Flute	119. Synth Drum
34. Electric Bass (finger)	77. Blown Bottle	120. Reverse Cymbal
35. Electric Bass (pick)	78. Shakuhachi	121. Guitar Fret Noise
36. Fretless Bass	79. Whistle	122. Breath Noise
37. Slap Bass 1	80. Ocarina	123. Seashore
38. Slap Bass 2	81. Lead 1 (square)	124. Bird Tweet
39. Synth Bass 1	82. Lead 2 (sawtooth)	125. Telephone Ring
40. Synth Bass 2	83. Lead 3 (calliope)	126. Helicopter
41. Violin	84. Lead 4 (chiff)	127. Applause
42. Viola	85. Lead 5 (charang)	128. Gunshot
43. Cello	86. Lead 6 (voice)	

Table 8.1 *The instrument mapping for the General MIDI specification.*

MIDI Software Varieties

Once all of the connections are made, it's time to power up the PC and attached MIDI instrument and install the software. Depending on the sound card or stand-alone MIDI interface you've chosen and its manufacturer, you will have received any of several different MIDI software packages currently available on the market. Very often these are special versions that are designed for and bundled with specific hardware products. Hence, you must follow the software installation instructions specific to the package you're using. Generally speaking, though, you should install the software in its own subdirectory on your hard drive to keep everything orderly and accessible, including your music and "patch" (MIDI sound-settings) files. Virtually every software package also includes some form of test or demo file to make sure the hardware installation and jumpers are properly set.

A few words are in order here about the various types of MIDI software available for creating, storing, playing back and printing your music.

Sequencing programs (or *sequencers*) allow you to record musical passages along with MIDI-specific information. These include channel assignments, voices (the different instrument sounds), vibrato, reverb, and other special effects. Sequencers vary in the amount and scope of features they provide, but virtually all of them allow you to record, edit, and play back your MIDI tracks. Most sequencers also provide some form of "cut-and-paste" utilities to permit you to record a basic section of a tune, copy and modify it, and paste it into another section. By doing this with several musical sequences, it's easy to assemble complete songs.

More full-featured sequencing programs also allow you to insert system and channel event information along with the musical data so that instrument sounds, tempo changes, and other unique events can be included in the composition as well. Sequencers generally permit you to enter your musical data directly from the MIDI instrument or the computer keyboard. As a rule, however, they don't allow hard-copy printing of the musical score.

Simple *composition programs* (or *composers*) are less complex in scope and function in comparison to sequencers. They usually offer only limited composing, editing, and play functions. Some simple composers allow you to compose music through the MIDI instrument, PC keyboard, or a mouse, providing a screen display in true musical notation that looks like actual sheet music with treble and bass clefs.

While not providing all of the gusto and power advanced performing or recording musicians may require, composers are excellent for recreational MIDI uses and provide a means for learning and teaching basic music notation and practices.

Scoring (or *notation programs*) allow you to convert MIDI musical composition files into traditional printed sheet music that can be used by virtually any musician. Some of the more advanced programs permit automatic key transposition, adding lyrics under the staves and other professional features. Most dot-matrix and laser printers are supported by better packages, and most accept standard MIDI files created with virtually any sequencing or composing program. Packages running under Microsoft Windows utilize all of the resources available, including any supported printers attached to the PC.

Patch librarians are software programs that contain pre-defined instrument configurations that can be used as-is or modified. Some patch librarian packages also permit creating custom instrument patches and changing the instrument sounds in the patch itself. For example, some programs may permit you to change the snare drum sound of a preset patch while keeping all of the same cymbal assignments. Others may permit you to "swap" the "power drum" kit for a more mellow-sounding "jazz" drum kit.

Sample librarians provide actual sampled instrument sound patches for downloading to MIDI devices and wavetable-based sound cards to expand the type and number of available instrument sounds.

Music generators are software packages that provide pre-defined accompaniment styles for putting the basic elements of a song together quick and easy. These programs afford some amount of variation in preset patterns, and as with the other MIDI software varieties described above, are covered in more detail in Lesson 11.

Mixer programs are utilities that make modifying MIDI controller information a more manageable task, usually in real-time during playback of a sequence. They are useful for adjusting volume, panning, reverb, and other controls for enhancing playback.

Some Outstanding MIDI Products

Since there are literally scores of dedicated internal and external MIDI interfaces, sequencers, tone generators, and instruments available today, it is not only impossible to cover them all but also beyond the scope of this book.

However, I had the opportunity to use several MIDI products first-hand while researching this subject and also for the production of my own music, and I found these products to be superb examples of what is available.

I've included short reviews of these products here to spotlight their interesting and unique features and capabilities, and it should be noted that many of these products can also be used without a PC. For example, a MIDI keyboard can be connected directly to the Yamaha QY20 sequencer/tone generator module without using a PC. Adding a PC with an interface, however, expands the capabilities of any MIDI setup and permits extensive sequencing, editing, and control of multiple devices, all from one location.

On the following pages are some of the MIDI products I've used and found to be outstanding performers.

Product name: MIDI Maestro   *Suggested retail:* $189.95
Manufacturer: Covox, Inc.   *PC required:*   Yes
Description: Internal PC MIDI interface/software package

Covox's sound/voice cards are covered in Lesson 4, and the Covox SoundMaster II sound card has a built-in MIDI interface which is identical to the MIDI Maestro in features and operation.

The MIDI Maestro package consists of a UART-standard MIDI interface card, 6-foot Y MIDI connecting cable and *64 Track Sequencer* software. It represents a great value for getting into MIDI inexpensively. The powerful *64 Track Sequencer* program has lots of professional features that are usually found in more expensive packages, including 600 pulse-per-quarter note sampling resolution, pull-down menus, keyboard and mouse support, smart (automatic) *quantizing*, and graphic editing of functions like velocity, pitch bend, aftertouch, and controllers.

The package can hold up to nine music files in memory at the same time. Tracks can easily be cut, pasted, spliced, combined, rearranged, and quantized. Standard MIDI files are supported for reading and writing, and files can be exported to all popular scoring/printing programs. The *64 Track Sequencer* software supplied in the package is configured to work with the Covox MIDI interface, but an optional *Pro* version of it also supports the nonCovox MIDI interfaces (MPU-401 standard). Contact Covox for current availability and pricing information on the *Pro* version.

Product name: QY20 Compact Music Processor   *Suggested retail:* $599
Manufacturer: Yamaha   *PC required:*   No
Description: External sequencer/tone generator module

Yamaha's QY20 Music Sequencer is literally a palmtop music production system that features a built-in tone generator, sequencer, and auto-accompaniment capabilities, all integrated into a sophisticated control interface.

This compact device, shown in Figure 8.5, measures about 7.5"L x 4.5"W x 1"D and weighs less than one pound with its six AA alkaline cells installed. The unit can also be powered with the included AC adapter, since battery life is only about six-ten hours under heavy use.

An LCD screen is provided for viewing the controls and settings of various editing and instrument functions. Soft-touch controls are provided, and individual music notes can be entered directly from the QY20's keypad or from any external MIDI controller. MIDI IN and MIDI OUT ports are provided on the unit.

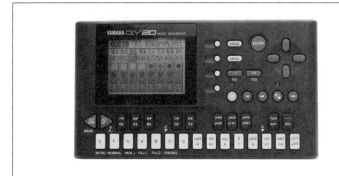

Figure 8.5 *The Yamaha QY20 provides extensive sequencer and tone generator capabilities.*

The QY20 uses Yamaha's AWM (advanced wave memory) technology to deliver 100 voices with outstanding sound quality, and eight different drum kits are featured. A 20-song sequencer is also built into the unit that has a 28,000-note capacity, and 32-note polyphony is supported on both record and playback, so intricate scores aren't a problem for the QY20.

The sequencer features are indeed impressive on the QY20. The sequencer is an eight-track unit divided into two 4-track groups. Tracks one through four are the sequencer tracks, while the remaining four tracks are the accompaniment tracks.

The first four tracks can be used with any of the 100 internal voices or eight drum kits (which provide 100 different voices to choose from) if the user wants to record via the QY20's own two-octave, polyphonic micro keyboard, or from an external keyboard using the MIDI IN connector.

The sequencer provides 100 preset patterns with six sections including Intro, Normal, Variation, Fill 1, Fill 2, and Ending that can be selected and used, as well as the ability to store up to 100 original patterns created by the user. These accompaniment tracks feature the advanced ABC (auto bass chord) accompaniment system by Yamaha which automatically harmonizes the chord and bass tracks according to the chords specified. The 25 preset chords enhance even the most basic of songs, and the QY20 can record in real-time or step mode.

The QY20 is also compliant with the General MIDI standard.

Product name: **Portatone PSR-510**   *Suggested retail:* **$689.95**
Manufacturer: **Yamaha**   *PC required:*   **No**
Description: **External 61-key multitimbral MIDI synthesizer**

The Portatone PSR-510 Electronic Keyboard from Yamaha is literally a one-person electronic orchestra that comes in a box. The features, preset patterns, realistic instrument sounds, and 61 full-sized keys make this instrument a joy to hear and play. And, since it can be powered by batteries or from AC wall current, you can take the Portatone and its music with you when you go—a big plus for the traveling musician.

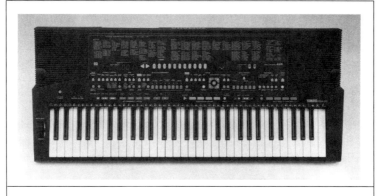

Figure 8.6   Yamaha's PSR-510.

The PSR-510 uses Yamaha's AWM (Advanced Wave Memory) to generate superb sound. Its 128 instrument voices comply with the General MIDI patch specifications and rival those of a live performance, but that's not surprising since they are actual state-of-the-art digital recordings of real instruments. The "orchestra" features acoustic and electric pianos, organs, basses and guitars, brass, woodwinds, strings, and tuned percussion, as well as a complete selection of modern electronic and sampled sounds. You can truly let your imagination run wild with such a smorgasbord of sound literally at your fingertips.

Excellent reverberation capabilities are also built into the PSR-510, giving you a range of eight digital reverb effects with depth adustment. There are also twelve delay-based effects that can give your music additional dimension and animation.

An innovative orchestration control cluster makes it simple to set up a range of split and dual voice configurations, permitting you to play different voices on the left- and right-hand sections of the keyboard or playing dual voices simultaneously over the full range of the keyboard. Single-finger and fingered chord modes are available for the various automatic accompaniment settings, and the unit also has on-board memory storage for songs, chords, voices, multipads, custom accompaniments, and overall control on four separate "pages," so there's plenty of internal storage for your compositions.

MIDI IN and MIDI OUT ports are provided on the PSR-510 and it can receive MIDI data (including velocity messages) over all 16 MIDI channels. It also features dynamic voice allocation for up to 28 notes at once as well as built-in stereo speakers.

The highly-sophisticated Auto Accompaniment section is very easy to use and can make anyone—even the totally tone-deaf—sound like an accomplished professional musician. In addition to offering General MIDI conformity to the GM patch chart, all of your musical creations generated on the PSR-510 can be exported as standard MIDI data to any other MIDI device or your software sequencer; naturally, any other MIDI files can also be played through the PSR-510 as well since it is GM compatible

The PSR-510 is an exceptional MIDI product worth a closer look.

Product name: **Miracle Piano System**   *Suggested retail:* **$479.95**
Manufacturer: **The Software Toolworks**   *PC required:*   **Yes**
Description: **External MIDI keyboard/piano teaching system**

If you've ever wanted to play the piano but didn't have the time or the patience to take lessons, take heart. The Miracle Piano System and your PC are all you need to learn how to "tickle the ivory" while having fun and making music at the same time.

Originally available for the Nintendo Entertainment System, The Software Toolworks has since adapted its Miracle Piano System for use with many popular home and personal computers including IBM-compatibles.

More than merely a keyboard with MIDI capabilities, the Miracle is a self-contained, self-paced instructional system for learning the piano using a personal computer.

The Miracle package contains a 49-key velocity-sensitive keyboard, an AC power supply for the keyboard, a foot pedal for the keyboard, a pair of headphones, an interface cable, manuals, and software. All you do is add a PC and you're ready to begin learning the piano—and making music right from the start!

Figure 8.7   *The Miracle Piano System.*

The Miracle doesn't require an internal expansion slot, since its cable plugs into the serial port of the computer. This makes it ideal for use with a notebook or laptop computer as well as with a desktop PC.

A pair of speakers are built-into the Miracle, so you won't need any external amplification to hear it. A pair of small, in-the-ear headphones are also provided with the unit for private practice sessions.

The Miracle is an excellent way to put some music in your life and many of the leading MIDI software packages support it with special mapping for playback through the Miracle keyboard.

Figure 8.8   *The Recording Screen/Sequencer from the Miracle System shows the current selections for instrument voices, tempo, and volume. The interface resembles the controls of a standard reel-to-reel tape recorder for ease of use.*

Product name: **CBX-T3**   *Suggested retail:* **$449.95**
Manufacturer: **Yamaha**   *PC required:*   **Yes**
Description: **External tone generator module with serial PC interface**

Yamaha's CBX-T3 is a stand-alone tone generator module about the size of an average hard-cover book standing on end (see Figure 8.14 on page 172). The CBX-T3 can also connect to a PC and/or to other MIDI devices for additional flexibility. The CBX-T3 has a total of 192 voices built in (including the 128 voices of the General MIDI Standard), and these can be accessed from its other operational modes. In addition to the General MIDI Level 1 mode, the Yamaha Disk Orchestra/Clavinova mode (a proprietary mode that supports Yamaha's *Disk Orchestra Collection* of music titles) and C/M mode for increased compatibility with popular desktop music systems.

Yamaha's AWM (advanced wave memory) technology is used on the CBX-T3, which endows it with the pristine sounds of the actual instruments that were sampled and stored in its internal ROM. Ten drum and percussion sets are available along with the 192 voices to provide an amazingly rich palette of sounds to work with. The unit is also capable of 28-note polyphony, so even highly intricate passages with multiple voices can be played back, and Yamaha's DSP-based reverberation effect is also provided in the CBX.

Supplied with the CBX module itself is a power adapter for using AC line current, an interface cable, two audio cables, a stereo plug adapter, an owner's manual, and a specially-configured copy of Passport Designs' *Trax* for Windows sequencer software (covered in Lesson 11).

The CBX unit interfaces externally to the PC, using the computer's serial port for communication. The supplied interface cable is outfitted with a 9-pin D connector on the PC side and an 8-pin DIN connector on its opposite end. The DIN connector plugs into the jack provided on the rear of the CBX unit, and MIDI IN, OUT, and THRU connectors are also provided for routing the MIDI signals. Additional connectors are located on the unit's rear for right and left line output as well as for the power supply connector. A three-position slider switch is also located here for selecting host operational modes: MIDI, PC, or Macintosh.

The front of the unit has 1/8 inch miniphone jacks for accepting headphones and audio input. Volume controls are provided for adjusting the audio input level as well as the master volume, and a red LED lets you know when the volume level is at its peak. Three yellow LEDs display the current mode, and 16 green LEDs above them show the active MIDI channel(s) in use. A push-button on/off switch is located on the front at the unit's top.

The installation is simple and quick, requiring only the connection of some cables and loading the software. The software automatically adds the required Yamaha CBX-T3 Serial Driver to the Windows control panel to make the device available for use by the PC. If desired, external MIDI devices can also be connected using the CBX-T3's ports.

The CBX's sound is superb, it is easy to install and use, and is General MIDI compatible, too.

Product name: **X-28H Multitracker**   *Suggested retail:* **$599.00**
Manufacturer: **Fostex**   *PC required:*   **No**
Description: **4-track 8-channel stereo cassette recorder with sync**

While MIDI provides creative freedom, compositional, and arranging possibilities that were never possible before the advent of digital electronics and sound synthesis, there are still times when you will undoubtedly want to use analog devices. Two of these occasions are when you want to add vocal tracks to your otherwise-MIDI compositions and when you want to overdub acoustic sounds on top of the MIDI sounds. The most accessible and affordable device to use for both of these applications is a good multitrack cassette recorder, and you'll be hard-pressed to find a better unit for the money than the Fostex X-28 Multitracker, shown in Figure 8.9.

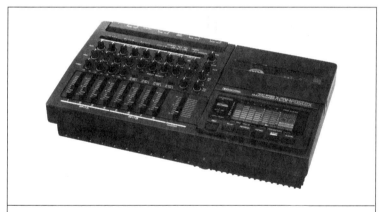

Figure 8.9   *The Fostex X-28H is the perfect analog complement to any MIDI studio.*

The X-28 is particularly attractive to musicians who favor MIDI, since it can accommodate eight inputs (it can actually accept ten inputs if you use the two auxiliary return inputs as well).

Tape sync is the process of using one of the tracks on the X-28H to synchronize operation with a MIDI sequencer, which in turn is used to control several instruments simultaneously. Virtually all of the MIDI sequencer software programs reviewed in Lesson 11 support external sync signals, so the X-28H's tape sync capability can be used to initiate software-based sequencers as well. Synchronization with MIDI devices is provided via an FSK (frequency shift keying) converter.

Since MIDI signals can't be recorded directly onto tape, an FSK-to-MIDI converter is required. This device converts the MIDI clock data from the MIDI sequencer into an FSK signal, which is then recorded to tape. In playback, the FSK signal is converted back into MIDI data for synchronization with the sequencer. Most modern sequencers, rhythm machines, and MIDI controllers have these FSK circuits built-in, but an external converter unit may be required depending on the individual equipment set-up.

Another handy feature of the X-28 is its ability to "punch-in" and "punch-out" for recording portions of tracks using the optional footswitch, and the tape can also be rewound and started using the foot-switch. The Fostex X-28H is a dual-speed machine for the best recording fidelity while maintaining compatibility with prerecorded cassettes. It also has Dolby B noise reduction, a tape memory, 6 LCD meters, and 15% plus/minus pitch control.

Product name: **MIDIMAN Interfaces**   *Suggested retail:* **$99.95-$119.95**
Manufacturer: **Midiman**   *PC required:*   **Yes**
Description: **Internal and External parallel/serial MIDI interfaces**

Midiman's MM-401 is an internal 1/3-size MPU-401-compatible interface card that easily installs in any 8-bit expansion slot. It works with any IBM-compatible PC from an XT-class machine right up through today's fastest 486 configurations.

The MM-401 is the only internal interface available that is backed by a lifetime guarantee, and it comes with $100 of free software including a *System Exclusive Archiver* program, a *MIDI Viewer Channelizer, Diagnostics*, and more. It also has the distinction of being the only 401-compatible interface with an on-board timer. The MM-401's UART mode has an additional timer that can be set via a System Exclusive message. Included with the MM-401 is a Y cable that provides jacks for MIDI IN and MIDI OUT.

Figure 8.10 *The MIDIMAN Portman PC/P (parallel) and PC/S (serial) interfaces are ideal for use with laptop and notebook PCs.*

If you'd prefer a MIDI interface that connects externally, MIDIMAN has this area covered as well. You even have your choice of whether you'd like the interface to connect to the parallel port or one of the PC's serial ports.

The Portman PC/P is the parallel model that attaches to any PC (Centronics) printer port using a standard printer cable. This leaves the serial port free for use of a mouse, a major point to consider with many of the laptop and notebook PC's that only have a single serial port.

The PC/P is not a transparent device, so you won't be able to keep the printer connected simultaneously with the interface (unless you have a second parallel port). A universal Windows driver as well as DOS drivers accompany the interface, and MIDI IN and MIDI OUT ports are provided for connections.

The Portman PC/S is the serial version of the external interface but it attaches to a serial port rather than a parallel port. As with the parallel version, universal Windows and DOS drivers are provided.

Both the PC/P and PC/S have suggested retail prices of $119.95 each and Windows help files for *Cubase*, *Cakewalk*, and *Mastertracks* are included with each. Both versions feature "smart buffering" to take the load off the software, making it ideal for system exclusive dumps.

MIDIMAN's external interfaces are housed in attractive, sturdy metal cases and are guaranteed for life. These external units also come with AC power adapters supplied for some PCs that do not have power available at their ports.

Product name: **MIDIATOR Interfaces** *Suggested retail:* **$119.95-$199.95**
Manufacturer: **Key Electronics** *PC required:* **Yes**
Description: **External parallel and serial MIDI interfaces**

Key Electronics manufactures what it calls "industrial strength" MIDI interfaces, and the products range in appeal to users from those with very basic needs to professionals who need control of up to 128 MIDI channels. Regardless of what your needs are, chances are excellent that there's a MIDIATOR that's right for you.

Figure 8.11   *Key Electronics MS-124 interface.*

The MS-101 is an external-connect serial interface that takes advantage of the programmable PC serial port features to allow full-speed MIDI communication. The MS-101 is housed in a sturdy aluminum case and weighs a mere six ounces. With dimensions of only 1.4 x2.6 x 4.2 inches, it's small and light enough to carry in a shirt pocket to your next MIDI "gig." A 25-pin serial port is located on one side of the interface, while MIDI IN and MIDI OUT ports are located at the opposite end. The MS-101 has a suggested list price of $119.95, and Windows driver software is included. An optional 9/25-pin one-foot serial cable kit is also available for $14.95 additional.

The MS-124 is a multiport MIDI interface that also connects externally using the PC's serial port. The MS-124 features one MIDI IN port and four MIDI OUT ports, each supporting up to 16 MIDI channels, to provide control for a maximum of 64 channels. The interface eliminates the need for additional patchbays, cable plugging, and channel assignment problems. It features totally new digital circuitry to provide maximum tolerance to both MIDI and serial port timing deviations, and Windows multimedia 3.1 driver software is included. The MS-124 carries a suggested list price of $179.95, and available optional extras include an external auxiliary power source ($16.00) and a 1-foot 9/25-pin serial cable kit ($14.95).

Key also offers the MP-128 parallel-connect interface for those MIDI users with "industrial strength" requirements. The MP-128 provides eight independent MIDI OUT ports that deliver a total of 128 channels. As with all other Key interfaces, Windows 3.1 driver software is included. The MP-128 lists for $199.95.

An optional MP-320 kit with dual MIDI IN and SMPTE sync is also available for stand-alone use with laptop, notebook, and other slotless computers. The price of the upgrade kit is $119.95, or the MP-128 can be purchased with the upgrade already installed (designated the model MP-328) for $299.95 list price.

Product name:	SH-075 MIDI Guitar Converter	*Suggested retail:*	**$699.00**
Manufacturer:	Shadow Electronics	*PC required:*	No
Description:	MIDI controller for guitars		

Up to this point we've only spoken about synthesizer keyboards as the principal means of MIDI input and sending control messages, but there are lots of other options available. In addition to keyboards, MIDI breath controllers are available for wind instruments, MIDI microphones convert vocal pitches into MIDI signals, percussion-pad controllers allow the use of drumsticks, and for guitarists (the author included) there are MIDI controllers for guitars. The SH-075 from Shadow Electronics is one of the best and most sensitive MIDI guitar controllers I've used.

The SH-075's main unit attaches to the tail of the guitar using the guitar's strap button screw to hold it in place. A hex pickup mounts under the strings directly in front of the bridge and connects via a thin cable to the SH-075 unit (the hex pickup can mount either with adhesive putty or screws, both supplied).

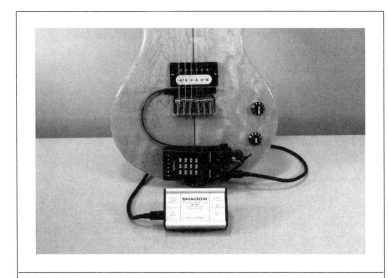

Figure 8.12 *The Shadow SH-075 MIDI Guitar Converter shown mounted on a hand-made Kramer prototype built by Paul "Unk" Unkert (The Guitar Guy). Photo: Liz Benford*

The SH-075 does a remarkably good job of converting an analog string vibration into a MIDI control signal. Many other guitar/MIDI converters have slow tracking—a slight delay between the time the guitar string is plucked and when it is reproduced as a MIDI-generated note on a synthesizer. This lag time can be quite disconcerting and is a major drawback of other guitar/MIDI units, but it isn't a concern with the SH-075.

The SH-075 has a highly-sensitive hex pickup and state-of-the-art electronics in its control unit to provide tracking, sensitivity, and string response that is as close to analog guitar playing as you're likely to find. The guitar can also still be played through an amplifier, either by itself or simultaneously while MIDI is being used, so thick "chorusing" is possible.

In addition to providing a built-in tuner, the SH-075 can operate in poly mode (all strings are assigned to a single MIDI channel permitting chords to be played) and mono mode (each string can be assigned to a different MIDI channel permitting six different voices to be assigned). The unit also supports pitch-bending up to eight semitones total, so even the wildest "licks" can be played through MIDI. MIDI notes can also be transposed up or down three octaves from the unit's control pad.

Included with the interface is the hex pickup, adhesive putty, mounting screws, a small screwdriver, and AC power adapter. If you're a guitarist looking for the best of both worlds, check the SH-075 out on your favorite "axe."

Product name: **MIDI Kit**   *Suggested retail:* **$119.95**
Manufacturer: **Midisoft**   *PC required:*   **Yes**
Description: **MIDI breakout box/cables/software for sound cards**

While most of the PC sound cards currently available provide full MIDI support through Windows, very few of them provide the additional accessory items you'll need to get the full benefit of MIDI possible by attaching external keyboard controllers, synthesizers, tone generators, and other MIDI devices. The folks at Midisoft realized that these required items are usually not included with standard sound card packages and decided to do something about it. The result is Midisoft's MIDI Kit, which contains everything you need to explore the world of MIDI with external devices connected to your PC.

Touted as the universal MIDI solution for Windows PC sound cards, the MIDI Kit's breakout box attaches to the D connector of popular sound cards including the Media Vision Pro Audio series, the Sound Blaster Pro, the Turtle Beach MultiSound, and the Advanced Gravis UltraSound, as well as several other cards using the popular 15-pin D configuration for MIDI adapters. Two good-quality six-foot MIDI cables are also provided in the kit for connecting the external device to the breakout box.

In addition to the hardware components of the MIDI Kit, a copy of Midisoft's *Recording Session* software is also included (see Lesson 11) along with a selection of fully sequenced MIDI songs voiced to support a variety of sound cards. It's the perfect PC/MIDI accessory kit.

Product name: Novation MM-10X   *Suggested retail:* $239.95
Manufacturer: Music Industries Corp.   *PC required:*   No
Description: External MIDI keyboard controller for Yamaha QY20

The Yamaha QY20 is such a versatile little device that it is a natural for use with an external keyboard. Novation's MM-10X is the perfect companion for the QY20, and it greatly enhances the device's playability, versatility, and practicality. It also makes an ideal compact portable MIDI controller.

The MM-10X features a two-octave velocity-sensitive keyboard that comes with a cable adapter for connecting it to the Yamaha QY10 (Yamaha's older tone generator that has been replaced by the QY20), or it can be connected to the QY20 with the optional ADP-1 adapter ($19.95 suggested list). The MM-10X even has a handy tray built-in for holding the QY unit while it is in use, as shown in Figure 8.13.

Figure 8.13   *Novation's MM-10X MIDI keyboard controller, shown holding a Yamaha QY20 Compact Music Processor. Photo: Liz Benford*

To keep you updated on the status of the MM10-X, a custom LCD is built into the unit that provides continuous information on all settings, such as MIDI channel, octave, program change, transpose, controller functions, and low-battery indicator.

The keyboard is equipped with full-size keys that are transposable over eight octaves. An optional sustain pedal can also be used since the MM-10X is also outfitted with an input for this purpose. Some of the other noteworthy features include velocity sensitivity, a pitch wheel, and programmable multi-function controller wheel. Overall it is a good keyboard controller for just about any MIDI use.

Powered by six alkaline cells, the MM10-X provides an average of more than 80 hours of battery life with normal use. A pair of strap holders is installed on it, so it can be used as an easy-to-handle remote keyboard controller, worn and played guitar-fashion, if preferred. And, since it is battery powered, it is totally portable and can be used with the QY20 in cars, planes, trains, buses, or virtually anywhere without having to worry about the availability of AC power.

Other optional accessories available for the MM10-X include a carrying case ($29.95) and a regulated AC adapter ($14.95) if you don't want to use battery power.

If you're using a Yamaha QY tone generator, you'll wonder how you got along without the MM10-X. And if you're using the multimedia capabilities of your PC's sound card and want to use an external keyboard controller for your MIDI input, the MM10-X makes an excellent choice as well.

Product name: Novation MidiCon   *Suggested retail:* **$169.95**
Manufacturer: Music Industries Corp.   *PC required:*   No
Description: External MIDI keyboard controller for PC sound cards

If you've been looking for a good external keyboard controller to get the most from the MIDI capabilities of your PC's sound card, your search may be over with the Novation MidiCon.

Designed specifically with the multimedia PC user in mind, the MidiCon is finished in an off-white, putty color that perfectly matches the PC equipment in any computer musician's setup. That, combined with all of the solid features the MidiCon has built-in, results in an affordable way to get in control of MIDI.

Many PC users with sound cards would like to explore the world of MIDI more fully, but the extra "bells and whistles" most stand-alone keyboard synthesizers come with keep their prices well beyond what the casual or curious PC musician may want to spend. With a suggested list price of under $170, the MidiCon provides a solid keyboard controller that has all of the necessary features without the extra goodies that aren't required for using it with a sound card. The result is a useful product that is priced right.

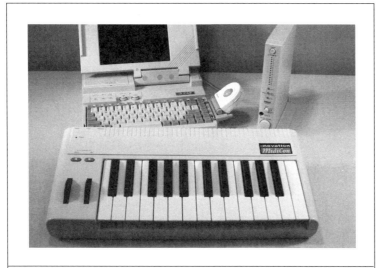

Figure 8.14 Novation's MidiCon, a good controller for sound card MIDI use. Note the Yamaha CBX-T3 Tone Generator in the background. Photo: Liz Benford

The MidiCon has full-size keys, a two-octave keyboard range, velocity sensitive response, two on-board switches providing an additional eight-octave range, pitch and modulation wheels, a new sustain input with a built-in auto-polarity feature, and one MIDI OUT port. Since the keyboard itself contains no tone generating source, there is no need for a MIDI IN port.

The keyboard is powered by alkaline cells that yield an average battery life of 250 hours, or it can be powered by an optional AC adapter. Since strap pegs are also provided on the MidiCon, it can also be used as a strap-on remote controller for mobility around the studio or for live performances on stage.

Accessory items are available for enhancing the MidiCon, including a carry case ($29.95 list) and a regulated AC power supply adapter ($14.95 list).

If you're into PC sound and you want an affordable, full-size touch sensitive keyboard controller available, this may be the product you're looking for.

Glossary

aftertouch   A type of keyboard touch sensitivity that permits the player to control the sound after the key has been pressed and while it is being held down. Aftertouch adds additional dynamic expressiveness to the music.

byte   A unit of information used in computer processing and storage consisting of 8 bits which, by their order, represent a single character.

channel   Any of the 16 communication paths MIDI provides for data transmission. Each of the channels carries its own separate and distinct messages over the same cable, which makes it possible to play several different musical parts on the same instrument or control different MIDI instruments simultaneously.

daisychaining   A term that describes two or more devices linked together through each other to the same PC. The first device is connected directly to the PC, while the second device is connected to the first. The third device is connected to the second, fourth to third, and so forth. Signals are passed through the "chain" back and forth from the computer to the desired device. To avoid confusion or conflicts, each device in the chain is given its own unique channel for communication and ID.

event   A term that refers to any status, system, or control message sent or received over a MIDI channel. These messages play notes and control MIDI equipment.

General MIDI   An update and enhancement of the MIDI 1.0 standard that provides greater compatibility between different manufacturers' MIDI equipment when transferring MIDI song files.

humanize

An effect that introduces slight timing, velocity, and volume variations to a MIDI track to simulate the "feel" of a live performance.

message

A collective term that refers to the words (or bytes) of MIDI control data. Messages typically consist of one or more words that include a status byte and one or two data bytes.

monophonic mode

In mono mode a MIDI instrument assigns incoming channel voice messages monophonically, permitting only a single note to be played at a time. Since the voices are each assigned to different channels, however, playing a chord results in three, five, or more different instrument sounds playing individual notes simultaneously (see *polyphonic mode*).

pitch-bending

A capability of many MIDI keyboards and other controllers used to simulate the way a guitarist stretches a string to alter the pitch of the note.

polyphonic mode

The ability of a synthesizer to play more than one note (chords) simultaneously. In poly mode, all notes are voiced the same and sent via the same MIDI channel (see *monophonic mode*).

quantize

Also sometimes called *auto-correction*, this refers to the process of correcting slow and fast timing variations to align the tracks with the tempo beats. Quantizing can make sloppy playing sound tighter, but overdoing it can make the composition sound too rigid and mechanical (which could then be corrected by humanizing).

SMPTE

An abbreviation for the *Society of Motion Picture and Television Engineers*, SMPTE refers to the synchronization standard designed by video engineers to synchronize different pieces of video and audio mixing equipment together. In MIDI, SMPTE is used to sync sequencers and other MIDI equipment as well as multitrack recording equipment to video, and it is used for creating sound tracks and other high-end applications. SMPTE is a time-based code that marks the passage of time as hours, minutes, seconds, and frames.

velocity

A synthesizer and MIDI term that means how hard the musical key is pressed or released. For keyboards having velocity control, this can affect the loudness or other tonal quality of the sound.

word

The native unit of storage on a particular machine. Depending on the microprocessor, a word can be an 8-bit, a 16-bit, or a 32-bit quantity.

LESSON NINE:

Professional Perspectives on MIDI

Some of today's leading contemporary electronic musicians share their experiences and insights on making music, using MIDI, and computers:

- Les Paul

- Jay Chattaway

- Suzanne Ciani

- David Arkenstone

- John Archer

- Fowler & Branca

Les Paul

Les Paul is a pioneer in the development of the electric solid-body guitar, the high-speed cutting lathe, multitrack recording, the echo chamber, reverberation, close miking, music synthesizers, and more. He and his wife, the late Mary Ford, were familiar household words and top recording stars at Capitol Records as well as on the radio and television from the late 1940s through the 1960s. This 78-year-old living legend still plays two 1.5-hour shows of nonstop guitar music at Fat Tuesday's jazz club in New York City every Monday night, which is where the following conversation took place.

Figure 9.1   *Author Tom Benford (l.) talks about guitars, music, and electronics with living legend Les Paul prior to Les's first set on a Monday evening at Fat Tuesday's jazz club in New York City. Photo: Liz Benford*

Tom: Les, how did you get started in "electrified" music?

Les: In the late 1920s and into 1930, right in that time period, I was a young kid working at a little barbecue stand halfway between Rockashaw and Milwaukee up in Wisconsin, but it was on the highway, and I played my harmonica, guitar, and I sang. Well, one of the people who worked in the place said that "if the people eating and drinking in their cars could hear you louder I'm sure that the tips would go up." And so I figured well, I'll grab my mother's radio, take a telephone, and if you can talk into it, there must be a way of hooking it up to the radio and the speaker. Well that was very easy. And so I used my mother's telephone, and I'd take it apart for the night, and give it back to her all put-back-together again the next day. But I had a microphone and my mother's radio, which had batteries and a battery charger.

Tom: About how old were you at this time?

Les: Oh I was almost 15 years old. So what happened...the tips went up! And a critic out there complained that the guitar wasn't loud enough, so I figured well I'd better do something about the guitar. The logical thing to do is to just take a phonograph needle, take the cartridge and tape it on the bridge of the guitar and just plug it in there and turn it on—only instead of playing a record I'm playing my guitar and it's amplified. I'm telling you now I had to have my father's radio for that. So my mother's radio was a telephone and a radio and a speaker, and across the other side was the amplified guitar, now I've got *stereo*.

I've got the whole thing running and the tips were going great and everything but I ran into a problem. When I turned it up loud I got feedback. So to counter the feedback [caused by the vibrating guitar body's resonance], I chucked some towels in it, and finally I'm pouring in black Plaster of Paris—I tried everything to dampen down the thing so the top didn't vibrate. It seemed logical to me that if the top vibrates, you're presenting a problem—only the string should vibrate. So the other half of the telephone came into use because it was a magnet and coil. I put that up by the strings and lo and behold if I didn't hear a sound come out of the guitar. I realized then that you don't need the body of the guitar to produce sound.

Les continued to experiment using magnetic pickups that evolved from the basic coiled-magnet idea used in telephone mouthpieces. In these experiments he stretched steel guitar strings on everything from sections of railroad track to pieces of balsa wood and all sorts of other items while he learned by doing—after all, this was new ground he was breaking and there were no books to refer to.

Realizing that the guitar body was not required for producing and amplifying the sound, Les stayed with traditional guitar body shapes for his experiments mostly, often having custom bodies built to his specifications over the next few years.

Les: So I started going to fellas who made guitars and they thought I was nuts asking for a guitar with no holes in it! "Where's the sound going to come out?." The last thing these old timers wanted was to be with some guy that's infected—and to them I definitely had a disease. They just said, "We don't want to say you're stupid but you surely aren't very bright . . . if you don't put a hole in it you're not going to hear anything!" Well, I'm telling them that I'm going to amplify it, and that turned them off, too.

So over a period of time, it was progressive, I finally got down to Chicago. In my long career it seemed like ages to get into the big-time. And I'd get guitar makers—National guitar, Larsen brothers, and many guys who made guitars—and ask them to make these guitars. Reluctantly they'd make this beast that had no holes in it and a half-inch top of wood, and this went on from 1933 until 1941, when I decided I was going to settle it once and for all.

So I went to the Epiphone Company which was on 14th Street in Manhattan. Every Sunday they let me have the whole place to myself, along with the watchman. And I built what was called 'The Log' (literally a piece of 4 x 4 with a neck, bridge, strings, and magnetic pickups). When I finished it, it was viable—no longer a railroad track. Now we had to lighten it up, make it look smaller, sweeter, nicer, arch the top and not have it so log-ish. So I did just that, and the Epiphone people were the first to see it because that's where I made it.

And they looked at it and curiously asked me some questions—like why in the world would I do something like that—but they weren't interested. I took it to Gibson and they called me the character with the broomstick with pickups on it.

Tom: Did you get a patent for The Log?

Les: The Log proved to be the answer but it took exactly ten years to sell Gibson on the idea. I took it to the Gibson people in 1941, showed it to them, asked them to build me one so forth and so on, which they did. They built me a solid-top guitar. And we varied and monkeyed-around with it, but I didn't patent it. I've gotten two patents in my life, and both of them are minor and irrelevant, nothing to do with what I'm doing here. I just never bothered—inventing was a thing, a necessity for me. I never patented the 8-track (recorder), I never patented echo, I never patented anything. I just, didn't bother.

Tom: You also invented the high-speed cutting lathe for phonograph records, didn't you?

Les: Yeah, I gave that a shot—I used a flywheel from a Cadillac for the first one because of its perfect balance. I sold that to the Marx Brothers. They had a machine shop and Groucho saw it in my shop window when I was building it and he said "What is that?" I said "It's going to be a cutting lathe." He said, "What's a cutting lathe?" I told him, "You make records with it." Groucho said "My brothers might be interested in that."

So they came over and looked at it and asked "What do you want for it?" I said, "Build me one and you can have it." They said "Well, we'd like to build them commercially," and I said, "I'll tell you how to improve on it—I already know what mistakes I've made." And I helped them improve on it and then Sherman Fairchild, a very famous man (Fairchild Airplanes, Fairchild Cameras, Fairchild Recording Equipment) copied my lathe right down to the flywheel.

Tom: But you didn't have any patent on it.

Les: No, I never patented nothing. So when the guitar came along, I went to the Gibson people and we used the same lawyer. I didn't even have a lawyer—I used Gibson's lawyer and we spoke together at that time. And at that time they said, "Well, now how do you want to do this?" and I said "Well, why don't we split it fifty-fifty, and we'll share the patent together and the rights to the thing and that'll be it." Well, Mr. Berlin, who was the chairman of the board, said okay.

Tom: So that's the deal you struck, fifty-fifty with them . . .

Les: Fifty-fifty but it didn't go down fifty-fifty. They patented the whole thing. (*laughs*) But I didn't know about it until many years later when, to my surprise, I saw it in *Guitar Player* magazine. I threw a fit, I called *Guitar Player* magazine, I called Gibson, I threw a riot act. By that time, he [Mr. Berlin] was no longer with Gibson, but he held the rights to it.

Tom: Oh my gosh . . .

Les: But that goes with the dinner too, you know. Maybe he misunderstood when they told him, for all I know. I don't know—it wasn't important to me.

Tom: Well you must've wound up with something . . .

Les: Oh yeah . . . they gave me an agreement that I would receive a royalty for anything that had a pickup under it. Everything . . . a banjo, a violin, a bass, no matter what it was, as long as it was amplified, I got my royalties, but I get another royalty if it bears my name. Oh, the royalty arrangements, everything, the money was exactly the same, there was no problem with the money. The only thing that I felt a little hurt by was the fact that here I picked the color of it, I picked the shape . . .

Tom: Just so that we can get the record straight, you invented multitrack recording that revolutionized the record and music industries. How did that come about?

Les: The first thing was that I convinced Bing Crosby that he should go from the disc (recordings were made directly to acetate disc in those days) to tape. He ended up with Ampex, and he gave them $50,000 to make a tape machine. When it was finished, Bing was very grateful for it, and he came over to my house one day, saying "I've got something in the back of the car for you." So I figured it was either a case of liquor, or a Philco radio (one of Crosby's sponsors), or I'd have enough Kraft cheese (another sponsor) for the next 500 years. I never thought I would see a tape machine. I said, "Mary, I don't think we have to stay home anymore, we can go on the road because we don't need the garage recording studio anymore." I worked a way out to do sound on sound, but I only drew it out on an envelope.

And so we packed our stuff up and took the tape machine with us. I called the Ampex people and told them that I had ruined the playback head and needed another head. I didn't want to tell anybody what I had in mind.

We were in Chicago, and Mary said, "But what if it doesn't work?" I said "It'll work, it'll work," and I was confident that it would work. Mary was not quite that convinced. Well, sure enough, the mailman brings up this special delivery package to the hotel and it's this box with a new head in it. I called a guy in the Yellow Pages to come over and drill a hole "right there" and he drilled a hole right there in the Ampex machine, and we didn't look underneath! We could have drilled through 15 wires and rods and all this stuff, but we were the luckiest people in the world, there was nothing there! And we mounted the head there and turned it on, and I said "Hello, hello, hello," and I played it back. Now I pressed the record button and I switched heads so that the playback head is first, then the erase head, then the record head. And, lo and behold. I say "Hello there, hello there," and with that I say "Hello yourself, hello yourself, hello yourself." It comes back with "Hello there, hello there, hello yourself, hello yourself," all mixed together. Mary says "It does work," and I'm the happiest guy in the world. And that was the invention of sound on sound.

Tom: You came up with some ideas for guitar synthesizers while you were healing from a bad car accident some years ago, didn't you?

Les: Yes. That accident was in 1948, and one of the attending doctors said, "We may have to amputate this arm."

There were two doctors, and they were arguing. One says "You know, he's not driving a hayride, this guy is a guitarist, he's a musician, we don't want to take that arm off." And the other one says, "It's got to come off." And I thought to myself, either way, whoever wins, I'm going to find another way of playing the guitar. So I started to design the music synthesizer, and it was very simple and based on a guitar. I already invented an oscillator, and a note is just a sine wave with some harmonics, and this is going to make your tone. And I'm saying now, the first synthesizer I designed in 1948 on a drawing was very simple. I just ran switches so that I cut the frets up, so that whatever string you push down on whatever fret, that's the note that played. Nurses would come in and say "How are you doing with your one-armed guitar that you're going to build?" We didn't even call it a synthesizer at that time. So it wasn't long before I had the whole thing planned out in 1948.

Now it wasn't until 1951 or '52 that I moved from California to New Jersey because Listerine (the sponsor) wanted to do a show. And in filming the show, *Les Paul and Mary Ford from Their Home in Mahwah, New Jersey*, that I had to put aside the synthesizer and some other ideas I'd been working on. But before I shelved the synth I got a draftsman to understand what I was talking about and draw it all out— had witnesses, too.

In 1952, I said, "I'll apply for a patent on it." A carpenter working in our house said to me, "The wall you've got in the office here cuts straight across—it don't go to the corner and you're wasting all that space." I told him I wanted to put some nice playback equipment there in my office, and he said "Well, do you want me to put anything in there?" I said, "Well, there's a lot of junk that I'm not going to be looking at for a while," so I rolled all my papers up, put them in tubes, put them in there, and he sealed the wall up. And that's where they are.

Tom: Really? Sealed inside the wall?

Les: Yeah. And behind it are the plans. I want to send them first to Robert Moog, because he's the guy who will appreciate them the most.

Tom: Maybe you can get Geraldo Rivera to cover "The opening of the wall and the recovery of the lost Les Paul papers?"

Les: (*laughs out loud*).

Tom: When it was clear that they weren't going to amputate it, didn't you ask to have your broken arm set in a position so you'd still be able to play guitar?

Les: Yes, aimed at my navel. The doc said, "Where do you want it," and I said "Aim it at my navel and it'll be okay." Yup. I invented the synthesizer in 1948, never patented it, the drawings are all in my wall at home, they're all set in there. Robert Moog (father of the Moog Synthesizer) said, "When did you invent the synthesizer?" I said "1948."

Tom: Amazing. Modern electronics, the personal computer, sound cards, and MIDI are all providing very powerful tools for people who may not be naturally gifted in music. Do you think that is a good thing or a bad thing?

Les: I think it's half and half, it's a blessing, and then it can be a curse, too. Because if you take someone, hand him a synthesizer, and he locks himself in a room for two years and he comes out playing like a vibe player, that's a shame. That's a damn shame...use the technology as an instrument and master it—don't let it master you.

Jay Chattaway

Jay Chattaway is a renowned composer of musical scores for film and TV in addition to creating orchestral jazz arrangements that are widely used in schools throughout the country. If you've ever watched the popular television series Star Trek: The Next Generation *or* Star Trek: Deep Space Nine, *you've probably heard Jay's work without realizing it. Jay has also scored several National Geographic Society and Jacques Cousteau TV documentary specials, and he received an Emmy nomination for his music on an ABC television production,* The Shark Chronicles. *He also composed and produced the music for 26 feature films including the Chuck Norris* Missing in Action *series, Stephen King's* Silver Bullet, *and the film* Red Scorpion. *Jay also created the music for the critically-acclaimed PBS television series,* Space Age.

Figure 9.2   TV, movie theme, and orchestral composer Jay Chattaway standing on the bridge of the Starship Enterprise on the set of Star Trek: The Next Generation.

Tom: Based on your accomplishments, I would think it's a safe bet to assume you're a formally-trained musician, is that right?

Jay: I have degrees in music composition, and all that sort of stuff, so I'm a certifiable music major I guess.

Tom: Is it also safe to assume that you use MIDI in your creative and production work?

Jay: All the time. But, just so you know though, our shows *Star Trek:The Next Generation* and *Deep Space Nine*, in addition to using electronics, are probably the only regular television shows left that have a substantial orchestra to go along with all that.

Tom: I'm glad that you brought that up. So the music isn't all synthesized?

Jay: No, my orchestra has about 45 members, acoustic players, and two or three, sometimes four electronic players in the actual orchestra that's recording. Generally two keyboards, one electronic wind instrument, and one percussionist who is doubling on a MIDI-based percussion rack system where he's able to trigger all sorts of samples and sounds, using MIDI and using a MIDI-controller made specifically for mallet and percussion parts.

These guys don't replace other sounds necessarily. For example, the electronic wind player comes up with unique sounds of his own, well, of his or my design, and then he's able to trigger them as though he were an acoustic musician. So he would have much more emotional control by using his breath or velocity or that sort of thing in order to make the music not sound like it was just electronic music performed on a keyboard. That always has been the sort of thing that tells electronic music apart form acoustic, and that is the lack of expression that takes place. Plus the fact that there's usually one person playing all of that stuff as opposed to having 50 or 60 different people interpreting what you've written, and therefore you get a little wider sense of response and emotional feeling.

Tom: That's an interesting observation. So even with the velocity control and the pitch-dynamic controls that are in today's MIDI devices you still feel that the dynamics of a live player as opposed to someone playing a wind part on a keyboard are integral to giving it that ultimate realistic sound and ambiance?

Jay: Oh absolutely, and the other thing, too, is that by just adding acoustic musicians my MIDI-based projects are embellished. The *Space Age* album is an example. I think it only has four live players on that project yet it still has a very natural sound, and part of that comes from the fact that I've been trained and I work mostly with acoustic players. We've been able to analyze the fact that if you have a string section, three players are not going to play as precisely on the downbeat as a synth would, and if you were able to make a string track or a string pass on your MIDI sequence, the way that you could make it sound much more realistic is to offset various tracks of the strings so that they're not all playing precisely on the downbeat. Sometimes a string section will play up to 100 milliseconds later than the downbeat, and that's why it sounds so big, because everybody else is playing at a different time. It's like the inaccuracy factor is what contributes to the natural grandeur of the whole thing, whereas with MIDI music, with the exception of some minor MIDI delays, everything happens exactly at the same time. People have worked real hard to make it that precise, you know.

Tom: What kind of computer are you using?

Jay: I have a small MIDI studio here in my home, it's Macintosh-based, Mac SE, and basically I have that system because of a particular piece of software that's integral to the way I work. I don't want to give a rave plug to these guys, I had to actually buy it . . .

Tom: We won't mention them by name, then.

Jay: Okay, but that's the sole reason that I went to the Macintosh system. The way it works is like this: the music editor actually supplies me with information that's on disks, and I'm able to insert those disks into my computer and manipulate the tempos of the cues, and do everything, including having the computer print out the score paper that I actually write the music on. Then I take the computer to the session as well, or use the computer that's there, and the computer is what drives the entire show, it generates the clicks, it generate the streamers, if there are changes that have to be made, I can manipulate them instantly on the computer screen, and that's how we're able to generates as much music as we do in such a short period of time.

When I do a large-scale electronic project, I'll go into a studio, such as where *Space Age* was done, supported by most of my MIDI gear as peripheral equipment. You know, there are things that I have my own sounds on, or instruments which I'm very comfortable with, and that's how I like to work.

When we do *Star Trek*, I actually notate the parts, and sometimes there is some presequencing involved, sometimes we'll involve a Synclair and two other key-boards. I did a show where Data, the android, has a dream sequence, and I wanted to do a very electronic piece. Then when Data was dreaming that he was becoming more human the orchestra with natural elements came back in. It was very effective, though we did have to spend several days presequencing the electronics in order to make it work.

Tom: I also remember an episode where Data was playing a concert violin, apparently quite well. I assume that a live musician actually dubbed the track and it was overlaid in sync with Data's motions.

Jay: Well, actually the way it goes, it's sort of the other way around: we prerecord those tracks then the actor listens and practices with that. Then, when they're shooting the scene, they actually play back the prerecorded track and he pretends that he's playing along with that. Of course, he doesn't make any sound, or even if he does make a sound it doesn't matter because they're not recording his actual performance. Then if it still doesn't look quite right we go in and rerecord it yet again, and do a very complicated kind of click-track that will accommodate his nuances, so to speak.

Tom: Then there's always the cutaway shot just in case the actor can't get it close enough for a tight shot . . .

Jay: Exactly. But sometimes they do that and they cutaway out-of-sync, which makes it very difficult to make it all line up properly. If you were to look at the notation on some of those parts, especially the one where Captain Picard played the penny whistle, the notation makes it look like some alien kind of thing. But in reality he was just taking his own liberties with it and they made a few cuts within the actual piece, they just arbitrarily cut the music, they didn't say how they wanted to do it, so we had to then re-record the music so that it fit those strange cuts they had made, so it was a little bit of a challenge.

Tom: I think that was the same episode where Captain Picard had a love interest who had this wonderful roll-up keyboard that she had gotten on another planet.

Jay: The interesting thing about that keyboard is that the black and white keys were not exactly in the same order that they are on our keyboard.

Tom: I suppose you have to make allowances for the design of alien musical instruments. Tell me, do you use sampled sounds extensively when you're composing orchestral works?

Jay: Yes. I have in my rack a couple of the Proteus modules for doing woodwinds and some percussion things. I use them as an orchestral tool just to listen, you know.

If I'm writing a part and I want to hear what actually sounds like an oboe, that's pretty realistic, and certainly a lot cheaper than having an oboe player come to your house. In that respect, I've found it as a helpful tool in writing things, but I don't ever plan to totally eliminate the orchestral players that I use by using electronics. I don't think it will come to that, at least not in the real immediate future. One of the main reasons is that the musicality and the emotional quality of having live players is still superlative to doing it with one guy playing it out of a black box. The other thing is the speed factor. When we have to turn out as much music on television and films in a short period of time, there would not be physically enough time on the show that I'm doing to actually program the entire show and have it performed in the same period of time as it takes me to physically write it, have the parts copied and performed by musicians. We'll do the entire score for a weekly episode of the show in five or six hours.

Tom: Really?

Jay: If we were to program it, it would take five or six hours to actually program maybe five or six tunes of music. Sometimes we have 30 minutes of music and the producers just would not be willing to spend that much time in the music production process. They want to come hear the music live, watch it with the film, make their adjustments, and then leave to go to the next phase of their production process, whether it be sound effects, or mixing, or whatever. So, the time factor on a quality show is still much faster to do it with live players, and actually, it's much more economical, if you don't factor in the reuse factor.

Tom: Are you ever called upon to do any of the sound effects or are you strictly related to the music end it?

Jay: No, we steer away from the sound effect area, there's a team of people that work on the sound effects on each show, which also uses MIDI. They use the Synclair system and everything is done through samples and triggered through time codes. We generally try to stay out of each other's way, though many times we'll discuss things among ourselves. Like "What do these alien bugs sound like here," so I don't have something in my music that's doing the same thing—we try to steer away from certain frequencies and all that, but they try not to do music, and we try not to do sound effects. Because it's hard to tell what's what, they sort of run into each other (*laughs*).

Tom: Do you have any parting thoughts you'd like to give my readers about MIDI and the technology in general?

Jay: Well, I guess the best piece of advice is before they get so wrapped up into the technology they should get some sort of basic level of musicianship, whether it be elementary piano lessons, or whether it be some computer generated piano technique. What happens, in many cases, is that people learn so much about the technology that they never, ever get a chance to learn about what it is in music that makes things actually work. So, as a result, you hear a lot of very high-tech sounding music that has no roots, and no real plan as to where it came from. I think possibly somewhere in this series of books there ought to be a book that's like a basic musicianship book, but dealing particularly with the aspiring MIDI artist. It should be a book that tells them what chords are supposed to go where and what scales are, and what notes are good harmony notes—you know, the very basic fundamentals of music. And, just because everybody knows once they get a synthesizer how sound is made and what sounds waves are all about, they might not know that a C chord is supposed to go into an F chord, and that sort of thing. So I think a real fundamental music theory or music approach, maybe an interactive approach might be a good thing for *you* to start thinking about designing for the PC or whatever direction you're headed in.

Tom: I've thought about doing a book like that, but I haven't discussed it with my publisher yet. When I do, can I say that Jay Chattaway told me I should do this?

Jay: Sure. Absolutely.

Suzanne Ciani

Suzanne Ciani, a premier contemporary TV/film score composer and recording artist with seven albums to her credit, could justifiably be called "the first lady of synthesis." As a young child she taught herself to play Bach and Rachmaninoff before she knew what a piano scale was. A Grammy nominee and the head of a highly-regarded commercial music production firm, Suzanne helped electronic music get off the ground in the early days.

Figure 9.3   Private Music recording artist and TV/film composer Suzanne Ciani. Photo: Diane Rubinger

Tom: Tell me how you became involved with electronic instruments and MIDI.

Suzanne: Well, my first involvement in electronics was about 1968—about the time I came out to the West Coast for graduate school at U.C. Berkeley.

Tom: Were you majoring in music in college?

Suzanne: Yes, I majored in composition; well, actually, I majored in music in college and then I went to graduate school for composition. That's when I started getting involved in what was the beginning of analog synthesizer technologies and also computer technologies because Stanford University, at that time, was one of the two centers for computer music, the other one being at Princeton University. So that was my introduction to the whole field. I worked with Max Mathews, who is considered the father of computer music, and John Chowning, who is the father of FM synthesis, something which later became very important in synthesizers as we know them.

Tom: Sounds like it's been a long walk down the road of technology for you.

Suzanne: Well I know that I went through every single stage; I can remember using the Commodore 64.

Tom: Really.

Suzanne: I can remember retro-fitting my Prophet 5 [synthesizer] for MIDI and, you know, we retro-fitted whatever we could once MIDI came out. I have to admit that I didn't understand what the big fuss was over MIDI at first because a lot of the things that MIDI allowed us to do, we were *already* doing. We were sequencing, we were editing sounds, and so forth, and basically I saw MIDI, in my own life, as just an enhancement of the things I was already doing. I think the real impact of MIDI was that it happened on such a huge scale. For me, maybe it didn't make a whole lot of difference right away, but the fact that now so many more people were getting involved and a new market was created—that was the real impact of MIDI.

Tom: That's an interesting perspective. What kind of a computer are you currently using?

Suzanne: Ah, I'm currently using Macs, a Mac IIcx and a PowerBook 160. For many years I used IBM, and it was quite a changeover for me to go from one to the other.

Tom: What was your reason for changing "religions," so to speak?

Suzanne: Well, actually it was a geographical thing. I had worked in New York for so long and I had a studio with a lot of synthesists. We all used IBM and I think the desire was to be compatible, but then when I came to the West Coast to work on an album I couldn't find anybody to assist me 'cause nobody out here worked with IBM. So, in order to get assistance in the tedium of production I switched to Mac.

Tom: Does MIDI merely reduce the production tedium for you or is it also a creativity enhancer as well?

Suzanne: Well, not to talk about tedium, I think it definitely is a creativity enhancer because you get to work in the medium hands-on, like a sculptor, in the sound. Years ago composers wrote music and sometimes never heard it at all. So

I love it because I can use it all through the process of writing my albums. I'll write and then I'll walk away from it and have it play to get a perspective on it, listen to the architecture of the piece. It gives you feedback, plus it expands the whole pallet of sounds that are available to you. So not only do we have the wonderful acoustic families of sounds—the woodwinds, brass, percussion, strings, things like that—but now there's a whole realm of sounds . . . poetic sounds, maybe my idea of what a wave would sound like, a percussion sound that sounds like a wave, or sounds that I make. I like adding this whole new family of sounds and new control of the sounds, spatial control of the sound, a way to move sound and create imaginary environments and spaces. And, you know, the traditional limitations are not there to say that a breath can only be so long or a bow could only be so long. So now you can hold sounds for days, months if you want—it gives you new possibilities. I'm not a big fan of sampling sounds, so I don't think of this domain as replicating the acoustic domain.

Tom: Do you prefer to work with the sounds that are on hand or do you search for exotic samples?

Suzanne: I guess I'm kind of like, you know...Picasso made something out of a bicycle seat, you just use what you find basically. But also the creative process is you're looking for something, you're going in a direction, but the direction is kind of evolving as a function of the process itself. To go into it and say, "Gee I want the sound of Isaac Stern's violin pizzicato for this piece," well, I find that a little bit boring and dead. I mean, I personally couldn't stand to go through a bunch of sound libraries, I just would be bored. For me, even from the very beginning I would have to say honestly it wasn't the sound. I love the sound, but it was what I could do *with* the sound that fascinated me the most. How I could interact with the sound—that was important for me.

Tom: We touched on this lightly before when you said that you were surprised at the way MIDI took over *en masse*. Is that good because now nongifted people can make music or is it bad because of that very fact in itself?

Suzanne: First of all, let me just say I think it's a good thing. To me, music is a language and this will also create good listeners. I'm not worried about the record companies getting too many tapes. I think that if more people are going through the process and creating and becoming familiar, they will develop an ear and listening is an educated response. I think any involvement with the materials of music is positive and this will enhance our ability to appreciate music.

Tom: Lots of contemporary artists are using full digital equipment in their own homes, and bypassing the studio completely. Is that what you're doing now or are you still part of the traditional studio setting some or all of the time?

Suzanne: My album *Pianissimo* was done direct to DAT, and an album like that could be done directly to DAT because it was a piano album. In general my albums tend to go to the width and breadth of high-expense technology and I have to go all the way. If, to get that last 10% of quality, it means going into a huge studio and spending whatever it takes and using two digital multitracks, I will do that because I'm really committed to making a quality product. I'm very happy when I can get that quality in a very simple way. If the album can be done by those methods then I'm really happy because its expensive, of course, to do them in a studio. On my next album I want to use an orchestra and I'll be combining the synth with this new thing that's a little LED "conductor." It runs off the sequencer and puts out a conducting pattern for the orchestra to follow. So I'm really excited about that.

Tom: That will be interesting to have human players quantize to conform to the synths.

Suzanne: Actually, what it means is that I can put all the variations of tempo that I want in and get it the way I want, and the orchestra can follow it even though its changing.

Tom: Are you currently working on that album or is it still in the planning stages?

Suzanne: Yes, I'm almost through with the writing.

Tom: What's the next step in the process?

Suzanne: Well I go through the writing stage. I'm very sloppy, I just make sure the architecture is right and I don't worry too much about the notes. Then I go back and clean it all up, fine-tune the sounds and make it all presentable. The next day I just do the orchestration, the written part.

Tom: Do you feel that its conceivable that acoustic instrumentation is really going to take a backseat as electronics become more and more prevalent?

Suzanne: On the contrary, I think that acoustic instruments will become more valuable and I would hate to see us lose all the years of evolution it has taken us. I think that the idea of seeing electronics as a replacement of acoustic sounds because of sampling leads us to the false conclusion that we don't need them any more. There are two families of sound, we just expanded the families of sound available the same way now you can watch a movie on TV but you still go to the movie theater. Its just different.

Tom: How would you counsel those reading this—to give them some encouragement and, perhaps, even to inspire them ?

Suzanne: Well, I thought about this and I think the whole thing is not to be afraid. Don't be afraid, just jump in. People think that there are types of people that have technical minds and other people don't have technical minds. I say you learn by doing, so get to know the personality of the program you're working with, get to know how it thinks, like getting to know a friend, use your intuition. To learn you just go up and touch and move it and you find out what it does, and you learn in the process. And then I would also suggest reading publications like *Keyboard* magazine for keeping up to date with both the manufacturing and the use of this technology.

David Arkenstone

David Arkenstone is a leading composer and synthesist producing contemporary music on the Narada label. His albums Valley In The Clouds, Island *(with guitarist Andrew White) and* Citizen of Time *all reached the Top 10 of Billboard's New Age Sales Chart. His* In The Wake Of The Wind *album was nominated for two Grammies, and his latest album release, an anthology called* Chronicles, *is destined to be another best-seller. David has used MIDI extensively in his composing, arranging, and recording since his first album was produced in 1987. Here he shares his experiences and insights with MIDI.*

Figure 9.4 *Narada recording artist David Arkenstone.*

Tom: Let's start with the basics—when did you first become aware of MIDI and start using it in your creative or production process?

David: I guess it was about a year before I started recording *Valley In The Clouds,* which was in July '86. I had a DX-7, one of the early MIDI synthesizers. But until I got something in the mail, I didn't know what MIDI was about, I guess. It was a mail-order offer for a Commodore computer with a MIDI-interface that lets you record everything. So I bought myself this little Commodore SX-64 portable computer with a tiny screen and I got started in MIDI.

I had a primitive sampler called a Mirage by Ensoniq, and I got that going with my DX-7 and my 8-track tape recorder and started making layered music. I guess that's when I really became aware of MIDI and I started to see that the potential was just unbelievable. I moved to more advanced synthesizers and started to program my own sounds a lot more and I realized that this is my calling. The more synthesizers I get, the more of an orchestra I can have at my disposal.

Tom: In sculpting your voices do you sample your own live sounds or tweak library samples to your own liking?

David: Because the recordings are so good, it's easier to find sounds that are close to what I need and then tweak them or blend them together with other sounds. I've found that to be pretty; I get real nice hybrid sounds like that.

Tom: What computer are you using to control the MIDI setup?

David: I'm using a Macintosh. I used to use the Commodore, but then I outgrew it. Then I moved to a Roland Music Computer whose sole function was sequencing, and I used that for a few years until I got the Macintosh.

Tom: Let's get your views on MIDI in general. Do you feel that MIDI enhances your creativity or does it just make the chores of producing music less tedious.

David: I think absolutely it's a creativity enhancer, without any question. I remember when I was doing the song *Valley in the Clouds* I was actually transposing whole sections as I composed the song. Because of MIDI and the computer interface, I was able to have more than one synth and I was mixing and writing at the same time. I just couldn't have done that with one synthesizer. MIDI makes it possible to combine sounds in a way you never could before because you'd need to have five hands or ten guys in the band—all playing the same thing. And through MIDI you can come up with new mixed sounds that you just couldn't do before, it was just impossible.

Tom: Are you strictly a keyboard person?

David: No, I play guitar and flute.

Tom: Are you MIDIed up with those instruments as well?

David: I haven't found a good MIDI-guitar thing yet. A keyboard is still a better controller, although I love to play guitar, and it'd be really nice if it worked correctly. There's so many things that they have to do electronically because the guitar has so many more nuances than a keyboard. With a keyboard either you strike the key or you're not striking the key, how fast you struck the key, then aftertouch—there's not too much. But on a guitar, there's the way you pick, the way you move, the bending of the string—there's more stuff that has to be processed.

Tom: What do you think MIDI's greatest gift to the masses will be?

David: It's really exciting for people who don't have a lot of musical training who can now sit down and make music because of this new technology. I think it's incredible, I think it's exciting and it's rewarding and more people will be doing music, that means more people will appreciate music and more people will appreciate the detail in music. Which is why I try to put a lot of things to listen to in all my records—you know, a lot of ways to journey through the album. I also think people have raised their standards as to what they will accept as good music and music that has been recorded well.

Tom: Do you have any advice, suggestions, or thoughts that you'd like to give those stepping boldly into the world of MIDI music now?

David: Well, I think it's important to avoid getting frustrated. I've been frustrated so many times, but I have music burning inside me strongly as a creative force. For people who don't have this fire it could be frustrating. The good thing is that it's becoming much easier to make music, and it's important to try to find your own voice—because in the end I think that's what will make you happy.

John Archer

John Archer is a cofounder of the duo Checkfield. Checkfield's first nationally released album was Spirit *in 1982 on the Pausa label. The duo's debut album on American Gramaphone was* Water, Wind and Stone, *followed by* Distant Thunder, *then* Through The Lens *and the latest release is* View from the Edge. *John was also the head of production at Network Music for eight years with over 60 albums in total to his credit. John also composes and arranges as well as functioning as the chief of production for American Gramaphone. His work can also be heard on the* Day Parts *series of albums from American Gramaphone.*

Figure 9.5   *American Gramaphone recording artist John Archer.*

Tom: Let's get a little background on how and when you formed Checkfield with Ron Satterfield.

John: Now let's see if I can come up with a short answer on that. In 1970 I moved out to San Diego from Detroit and coincidentally that's the year Ron moved out to San Diego from New York City, and we met in a music class in college within months after we both got there, and we kind of bonded a little bit because we had a music theory professor that we both detested and fought with constantly. We kind of hung out for that year a little bit and then we both went off and did other things for four or five years, and I didn't speak to Ron that much. Then one day we ran into each other, and just coincidentally we ended up living about a block from each other in a little town north of San Diego called Ensalitas. Also coincidentally, we were both working in guy/girl duos at the time in the little steak houses and bars up there. We started getting together after the gigs to play and listen to music till the wee hours of the morning—sometimes till daybreak—and started writing. That's how we got together.

Tom: So you're a formally-schooled musician rather than just a "gig" player?

John: Well, actually, I went at it kind of backwards because I started my schooling back in Detroit, went to college to be an electrical engineer, and decided that wasn't what I wanted to do. Then after I came out to San Diego, I decided that I wanted to be a musician, and up to that point (I was 18 or 19 then) I really had not seriously played any musical instrument. I just tinkered a little bit with the piano and the guitar, but had never seriously trained or studied, and at the ripe old age of 19 or 20 I decided that's what I wanted to do. So I basically locked myself in a room and practiced my ass off for a couple of years. Then, when I was 21, I started working the bar scene, and worked as a professional musician until I was about 26. At that point I decided to go back and find out what it was I was doing and so I entered the music program as a composition major at UCSD.

Tom: So how did you get started with MIDI?

John: Okay, actually, MIDI to me is just one step in the whole evolution of electronic instruments. I became fascinated when synthesizers came out and bought one of the first Mini Moogs, and then when I was at UCSD they had a marvelous program, one of only a half-dozen in the country that was dealing with electronic music, and it had the Center for Music Experimentation.

Back then doing an electronic composition was a lot different than it is now. I would work for two or three weeks doing punch cards, and then I'd take them down to the main administrative computer center where we used the main Burroughs machine to actually do the music, because that was the only computer we had available. So I'd take in my shoeboxes full of punch cards, and they would feed them into the Burroughs, and then at 3 AM, when there was some downtime on the computer, my little 15-second composition would pop out a port at the Music Experimentation Center, so I was in on some of the real beginning stuff there.

Then while I was working as the head of production for Network Music in San Diego, we decided to bite the bullet early on and we bought one of the first Synclaviers. That was a dinosaur machine, it had massive bugs. I used to spend about every third week back in New Hampshire trying to work the bugs out of the machine so we could use it in our music production. But once I got my hands on an instrument like that there was no going back. Then I started amassing MIDI instruments, and I think my first MIDI-instrument was a Memory Moog. In fact, soon after that we got a MIDI port on the Synclavier, and just started working from there.

Tom: In addition to playing keyboards you also pick up a guitar now and then. Have you MIDIed the guitar at all?

John: Actually, it's the other way around. Over the years I specialized more in guitar than keyboards, specifically acoustic guitar. I have a Roland GR-50 (guitar MIDI synthesizer) and pickup on the guitar. I don't use a lot of it even though I have better technique on guitar than I do on piano; I feel the guitar-MIDI interface is kind of primitive for the most part. If I want an expressive line it's easier for me to do it on keyboard than on guitar. I use the MIDI-guitar occasionally, but the glitches, the mistracking, and the delays all make it less useful than I'd like.

Tom: Did you start using a computer for your MIDI sequencing or did you use an external unit for that purpose?

John: My first sequencer was a dedicated hardware unit, a Yamaha QX-1, that I picked up right before we started working on the *Distant Thunder* album, and as most people do with new toys, we ridiculously overused it. We ended up spending hundred of hours going in and tweaking notes that probably didn't make any difference, but we did it because we could. That was the first sequencer I had, and we used that for both *Distant Thunder* and *Through the Lens*. If I remember correctly, right after that I decided to go with a computer-based sequencer.

Tom: And you're using an IBM compatible, right?

John: Right. Actually, I'm still using an old 286 with Voyetra's *Sequencer Gold* software and interface. It has worked out well for me because they did a good job of making it glitch-free and it's always very dependable. I probably should have upgraded my processor years ago, but it's always worked so well I just never found any need to.

Tom: Do you find that MIDI enhances your creativity?

John: I guess I'd have to say a qualified yes. I've gone through a curve that isn't unusual when you first get some of these toys, in that you tend to use them in kind of a superficial way. When you get the samplers you're playing all the parts through the keyboard and then, after a while, you look back and you know all of these oboes and strings and everything else may sound *close*, but not as the instrument would be played since I'm basically playing it on a keyboard. The same is true with arranging. For a while after I got the stuff I would try to do my string arrangements on the computer so that I could hear them before I actually gave it to the string section, you know, which is nice. Especially with the cost of running a string section, it's nice to "debug" your part beforehand. But, on the other hand, if you arrange strings on a piano it sounds like piano and you're not using the strings to their fullest ability. So now when I do orchestral arrangements, I've gone back to score paper and then, if I'm unsure, I might try some passages in the sequencer just to make sure they work. But I no longer write orchestrations at the keyboard because, again in retrospect, I looked back at some of the pieces and said, "that's not great string arranging."

Tom: Do you think the ease of access to MIDI and MIDI music brought about by PC sound cards may cause the music industry to be deluged with demo cassettes from computer musicians?

John: Well, to be perfectly honest, I don't think any technology could bastardize the music industry as much as the record companies have. The fact is that I'm a great fan of participatory art, and I think some of the best music is the music that people make themselves. So I don't see it as a negative thing in the music industry, because again, the fact is that people are trying it and getting some enjoyment out of it. I'd rather have them do that than have them buy some of the knuckle-headed b-s they've got on the airwaves.

Tom: What advice would you give anyone who wanted to get seriously involved with computers, electronic music, and MIDI—perhaps to go into it professionally, as you've done?

John: I have found personally that a good solid foundation in both electronics and music has been a great help. Especially, with so many boxes [synth modules, effects processors, and so forth] on the market right now, the real trick with all of them is using them to capacity and beyond. And that's something where it's not just a matter of roaming through presets—it's knowing what the instrument is doing and how it's doing it, and trying to make the instrument do more than even its designers had intended. Because most of these boxes aren't all that terrific until you kind of hot-rod them a bit, always pushing to get that last full bit out. A good background really is valuable so that it's not just a box with knobs.

Fowler & Branca

Bob Fowler and Steve Branca, who record on the Silver Wave Records label, have been involved in writing music for over ten years and several of their tunes have been recorded by artists including Tim Eyerman and Michael Pedicin Jr. Their first album, The Face on Cydonia, *was a best-seller on the Adult Contemporary charts for several months, and their latest album release,* Etched in Stone, *has been comfortably nestled in the AC Top 10 for several months now as well. Bob and Steve use MIDI in their work and talk about it here.*

Figure 9.6 *Silver Wave recording artists Fowler & Branca.*

Tom: I know that MIDI plays a big part in your creative and production process, and I know that you use an Atari computer to manage the MIDI devices and sequencing. But I don't know how you actually got involved with MIDI...

Bob: Well, we started back seven or eight years ago with, I think, with the first Yamaha, a QX-7 or something, and that was a one-channel-at-a-time sequencer—by today's standards, very antiquated. And then we went up to an 8-track sequencer, and that was a big step up, that was really fun. At that time we only had maybe one or two synthesizers, and then our biggest step up from there was running MIDI time code onto tape. That made it possible to have more than one part play at the same time and without committing anything to tape—that was pretty exciting. It wasn't until four or five years ago that we actually went to the computer and started using software.

Tom: Now you guys have apparently been working together for quite a while already?

Steve: Oh yeah. We played in club bands together for a number of years. And we've known each other how long Bob?

Bob: I don't know, 13 years, 14 years.

Steve: Yeah, at least. It was a good eight or nine years that we were working together and writing music before we landed the contract with Silver Wave, and we had written a few tunes that were placed on other record labels. We were really attempting, in the beginning stages, to write more popular or dance music and we found that arena to be pretty overcrowded. And having some of our roots in jazz and fusion, those were the styles of music that we enjoyed listening to, so we decided to try our hand at doing that, since both of the songs that we had written primarily as dance songs were placed on jazz albums. Bob approached me one day saying, "Why don't we just try to write this stuff?" So we did.

Bob: Yeah, it took quite a while for us actually to believe enough in it to send it out.

Tom: Is MIDI playing a significant role in the creative or production end of your writing, or both?

Bob: Oh, I think it very much aids you in the creative process because you're able to do things that you could only dream of before. You can cut and paste parts, you can invert phrases and lines that you probably would have never thought of playing, and especially the accessibility of the sounds themselves. I know not only Steve and I, but a lot of people I talk to who work with MIDI wind up writing the song around the sound they liked. That's a really fascinating thing when you can get a sound that you like, then you can just call up another multi-timbral sound on a synth and just keep writing. So, theoretically, if you are feeling inspired there's no holds barred. It's not like you have to go call up a drummer and say, "Hey could you play this groove for me?" and then go find a bass player and this and that. I mean, you can just sit there and go.

Steve: And sometimes it works in the opposite way. There's a couple of times we've written songs entirely using synthesizers and MIDI and then turned around and replaced some of those parts with actual acoustic instruments. Thereby, you know, the MIDI allowed us to set the stage for writing a song—a song that maybe we wouldn't have sat down with acoustic instruments to begin with and written. So it just gives you this enormous palette now. Instead of me just sitting there with a guitar and listening to the twang of my strings, I can hear other instruments play the part that I'm playing, so I don't necessarily have to be confined to being just a guitar player or Bob just a bass player.

Bob: Which brings up the next, I think really important point. For most people, you don't have to be able to play an instrument that well to be able to have a finished or a really good sounding product using MIDI.

Tom: And do you see that as a positive effect?

Steve: Yeah, just look at what multitrack recording did for the quality of music—you know, from the old days, like in the 50s when they recorded everything on two tracks, or even one track, everyone sat in a room and played together. Then multitrack came along and they were able to edit, it made it easier for groups who couldn't really play that well to sound a lot more professional and better. I think as each phase happens there will be more people who have access—to be able to write where they normally wouldn't be able to. I think what will be the deciding factor as to whether or not your music is listened to or not will be in the actual creation or the writing of the music, not just the technical aspect, the playing of it, but ideas, so I think there's still going to be that common denominator, what's good and bad...it's really no different than what's happening with the art applications and desktop publishing. People that couldn't draw are able to create works of art, but it still comes down to a matter of taste.

Bob: Yeah, and true ability. I think a lot of people were concerned when MIDI became so accessible to everybody that there was going to be a big flood, and there will be a big flood. But you know, I think the people who really do have something legitimate to say are going to come across no matter what they work on.

Tom: Have any advice, suggestions, or thoughts you'd like to give my readers who are now entering or contemplating this exciting world of MIDI and electronic music?

Steve: Wow, that's a tough one. I think you've got one life to live and there's a whole array of colors there, so why be limited to red, green, and blue? If you're an artist you'll be able to use whatever tools that are available to you and create something that's, hopefully, beautiful.

LESSON TEN:
Other Sound Uses

- Sounds and system events
- Voice annotation
- Multimedia presentations
- Speech synthesis
- Some additional terms and definitions

Using Sound in Windows

The Control Panel, located in the Main group of the Program Manager, is the nerve center of Windows from which you can change the environment settings as well as those of the peripherals and devices connected to the PC. The Control Panel also includes an icon for the sound settings that permit you to assign sounds to various Windows system events. This icon is only accessible if a sound device and the appropriate drivers are installed in Windows 3.1. If the device and drivers aren't installed or configured properly, the sound icon is "grayed-out" and is not accessible if you click on it.

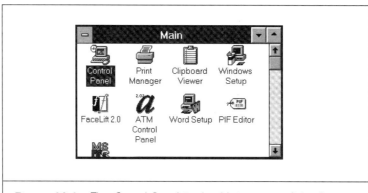

Figure 10.1   *The Control Panel in the Main group of the Program Manager.*

The Sound icon assigns sounds to system events. These are depicted in Figure 10.3 on the left, while the sound files available are shown in the column on the right. In this illustration, the Asterisk system event has been assigned the TADA.WAV sound file, so anytime Windows 3.1 or any application displays an Asterisk dialog box, the TADA sound file automatically plays. Sounds can be assigned to any of the events listed on the left of the display, and clicking on the **Test** button allows you to hear the sound file directly from the Control Panel to audition it.

Figure 10.2   *The Sound icon in the Control Panel is only accessible if an audio device and the required drivers are installed.*

Windows 3.1 comes with four standard sounds included as part of the standard code:

- CHIMES.WAV
- CHORD.WAV
- DING.WAV
- TADA.WAV

Adding sound to system and application events adds a new dimension to the act of computing, and even such routine tasks as word processing and using a spreadsheet can get a boost from sound. Instead of silent dialog boxes to alert you or request input from you, now you can have your choice of sounds to accompany these on-screen messages.

The four sound files included in Windows is a good starting point that gives you an idea of how sound can be used and assigned to system events, but you'll soon want to give your system the custom touch—or should we say custom sound—that makes your computer unique.

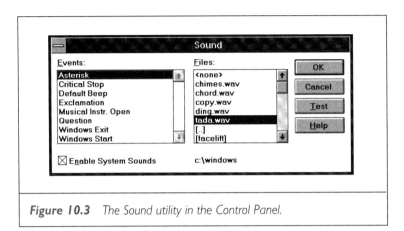

Figure 10.3 *The Sound utility in the Control Panel.*

To give you an idea of what it's like to have audio prompts in addition to visual cues, consider that virtually anything you can hear (and record) can become a viable *sound bite* .WAV file that you can use for any of the attachable system events.

In addition to recording sound bites in your own voice, you can also use a VCR, cassette player, or other device producing line output to the soundboard's input jack to record sound from these sources.

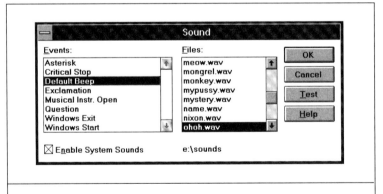

Figure 10.4 *Building a sound-bite library can be fun, and assigning sound to normal system events lightens up the computing environment. The author's system setup, shown above, uses a humorous "uh-oh" sound as the default system beep, while former President Nixon proclaims "I am not a crook" when Windows is exited.*

In the Files column of Figure 10.4 are lots of .WAV file types that comprise my ever-growing sound bite library. I've found many terrific snippets of sound on TV that make humorous "quickies" to add a little lightheartedness to my computing sessions. I simply record TV shows on my VCR that are likely to produce some real sound-bite winners (*The Simpsons* is a treasure trove, as are old *Three Stooges* and *Laurel & Hardy* movies), and then use the Sound Recorder accessory while I play back the portions I want to capture. TV commercials are another great source of sound samples.

For example, my MONKEY.WAV file is a sound bite of a Scotsman saying *I don't give a monkey's chuckee* in a thickly-brogued accent, MEOW.WAV is a pussycat's vocalizations, NIXON.WAV is the former president proclaiming *I am not a crook*, and so on. You can get really creative and your imagination is really your only limitation. You'll also find that you develop an "ear" for picking up good sound bites the more you get involved using sound.

As we learned earlier, sound bites can be up to 60 seconds in length when recorded from the Sound Recorder accessory itself, although virtually every sound card and audio port device comes bundled with software that permits recording longer .WAV files. For most sound bites, however, a full minute is more than you'll need since some of the best sound bites are the under-three-second quickies. And don't forget that sound files take up disk space: the NIXON.WAV file has a length of .77 seconds and occupies 8,590 bytes.

There are some audio software packages currently available that permit attaching additional sounds to other actions and events beyond what is possible from the sound accessory itself. For example, some of these packages permit assigning sounds to the activity of resizing a window itself, and may permit other sound files (such as MIDI music) to be played in response to an event or action. These packages and utilities are covered in Lesson 9.

Voice Annotation

While attaching sound to the system events exemplify some of the fun things you can do, there are also many practical uses for recording and using sound in Windows applications themselves. You can add audio memos to your word-processing documents and spreadsheets, include audio on-line help in your applications, and much, much more. Attaching sound (usually verbal sound bites) to your documents is called *voice annotation*, and it is one of the practical business uses for PC audio made possible through the Windows 3.1 environment. Voice annotation is like having audio Post-It notes that you attach to your documents, spreadsheets, or databases. You can increase the effectiveness of your documents and enhance communication by using voice annotation to ask questions, add comments, or draw additional attention to an item by clicking on a sound icon. The nicest part about voice annotation is that the voice messages "travel" with the host document, so there is no need to open up an additional utility or application to use them.

To illustrate how voice annotation works and how easy it is to use, we'll use this manuscript as an example. I am writing this book using Microsoft Word for Windows and voice annotation is supported by this application. At this point, let's say that I decide I'd like to include a voice annotation that gives some additional commentary.

I simply click on the **Insert** menu (see Figure 10.5), then click on **Voice Annotation**, and the dialog box shown in Figure 10.6 is displayed.

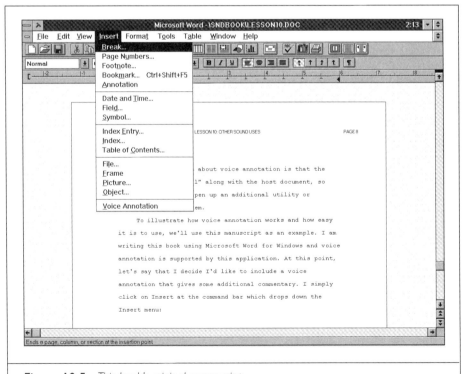

Figure 10.5   *This book's original manuscript.*

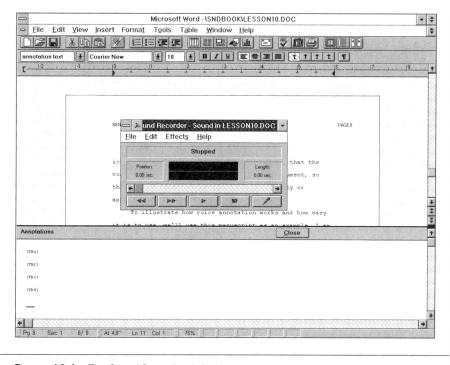

Figure 10.6 *The Sound Recorder dialog box.*

When a voice annotation recording is completed, a small microphone icon appears next to that entry in the annotation window. Clicking on the microphone icon again invokes the Sound Recorder accessory so the corresponding voice annotation segment can be played, edited, or moved to another location.

Five of the six annotation entries shown in Figure 10.7 on the next page are "blanks"—there is no audio information in them, but they were inserted to receive additional commentary at a later time. Since there is no audio file associated with them, no microphone icon is displayed.

The integration of the voice annotation and the word processing document is said to be *seamless*, since they are joined together through the data sharing, linking, and embedding capabilities of the Windows environment.

When a voice file is annotated to a document, it is said to be a *secondary messaging medium*. The document itself is the *primary medium*. However, you can use voice messages as the primary medium if you desire by simply recording your voice files

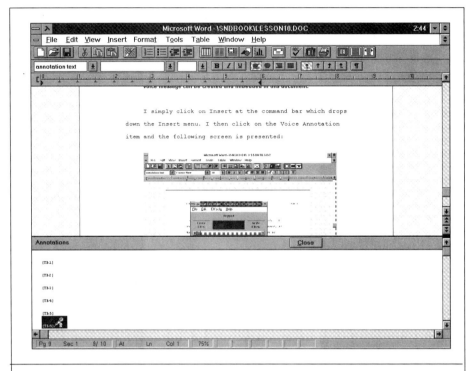

Figure 10.7 *Annotations are signified with a microphone icon.*

to floppy disk, which can then be sent to other PC users instead of a written document. The uses for voice messaging and adding sound to your applications are virtually unlimited, so be creative in your thinking to get the most enjoyment and benefit from the sound capabilities built into Windows.

Multimedia Applications

Multimedia is a combination of sound, graphics, animation, and video, and it is currently the hottest software development area. As more PC users add sound cards and audio port devices to their computers, multimedia applications will continue to get more popular and we can look forward to lots of exciting, interesting, and highly productive applications coming our way in the future that will all take advantage of the benefits of multimedia.

While it is beyond the scope of this book to go into detail about all of the sound and audio aspects of multimedia, here are a few of the key areas in which sound plays a major role:

- A voice narration (.WAV) file can be played simultaneously while a music (MIDI) file is playing in the background.

- Graphics can have voice annotation files attached to them in addition to or instead of text captions.

- Video and animations can have narratives and synchronized sound effects in addition to music.

- Standard audio CDs can be played through a PC's CD-ROM drive and the audio output merged with other audio files (.WAV and MIDI, for example) for combined output.

- Music and sound-effects files can be attached to program actions to give additional emphasis or direct the user's attention.

- Other uses are limited only by your imagination.

For a more complete understanding of multimedia, its uses and how to get the most from it, I highly recommend *Welcome To...Multimedia* by Linda Tway (MIS:Press, 1992), as well as *Welcome To... CD-ROM* by Tom Benford (MIS:Press, 1993).

Speech Synthesis

Computers can't speak, but they can run software that assembles and approximates synthetic speech, thus giving the PC the ability to produce "spoken" words. Computer speech can be produced either by splicing prerecorded words together, or by combining the individual sounds that make up individual words. Computer-generated speech, however, lacks the inflection and cadence of live human speech and, as such, sounds very monotonous and mechanical. It is used widely for interaction with the handicapped and for other special purpose applications, and it is also gaining in popularity as an automatic proofreading device.

A speech synthesizer is included in the Microsoft Windows Sound System, and can be used to have data proofread aloud in Microsoft Excel or Lotus 1-2-3 for Windows spreadsheets. If you've ever had to verify long columns of data in a spreadsheet, you can appreciate how useful it is to have two people working together—one looks at the data in the spreadsheet and the other reads the original numbers aloud. Now you can have your PC do the reading, so you won't need a second person to verify the integrity of your data.

There are other speech synthesis programs available such as *Monologue for Windows*, and these are also covered in depth in Lesson 9.

Some Other Sound Goodies

In addition to providing a hardware and software combination for recording and playing back sound, the Microsoft Windows Sound System provides some other features and capabilities that were only briefly mentioned in Lesson 6. Here's an opportunity to take a look at what other components make up the complete package.

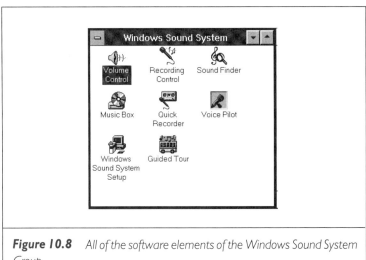

Figure 10.8   *All of the software elements of the Windows Sound System Group.*

The icons shown in Figure 10.8 are used for invoking various elements of the sound system. Their associations are as follows:

- **Volume Control.** Clicking on this icon adjusts the volume and the right/left channel balance. It can also quickly mute all sound, and provides a means for controlling the volume and balance for all of the individual sound sources (CD audio, microphone, line input).

- **Recording Control.** This is used for specifying the recording source (mike or line input), and it controls the input level for recording sounds with Quick Recorder or for voice commands with Voice Pilot.

- **Quick Recorder.** This is used for quick recording and playback of sound, including voice messages. It is also used for editing sound, adding effects to sound, and adding pictures, text labels, and descriptions to sound files, in addition to attaching sounds to other documents.

- **Sound Finder.** This is a handy utility for managing sound files. It permits you to browse and preview (audition) sound files as well as edit them. It is also useful for converting files from other sound formats and for adding pictures, text labels, and descriptions to sound files.

- **Voice Pilot.** Covered in detail in Lesson 9, this is used for controlling the computer with voice commands.

- **Music Box.** A utility for controlling the playback of audio CDs in a CD-ROM drive if one is installed in the PC. It also permits assigning CD and track titles as well as setting up custom play lists.

- **Sound System Setup.** This permits adding or changing Windows Sound System components, as well as setting the preferences to your liking.

- **Guided Tour.** A multimedia guided tour of the Windows Sound System that acquaints you with its features and demonstrates their uses and effect.

The hardware features of the Windows Sound System are covered in more detail in Lesson 4.

Covox Features

The Covox Voice Blaster comes with a recording utility, in addition to its recognition software, that permits recording and attaching/embedding sound files.

The SyncRecorder uses the same friendly user interface based on consumer products like cassette decks and CD players, so it is very easy to use and doesn't require any special skills. Unlike the Sound Recorder, which is limited to a

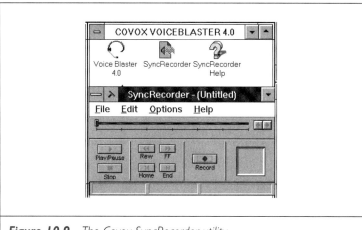

Figure 10.9 *The Covox SyncRecorder utility.*

maximum sound file length of 60 seconds, SyncRecorder can record continuously up to the maximum capacity of your hard disk. Covox's audio hardware products and other Covox software is covered in more detail in Lessons 4 and 9.

Glossary

attach   The process of linking one type of data seamlessly to another, as in the attachment of a sound file to a word-processing document. When an item, such as a voice file, is attached to a document, the voice file becomes coupled to the document file, much the same as if the sound file was a Post-It note attached to another sheet of paper.

embed   The process of building an item into another item as opposed to attaching it. An embedded sound, for example, becomes a part of the document file in which it is embedded, rather than remaining a free-standing entity that can be unattached.

primary messaging medium   A word-processing document, spreadsheet, or database file that is the carrier for any secondary messaging medium such as a sound, graphic, or video file. (See *secondary messaging medium*.)

seamless integration The result of hardware or software elements working flawlessly without requiring program adjustments or exceptional effort. Ideally, seamless integration refers to multiple applications all sharing the same resources (such as a sound card and audio files) without conflict or without requiring additional loading on the part of the user.

secondary messaging medium Any auxiliary data format that acts as a supplement to the primary messaging medium. For example, a word-processing document would be considered the primary messaging medium, while its attached or embedded sound file would be the secondary medium. (See *primary messaging medium*).

sound bite An informal term that refers to any small audio segment used in broadcast, recording, or multimedia applications, either by itself or in conjunction with text or graphics.

speech synthesis The ability of a computer to produce "spoken" words. Computer speech can be produced either by splicing prerecorded words together, or by combining the individual sounds that comprise individual words.

voice annotation The capability to add vocal sound bites including questions, comments, emphasis, and auxiliary information by either attaching it or embedding them in a document, spreadsheet, or database.

LESSON ELEVEN:
Software Reviews

This chapter contains hands-on assessments of over 50 software packages.

The Software Factor

While a sound board or audio port device can indeed open up the world of sound to you and your PC, finding the right software package for the specific tasks and objectives you have in mind will expand your horizons even further.

Let me preface these reviews by saying that you won't find a bad review included here. That is by design, not by accident. The truth of the matter is that the space for this chapter was limited and I didn't want to waste it by covering anything that wasn't a first-rate product. Therefore, every one of the titles you see included here is definitely worthwhile. Here's a listing of the titles I've covered in this lesson:

260 Instant Drum Patterns	Mr. Sound FX
AudioClips / 2001 /orig. StarTrek /Next Gen.	Multimedia Music Library
AudioView	Music Mentor with Recording Session
Band In A Box	MusicBytes
Best of MIDI Collection Vols. I & II	MusiClips Collectors Edition Bundle
Best of Sound Bytes Vol. I	MusicTime
Cadenza	Nautilus Monthly Magazine on CD-ROM
Cakewalk Pro for Windows	Pianist, The
Composer Quest	Play It By Ear
Dr. T's Sing-A-Long	Power Chords
Drummer 2.0	PowerTracks
Encore	Rhythm Ace
EZ Sound FX	Sequencer Plus Gold
Interludes: Ear Play	Soloist
Interludes: Note Play	Sound Forge
Interludes: Rhythm Play	Sound Impression
Interludes: Sound Sculptor	Studio for Windows 3.1
Jammer Pro 2.0, The	SuperJAM!
Jazz: A Multimedia History	Synergy
MagiClips Music	Trax
Master Tracks Pro-4	Trycho Tunes
Microsoft Musical Instruments	Turtle Tools for Multimedia, The
MIDI MaxPak, The	WAVE for Windows
Monologue for Windows	WinSong
Mr. Drumstix' Music Studio	World of Music Sampler

Title: **260 Instant Drum Patterns** **Media:** **Floppy disk**
Publisher: **Five Pin Press** **List price:** **$29.95**

Most non-drummers have difficulty creating rhythm tracks for song sequencing. This package provides a disk of patterns supplemented by a book. The patterns on disk are based on the popular René-Pierre Bardet book, which is included. The book documents the patterns in both music notation and grid form.

The instant patterns can be used with any software sequencer that reads standard MIDI files, and you can also use these patterns with *Drummer* 2.0 (also reviewed in this lesson) by CoolShoes Software.

Using a sequencer or *Drummer* 2.0, you delete, copy, and paste individual patterns to form complete songs or modify them to create even more drum patterns. The software's documentation details how to use the patterns and set them up properly for your particular drum machine, keyboard, or tone module.

The rich variety of contemporary styles and fill patterns includes: Afro-Cuban, Blues, Boogie, Bossa Nova, Cha-Cha, Disco, Funk, Jazz, March, Paso Doble, Pop, Reggae, Rock, R&B, Samba, Shuffle, Ska, Slow, Swing, Twist, Waltz, plus Endings, and more.

Using the patterns couldn't be easier, yet it provides an incredibly rich resource for quickly building "killer" drum lines and percussion tracks for your MIDI compositions. Even the most intricate multiple-roll fills can quickly be copied, cut, and pasted to add those really distinctive touches to your sequences, and the General MIDI standard (and 15 others) is supported.

Title: **AudioClips Collections** **Media:** **Floppy disk**
Publisher: **Sound Source Unlimited, Inc.** **List price:** **$59.95-69.95**

If you're looking for a way to add some spice to your Windows computing sessions, Sound Source may have just what you're looking for with its AudioClips Collections. As of this writing there are currently three Collections available, but more are in the works and may be available by the time you read this.

The Logical Collection ($59.95) contains authorized digital samples of classic dialog, sound effects, and musical cues from episodes of the original *Star Trek* television series.

The Encounter At Farpoint Collection ($69.95) features popular dialog, sound effects, and music from the pilot episode of *Star Trek: The Next Generation, Encounter at Farpoint*.

The 2001: Collection ($69.95) features lots of HAL dialog, sound effects, and music from *2001: A Space Odyssey*, plus bonus clips from *2010: The Year We Make Contact*.

With each of the collections a Windows 3.1 utility called *Whoop It Up!* is also included. This program greatly increases the number of system events to which you can assign AudioClips. Additionally, .MID (MIDI) files can be assigned to play back at specified events, provided a Windows 3.1 MIDI device is installed.

And if you don't have a sound card or an audio port installed (yet), you can still take advantage of AudioClips since a driver is also included to route sound through the PC's internal speaker.

Title:	**AudioView**	*Media:*	**Floppy disk**
Publisher:	**Voyetra Technologies, Inc.**	*List price:*	**$129.95**

Relying entirely on graphics and an intuitive GUI front end, AudioView makes sophisticated sound mixing, editing, and effects handling incredibly easy, even for the casual sonic aficionado.

AudioView permits mixing multiple audio files such as voice, music, and sound effects with full volume control for each. Additional effects like fade in and out can also be implemented during the mix for highly professional results.

The program supports standard .VOC and Windows .WAV format sound files in mono or stereo, and it includes some very high-end features like trim, silence, and scale, in addition to the usual cut-and-paste functions. A selectable range control is also provided for zeroing-in on a particular section of a file and it affords highly accurate editing. Everything is graphically-based, including the visual representation of the sound file. A zoom feature permits viewing and modifying sounds at the finest resolution. Visual feedback via "LED bar display" graphics keep you informed of the input signal strength, the ability to "punch" in or out of recording mode, and a plethora of special effects including noise-gate threshholding, adding echo and reverb, inverting and reversing samples, and more all make this a truly outstanding package.

AudioView also comes with Voyetra drivers for just about any sound card you can think of, and they include custom MIDI-map setups that optimize the voices and channels for each card.

Title: **Band-In-A-Box** *Media:* **Floppy disk**
Publisher: **PG Music, Inc.** *List Price:* **$88.00**

One of the most interesting and useful pieces of software I've come across for quickly assembling songs and musical elements, *Band-In-A-Box* is an "intelligent" music accompaniment software program for any MIDI music system or PC sound card.

The program automatically generates a complete, professional-quality arrangement of piano, bass, drums, guitar, and strings in a wide variety of popular styles. Twenty-four styles are built into the program, and an auxiliary styles disk with more variations is also available for $29.00 additional.

With *Band-In-A-Box*, you can input a typical song in just a couple of minutes by simply typing in the chords for any song. Chord entry is simple and straight-forward, using standard chord symbols (like C, Fm7, or C13b9). Once the chords are entered, select the style you like and *Band-In-A-Box* does the rest. There are additional provisions for varying the style and even for custom endings. The included Stylemaker utility permits you to create your own styles or modify any of the built-in styles to suit your musical tastes. Different drum "kits" are also provided to find the right percussion sounds for your creations, and the program also features a built-in sequencer for recording your melodies.

Whether you're just getting your feet wet in computer music or you're an accomplished pro looking for a fast way to build musical foundations for songs, this program is a treasure.

Title: **Best of MIDI Connection Vols. I & II, The** *Media:* **CD-ROM**
Publisher: **Metatec Corp.** *List price:* **$49.95 ea.**

Like its sister products *The Best of Photography* and *The Best of Sound Bytes*, *The Best of MIDI Connection Volumes I and II* are a compilation of material which has been used in the *Nautilus* monthly CD-ROM magazine from Metatec, but there's lots of additional material here that is new and unique to this disc.

The CD-ROM is a hybrid disc so it plays correctly in either a Macintosh or an IBM-compatible computer (the files appear in two formats at discrete locations on the disc). Over 300 MIDI files are provided on each volume for use by both Macintosh and DOS/Windows sequencer software.

The selection provides a pleasantly rich variety of classical, ragtime, and contemporary compositions that vary in scope from single instrument pieces to full orchestral, multi-timbral works of considerable complexity.

Ready-to-use drum patterns and chord progressions are included as "building blocks" for the MIDI composer, and improvisation aids with EPS (encapsulated PostScript) printable sheet music are also useful features of this disc.

All of the MIDI files on the disc were saved in two formats: Passport Designs *MasterTracks/Pro-4* format and as standard MIDI files ready for import into your favorite MIDI software for playback, arranging, or editing.

Title:	**Best of Sound Bytes Volume I, The**	Media:	**CD-ROM**
Publisher:	**Metatec Corp.**	List price:	**$49.95**

Available in separate versions for both MPC and Macintosh computers, this disc is a diverse collection of music, sounds, audio tracks, and waveform sound files compiled from over a dozen issues of *Nautilus*, a Macintosh and Windows/MPC CD-ROM monthly optical media magazine service (see the *Nautilus* review).

Both versions contain twenty multimedia music beds, twelve sound effects, two 60-second spots. Sixty, thirty, fiftenn, and five-second multimedia music beds are also provided.

The Macintosh version contains files that are compatible with the DigiDesign AudioMedia System card or the Macromind/ Paracomp Soundedit System, and an interactive listing and "locator" front-end for the sound files is provided.

The MPC version has files that are compatible with all Windows-supported MPC-compatible audio devices. All of the sound files on this version are recorded in two formats: 22 kHz 8-bit (.WAV file format) and 44 kHz 16-bit (.AIF file format). A "locator" listing of all sound files on the disc is included.

Sounds include high quality recordings of such effects as bowling balls hitting pins and jet planes flying by overhead. Excellent musical beds in various pre-timed durations make assembling the background audio portion of a multimedia presentation or movie a snap. And all of the audio can be used royalty-free!

Title: **Cadenza for Windows Ver. 2** *Media:* **Floppy disk**
Publisher: **Big Noise Software, Inc.** *List price:* **$299.95**

This powerful Windows MIDI sequencer package has gotten better with the release of Version 2. The new version provides support for additional MIDI interfaces, provides SMPTE tape sync, it can handle up to 256 MIDI channels, and supports extremely powerful editing of MIDI.

Some of the package's outstanding features include music notation editing, chart printing, swing quantizing, auto saving of your files, and much more. The program supports up to 64 sequencer tracks and provides controls for adjusting the track patch, volume, and panning. "Smart" instrument setups, mute maps, full graphic editing, multiple block marks, and multiple editing views all combine to make this a superb package for any MIDI musician.

Sophisticated features like punch in/out, a chase lock and the ability to lock editing windows together make this a noteworthy (pardon the pun) package, and icon-based editing tool boxes take advantage of the Windows environment.

The program's on-line hypertext help is among the best I've encountered and the displays are large and easy to read. Must-have features like convenient transport control bars, controller edit faders, and multi-window design for easy organization are all here, along with zoom in/out, programmable quantizing and humanizing, speaker and MIDI note metronomes, multitasking, and more.

Title: **Cakewalk Professional for Windows** *Media:* **Floppy disk**
Publisher: **Twelve Tone Systems** *List price:* **$349.00**

If you're looking for a true industrial-strength MIDI sequencer that runs under Windows, *Cakewalk Professional* is probably going to fit your bill of goods.

Cakewalk Pro can handle up to 256 MIDI tracks, and it makes high-powered MIDI sequencing easy thanks to its variety of graphical views, excellent controls, and logical program layout.

You can view and edit MIDI notes in piano-roll, staff notation, or event-list formats. You can draw tempo changes, velocity levels, and pitch bends with your mouse, mix volume levels with graphic faders and, while your music plays back, change sound assignments, panning, tempos, pitch transpositions, and much more. You can even control digital audio cards and other multimedia devices synchronized to your MIDI sequences.

An ideal application for music composition, audio production, video or film scores, radio spots and multimedia applications, *Cakewalk Pro* makes sophisticated tasks simple.

A special feature is the *Cakewalk Application Language* (CAL), which is a built-in programming language that lets you create your own chord generators, patch editing routines, data thinners, drum maps, and other editing commands. Sample programs are also included, and additional CAL routines are available through Twelve Tone Systems.

Cakewalk may well be the only MIDI sequencer package you'll ever need— regardless of what your requirements are.

Title:	**Composer Quest**	*Media:*	**CD-ROM**
Publisher:	**Dr. T's Music Software**	*List price:*	**$99.00**

Composer Quest is an interactive exploration of music, history, arts, and sociological change from the year 1600 through the present day.

The program makes music history come alive by taking you on a tour through time to investigate the greatest composers in classical and early jazz music.

To make learning fun, *Composer Quest* features a game. Upon hearing a mystery melody, you board the Time Machine and travel back in time to find the composer who wrote the music you've heard. You'll meet some interesting people along the way in a race against the clock.

If you've ever wondered what was happening in general world history while Tchaikovsky was writing the 1812 Overture or when Picasso was experimenting with new art forms, you'll find these answers and more in the program.

You can listen to over 60 great musical performances, read biographies of important composers, scan news events from 1600 to the present, view high-resolution 256-color screens, take a quiz to test your knowledge and much, much more.

A quick index is also built into the program to help you find any composer quickly and easily. All sound cards that work with Windows 3.1 are supported, and an MPC-compliant PC is required to use the program properly.

Composer Quest is a fun, unique, and educational program that anyone who is interested in music will enjoy.

Title: **Dr. T's Sing-A-Long**   *Media:* **Floppy disk**
Publisher: **Dr. T's Music Software**   *List price:* **$49.95**

Billed as "Karaoke for Kids," *Dr. T's Sing-A-Long* uniquely combines music, captivating animations, song lyrics, and musical notation to make singing along a real treat for children and parents alike.

Each of the more than 25 classic children's songs has its own characters and an animated story, and there's even a master of ceremonies. The cast of colorful characters includes *Itsy Bitsy Spider, Old McDonald, Mary Had a Little Lamb, Yankee Doodle,* and more.

Older children can reinforce their reading skills and learn to read music before they know it. Younger children find the animations alone entertaining. Parents and educators will both agree that it's a delightful and fun way to introduce kids to the wonders of music.

The user interface features big buttons to make it easy for youngsters to control the program. There are options to repeat songs and turn the lyrics or the melody on or off. You're also given the capability of speeding up or slowing down the music as it plays, and the melody and lyrics scroll in time with the music.

Included with the software is a booklet that teaches the basic principles of music, and the program is capable of printing the music and lyrics to any Windows-supported printer. It's a terrific introduction to music for kids of all ages.

Title: **Drummer 2.0**   *Media:* **Floppy disk**
Publisher: **Cool Shoes(Inter-Galactic)Software**   *List price:* **$99.00**

Drummer 1.0 was probably the best-selling drum software program available, mainly because it was easy to use and it had a bevy of great features that made putting percussion tracks together a relative snap. *Drummer 2.0* improves on the basic functionality of the earlier version and, in the process, makes it much more powerful and easier to use than ever before.

The new version supports MPU, Key, AdLib, Sound Blaster, and other sound devices, plus it has the capability to save 11 different kinds of format 0, 1, and 2 MIDI files.

Real-time recording from any MIDI instrument is also supported with 2.0, as well as real-time control from other MIDI devices. A pattern swing facility makes adding variations easy, as do the expanded metric structures with start-time/ duration rescaling. This is particularly useful for making a certain sequence "fit" a desired time frame, as in video or multimedia presentation work.

Drummer 2.0 permits using twice as many patterns at once and it also features an integrated pattern librarian. A MIDI metronome, global channel assignment, score page looping with section selection, many new editing commands, and customizing options and improved file windows all make 2.0 a winner.

Other drum patterns, such as 260 *Instant Patterns* from Five Pin Press (also reviewed here) can be used with *Drummer* 2.0.

Title:	Encore	*Media:*	Floppy disk
Publisher:	Passport Designs	*List price:*	$595.00

A stronger and more comprehensive composition and score printing program than its sister product, *MusicTime* (reviewed elsewhere in this lesson), *Encore* shares all of the ease of use and intuitive interface features of its smaller sibling while increasing staff-handling capacity to 64 staffs. You can literally create and print the individual scores for a 64-piece orchestra with this package. If you have heavy duty composing and music publishing needs in your MIDI environment, this is probably the package you've been looking for.

Encore can transcribe music as you play it live on a MIDI keyboard, read a MIDI file created in any sequencer, or build a beautiful notation, one note at a time. Your score can have up to 64 staves and you can work on up to 16 files simultaneously, so the package is capable of handling the most demanding tasks.

Once entered, the page of music is completely interactive on the screen, and you can grab and move notes, staves, symbols, and other elements to edit the score in almost any way you could desire or imagine. You can also type in lyrics and text or import them directly from other programs. Professional page layout controls, automatic beaming, transposable guitar chord symbols, and sophisticated part extraction help you prepare printouts that exactly match your needs. Additionally, *Encore* can quickly transcribe sequences from any Passport sequencer or any sequencer that exports standard MIDI files for added flexibility.

Title: **EZ Sound FX** *Media:* **Floppy disk**
Publisher: **Future Trends Software** *List price:* **$79.00**

EZ Sound FX is a nifty collection of six easy-to-use Windows sound utilities that will add some pizazz to your sound card.

Master FX is a flexible and versatile sound editor that records, edits, and plays back your own sounds or any other sound. A real strength of the software is its ability to import and process sound files from sources other than a PC including the Macintosh, Amiga, NeXT, and Sun computers. *Panel FX* is an overall control panel for adjusting the sonic parameters of your system. Three main control sections are available from within Panel FX: Hardware, System, and Volume. *CD FX* is a utility for playing audio CDs through the PC's CD-ROM drive, and it uses a graphic control interface that resembles an actual audio CD player. *Digital FX* permits you to assign digitized sound samples to a variety of Windows-related events including starting and stopping an application, opening or closing a window, and so forth. *Music FX* is a music-playing utility that permits you to select sound files to compile a play list and then play them as a background task. Ten albums of synthesized songs are also included with the software with selections to suit just about every musical taste from classical to contemporary. *Synth FX* is similar to *Digital FX* except that it allows you to assign FM-synthesized sounds (instead of digital samples) to Windows events and system activities. A rich assortment of synth sounds are also included.

Title: **Interludes Series (4 titles)** *Media:* **Floppy disk**
Publisher: **Ibis Software** *List price:* **$39.95-$99.95**

Ibis' *Interludes Series* is a unique and specialized series of interactive music games and utilities that are perfect for musical novices of all ages.

NotePlay is a sight-reading game. Merely select your skill level and NotePlay composes an exercise for you. Note reading speed and accuracy improves while you keep trying to beat your high score. Thirty different skill levels are provided, and it features a fun, graphical interface (suggested list price of $49.95).

RhythmPlay is a rhythm-training game that makes learning rhythms fun and challenging. Perfect for beginners, the program features a visual metronome, 24 skill levels, sustain and timing accuracy, a high-score table, slow, normal, and automatic play modes, and more. The suggested list price is $49.95.

SoundSculptor is a graphical sound utility for sound cards that allows you to create and synthesize sounds in a graphical environment. You can create and save your own sounds by changing attack, decay, sustain, and release rates. It lists for $39.95.

EarPlay is a useful game for developing your ability to recognize intervals and melodies, and your skills will improve as you try to beat your own high score. *EarPlay* composes musical phrases for you based on your selected skill level, and it helps you develop your "musical ear" while having fun at the same time. The program has a suggested list price of $49.95.

Title:	**The Jammer Pro 2.0**	*Media:*	**Floppy disk**
Publisher:	**Soundtrek**	*List price:*	**$175.00**

The *Jammer Pro* 2.0 is a unique piece of MIDI software—in fact the package touts it as "the complete PC MIDI studio that includes studio musicians." While this may sound like its stretching the truth a bit, it does provide an incredibly automated means of producing background, rhythm, and even lead parts for your MIDI compositions.

Two hundred and fifty-six "built-in professional studio musicians" create drums, drum fills, drum solos, bass parts, rhythm guitars and keys, melodies, lead breaks, and chord progressions for you, entirely automatically if you so desire. You can control the style of each musician on each track as they crank out millions of different parts. You decide which tracks and measures to keep or redo.

The program is capable of handling up to 256 tracks of composing, live recording, sequencing, mixing, and producing. One hundred twenty-five band styles files including rock, pop, blues, funk, jazz, ballads, classical, bluegrass, Latin, Reggae, and many more are sure to provide the right tempo and backing for your songs, and you can enter your own chords at any eight-note boundary or let *The Jammer* create new chord progressions for you.

More than mere automatic accompaniment, using *The Jammer* is like working with a group of hip musicians in a recording studio environment, with you as the producer and ultimate musician. A standard version of *The Jammer*, which has slightly slimmed-down features, is also available for only $88.00.

Title: Jazz: A Multimedia History   *Media:* CD-ROM
Publisher: Compton's New Media   *List price:* $99.95

This disc is an educational introduction to and melodic journey through the world of jazz music. The disc is highly interactive and the user is encouraged to travel from the origins of jazz to the vibrant, electric sounds of today's contemporary jazz and fusion musical styles.

You'll be able to hear quotes and interviews from jazz musicians that will give you interesting insights into what the jazz scene is all about. You'll be able to see how early jazz evolved into what it is today, and you'll learn how to interpret the nuances of jazz while enhancing your appreciation—without knowing music notation!

You'll learn about the inventors and the innovators of different styles like ragtime, swing, bebop, fusion, big band, and soul. This disc contains a complete chronology of the music and masters complete with photos, sound effects, and jazz music from 1923 to 1991.

Duke Ellington, Charlie Parker, Louis Armstrong, and other founding fathers of jazz are biographied, as well as contemporary musical innovators like Herbie Hancock, Miles Davis, and Weather Report. Ella Fitzgerald, Carmen McRae, Al Jarreau, Bobby McFerrin, and others are covered as well in this rich musical tapestry, and selected recordings from these artists are also included.

If you're a jazz aficionado, or just a music lover in general, *Jazz: A Multimedia History* hits a high note.

Title: Magiclips Music   *Media:* CD-ROM
Publisher: Wolfetone Multimedia Publishing   *List price:* $89.95

Magiclips consists of professionally crafted original production music for computer, multimedia, film, and video presentations. The music is supplied in mixed-mode on the CD-ROM in formats that can be read by the computer and also played on an audio CD player.

The disc is designed to enable you to easily enhance your presentations with top-quality music in a variety of styles and lengths. "Que cards" are provided to help you locate just the sounds you want by *Feeling* (such as uptempo, inspirational, and success), *Musical Style* (funky, jazzy, Caribbean, and so forth) and *Use* (such as sports, product, travel). Fanfares, intros, outros, and beds, the essential building blocks of good production music, are all provided here.

You can use *Magiclips* music on any number of presentations, sell as many as you like and publicly play or broadcast your presentations (including advertising uses) without paying any additional royalties or having to comply with any reporting requirements. Once you buy this disc, the music is yours to keep and use any way you desire.

Thirty-five *Magiclips Music* segments are provided in the following formats: 16-bit mono .WAV, 8-bit mono .WAV, 16-bit stereo .WAV, 8-bit mono .WAV (22 kHz), 8-bit mono .WAV (11 kHz), 8-bit mono .VOC (11 kHz), and MIDI type 0, type 1, and *Master Tracks Pro* formats.

Title:	**Master Tracks Pro-4**	*Media:*	**Floppy disk**
Publisher:	**Passport Designs**	*List price:*	**$395.00**

This is the big brother of the *Trax* package also from Passport Designs (reviewed elsewhere in this section).

Running under Windows, *Master Tracks Pro-4* is a comprehensive MIDI sequencing package that encompasses all of the features and ease of use of *Trax* while adding many of the sophisticated features required by professional-level users.

Recording is simple with 64-multichannel tracks and familiar controls that resemble a tape recorder. You can record your music in real-time as you play, or step-enter it a single note at a time. You can then cut, copy, paste, clear, insert, mix, or delete information from any part of any sequence or song. A user-programmable preset palette lets you choose the right instrument sounds and audition them as your sequence plays. Industry standard MIDI files are supported.

You can view and edit your MIDI files in several different ways, and processing features including humanize, quantize, transpose, fit time, and strip data on tracks or entire sections of a song are supported. A unique global change filter singles out specific data types and locations of events to make complex editing chores a simple affair.

Master Tracks Pro-4 is a superlative all-in-one package that provides a simple yet powerful means for recording, composing, editing, and producing printed sheet music of your compositions. It's easy enough for the novice, powerful enough for the pro.

Title: **Microsoft Musical Instruments** *Media:* **CD-ROM**
Publisher: **Microsoft Corp.** *List price:* **$99.95**

More than 200 musical instruments from around the world come to life in *Microsoft Musical Instruments*, an MPC CD-ROM which is a real treat for anyone who loves music.

Articles are provided on each instrument that explore the history of the instrument while providing over 500 excellent photographs and 1,500 sound samples.

Familiar instruments as well as exotic ones from the farthest reaches of the globe—everything from accordion to zurna—are covered in great depth and details. You can zoom-in on information with a click of the mouse or jump from one section of the program to another, since all of the data is dynamically linked.

In the *Instruments of the World* section of the disc you can invoke a regional display of instruments from different areas of the world along with sound samples of each. Clicking on an instrument brings forth a full-page article.

The *Musical Ensembles* portion provides sound samples of different musical styles (chamber music to steel drums and everything in between) for listening and learning. The sound samples are full-fidelity recordings of professional musicians using the actual instruments.

Based on the highly acclaimed *Eyewitness Guide* book series, this disc takes you on a wonderfully interactive tour of music and the instruments that make it. It is an excellent program for anyone of any age.

Title: **The MIDI MaxPak** *Media:* **Floppy disk**
Publisher: **Big Noise Software, Inc.** *List price:* **$199.95**

The MIDI MaxPak provides a complete software solution for your MIDI studio needs. The product is really four individual programs that work interactively with each other to provide an incredibly powerful software environment for working with MIDI. The four programs are *LibMax*, *SeqMax*, *MixMax*, and *JukeMax*.

SeqMax is a 64-track sequencer that can record and play back all MIDI data. It allows easy editing with both text and graphic editing screens, and it provides support for multiple MIDI ports and tape sync support. Other outstanding features include variable quantizing, humanizing, swing, and more.

MixMax is a 16-channel automated mixer simulation that can record and play back movements of its on-screen controls as well as record and play back control changes from external MIDI devices. Each channel contains seven controls plus an LED simulation, and all controls are user assignable. *FadeMax* has all of the editing features of *MixMax*, but has only one control per channel, a fader. Essentially, it is a lighter version of *MixMax*.

LibMax is an easy-to-use patch librarian for many MIDI devices that lets you copy patches between banks to create new sets of sounds for your instruments. It knows how to communicate with instruments through special instructions contained in its Instrument Profile files.

JukeMax is a player utility that lets you assign song play lists. Combined, they make the *MaxPak* a great software package.

Title: **Monologue for Windows**   *Media:* **Floppy disk**
Publisher: **First Byte**   *List price:* **$79.95**

One of the first text-to-speech products to work with virtually all Windows-supported sound cards, *Monologue for Windows* provides an easy-to-use program that can enhance your productivity in several ways.

Any pronounceable combination of letters and numbers can be clearly spoken by the program, and it doesn't require any recording or speech training.

For data verification purposes, merely click the mouse to select a block of text and Monologue speaks that block for you. Used with spelling and grammar checkers, it's a great tool for ensuring that your documents are comprehensible and precise.

You can also use *Monologue* for proofreading, and it is particularly useful for checking spreadsheets and other documents that contain columns of numbers.

If you're interested in developing software, *Monologue* is macro-programmable using Windows Dynamic Data Exchange (DDE). For example, Excel macros, Word Basic routines, or Toolbook script can be interfaced with *Monologue* to add speech to your application.

Monologue is implemented as a background Windows application, and it is available on the desktop at any time through a simple click of the mouse. Speech parameters give you control over the sound, allowing you to set the volume, pitch, and speed of the speech. An exception dictionary is included that allows you to save your own preferred pronunciations as well.

Title: **Mr. Drumstix' Music Studio**   *Media:*   **Floppy disk**
Publisher: **Howling Dog Systems, Inc.**   *List price:* **$69.95**

If you have a youngster who's interested in music, *Mr. Drumstix' Music Studio* is an ideal way to nurture that interest while providing the child with hours of entertaining fun as well.

While primarily intended for entertainment, the games that are included in the program have been created with musical skill training in mind, and the input for the game concepts came from a highly experienced music educator.

Since children are naturally curious, *Mr. Drumstix' Music Studio* capitalizes on that curiosity by providing a positive environment in which they can begin exploring the world of music. The games and activities included provide a colorful setting in which children can express their creativity.

An assortment of tune files are provided with the software, although it can also play any song files created with *Power Chords*, also from Howling Dog Systems, Inc. (*Power Chords* is also reviewed in this lesson). It is important to note that this program will not play standard MIDI files, since it uses songs expressed in terms of repeating musical phrases. Standard MIDI files do not have this required information encoded into them.

Colorful graphics, good control layout, and an extremely easy-to-use interface makes this program ideal for younger children, although it is interesting (and challenging) enough to attract and hold the attention of parents as well.

Title: **Mr. Sound FX**   *Media:*   **CD-ROM**
Publisher: **Prosonus**   *List price:* **$29.95**

If you've seen any of the zany *Police Academy* movies, the vocal sound effects of Michael Winslow will certainly be familiar to you. Well, Michael has contributed his unique talents to this CD-ROM based collection of weird and wacky sounds from Prosonus that'll knock you out.

Winslow is *Mr. Sound FX*, and he likes to make noise. In fact, it's real hard to get him to shut up. Just when you thought you heard it all, he blows you away with yet another mind-boggling sound effect.

Mr. Sound FX is an excellent way of adding life to any Windows application. You can choose from over 150 sound effects to spice up your system sounds, add impact to graphics presentations, and attach special effects to your screen savers and custom icons.

The sound assortment includes violent explosions and machine gun fire, sirens and shattering glass, speeding planes, trains, cars and crashes, animal sounds and bird calls, cartoon voices, laughter and applause, sci-fi and electronic effects, sports, recreational and household sounds, musical sound effects and much, much more.

The program will work with any supported Windows sound card and it also comes with its own Windows Sound Driver for routing the sound effects to the PC's speaker if you don't have a sound card (yet). This one's sure to evoke lots of laughs.

Title:	**Multimedia Music Library**	*Media:*	**Floppy disk**
Publisher:	**Midisoft**	*List price:*	**$79.95**

Midisoft's *Multimedia Music Library* is a collection of music designed for use in multimedia presentations. Distributed on floppy disks in standard MIDI file format, the library is compatible with Midisoft's other products as well as with any other MIDI playback and editing software capable of reading standard MIDI files.

The music in the library is provided on a royalty-free basis for nonbroadcast use, which makes this package a cost-effective way to provide music for your multimedia needs.

Unlike other music library collections that provide unrelated musical pieces and leave you to pull it all together coherently, Midisoft's *Multimedia Music Library* organizes many of the pieces into smaller libraries unto themselves. In each of these smaller libraries you'll find an assortment of related music cues that you can use throughout your visual presentation. Under this arrangement, selecting related musical cues (such as introductions, fanfares, interludes, and lead-ins) is just as easy and straightforward as choosing the main theme.

The *Multimedia Music Library* comes with *MIDIBase*, an easy-to-use front end that lets you audition any piece in the library. Additionally, MIDIBase gives you information such as the title of the piece you're listening to, its file name and length, a description of the piece, its composer and comments. If you're working in multimedia, this package is a must-have resource.

Title:	**Music Mentor with Recording Session**	*Media:*	**Floppy disk**
Publisher:	**Midisoft**	*List price:*	**$149.95**

Music Mentor with Recording Session is the first Windows-based multimedia environment that combines music education and entertainment with the excitement of music creation in an affordable, integrated package. It's the perfect software for anyone getting started with computers and music, since it provides an introduction to the basics, it teaches about music history, and then it lets you take this knowledge and put it to use in making your own music.

The *Music Mentor* portion starts you at the beginning by providing simple definitions of melody, harmony, rhythm, and so forth. As each section progresses you are introduced to more challenging material. In addition to covering the six major topical areas there is also a section on the basics of reading music.

The *Recording Session* portion of the package provides an easy-to-use MIDI recording and editing program that displays music in standard notation. You can fine tune your music using the Score and MIDI Event List views, and you can enhance your skills as a recording engineer with the Integrated Mixing Board.

An ideal program for composing, recording, perfecting, and programming music for a wide variety of uses from business presentations to jam sessions, *Music Mentor with Recording Session* gives you the basic building blocks and the tools you'll need to make the most of this knowledge.

Title:	**MusicBytes**	*Media:*	**CD-ROM**
Publisher:	**Prosonus**	*List price:*	**$99.95**

MusicBytes is an excellent collection of multimedia music and sound effects clips that will add punch to your presentations, training videos, games, entertainment, and educational programs—or, you can just have fun with them!

Over 100 sound effects files are provided that run the gamut from commanding attention to hilarious. Twenty-seven original musical compositions are also included that include bebop, bluegrass, classical, corporate, fanfare, funk, fusion, industrial, international, jazz, new age, pop, orchestral, reggae, rock, and romantic styles.

The music selections are particularly noteworthy, since they are the works of several well-known artists who tour and record with the likes of Pink Floyd, The Doobie Brothers, Steely Dan, and Toto. The roster of artist credits includes Scott Page, Jeff Porcaro, Steve Kukather, Neil Stubenhaus, Jeff "Skunk" Baxter, Mike Lang, Dan Sawyer, Lee R. Thornburg, Steve Farris, Rock Deadrick, Kim Scharnberg, and Kevin Maloney.

A *Media Librarian* application is included with the package that provides a convenient and easy-to-use way of auditioning, cataloging, finding, cutting, and pasting from the collection.

Perhaps the best part of all is that all of the music and sound effects of *MusicBytes* are provided royalty-free. You don't even need a sound card, since you can play *MusicBytes* through your PC speaker.

Title:	**MusiClips Collector's Edition Bundle**	*Media:*	**Floppy disk**
Publisher:	**Voyetra Technologies, Inc.**	*List price:*	**$149.95**

MusiClips is a collection of over 150 songs in General MIDI format in five different volumes. Volume 1 consists of patriotic/ traditional/children's selections. Volume 2 contains holiday and religious/ethnic melodies. Volume 3 is a collection of classical favorites. Volume 4 is a compilation of 50 drum tracks complete with fills, variations, and licks. Volume 5 is filled with royalty-free production music for use in your own presentations and applications.

All of the song files were professionally created by accomplished musicians. The songs sound great when played through a sound card's FM synthesizer, and they are absolutely terrific when heard through a tone generator or external MIDI device.

MusiClips supports the SoundBlaster, AdLib, and any sound card that is compatible with the SoundBlaster or AdLib standards in addition to IBM's Music Feature and Roland's LAPC cards.

All of the MIDI files in the five volumes can be played directly through the Windows media player accessory, with the MIDI mapper set to General MIDI. You can also import these MIDI files into any software application (such as a sequencer, score printer, arranger, or mixer) that can utilize and process standard Type 1 MIDI song files. A player utility lets you play song files directly from the DOS command line as a background application, so you don't have to run Windows to use the files. The individual volumes are also available for $69.95 each.

Title:	MusicTime	*Media:*	Floppy disk
Publisher:	Passport Designs	*List price:*	$249.00

A desktop music composing and notation program for use with MIDI instruments or MIDI files played through a sound card's FM synthesizer under Windows, *MusicTime* provides an enjoyable, fun, and creative means of playing, composing, recording, and printing music. The printed output quality is that of commercially-published sheet music and you can add lyrics, the author's name, or other text anywhere on the staves. But there's more to this software than just its music-printing capabilities.

Music can be entered "from scratch" with the mouse or from a MIDI keyboard and played back through an attached MIDI instrument or through the sound card as soon as it is written. As the mouse is moved over the staff (treble or bass), the corresponding note on that staff position is played so you can "audition" the note before you select it. Sharps, flats, naturals, rests, dotted values, and other incidentals are all easily selected using the mouse from the seven note and symbol palettes and placed as desired on the staff sheet.

Commands to record, edit, and modify any aspect of the score and cut, copy, and paste individual measures or entire sections of music are provided, and note key transposition is easy to effect.

The program is very easy to learn, and its logical layout and intuitive interface make composing (and learning how to read) music a very pleasant and rewarding experience. It's a great program for anyone interested in music on a PC to learn and use.

Title:	Nautilus Monthly Magazine	*Media:*	CD-ROM
Publisher:	Metatec Corp.	*List price:*	$9.95/issue

Nautilus is a multimedia magazine published monthly on CD-ROM that provides information and software for Macintosh and PC/Windows users. Its content varies with each issue, but generally runs the gamut from utilities to programming tools to games and newly-released CD audio tracks. A typical issue might contain a collection of the best shareware and commercial demos, commentary and industry news, tech tips and tools, educational programs, multimedia pre-sentations, and "building blocks" such as photos, graphics and clip art, sound effects and production music, MIDI files, and desktop publishing components and tutorials.

Separate issues are published for Macintosh and PC users, thus providing the best material for both formats on a monthly disc dedicated to each machine format.

An annual (12-issue) subscription in North America is $137.40, which breaks down to $9.95 per issue plus $1.50 for shipping and handling. Metatec Corporation also has a "pay as you go" subscription option available.

A sample *Nautilus* disc is available for a shipping and handling charge of $4.95, and a three-disc "mini-subscription" (the *Intro to Nautilus* plus two regular issue discs) is also available at a suggested retail price of $29.95 if you'd like *Nautilus* on trial. Every issue is loaded with lots of helpful information, reviews, and other items that make it worthwhile.

Title:	**The Pianist**	*Media:*	**Floppy disk**
Publisher:	PG Music, Inc.	*List price:*	**$29.00**

A super bargain of a program that contains a huge collection of over 200 of the world's most popular classical piano pieces, performed by world-class concert pianists, a music trivia game, program notes, biographies, an on-disk music dictionary, and more make this one of the most value-packed musical software products available.

From the same folks who bring us *Band-In-A-Box*, *The Pianist* brings a wealth of music to the PC user with a sound card or a MIDI system. These music files can be used for presentations, for learning, for use in other musical applications, or just for listening.

All of the pieces were recorded in real time by concert pianists on an 88-note weighted MIDI piano keyboard. They aren't quantized or step recorded, so the resulting performances truly reflect the performances of the pianists who played them. All are complete artistic performances, professionally played, recorded and saved as standard MIDI files. You'll hear the music playing with CD-quality through your sound card or MIDI system, just as if the pianist was in your home.

The included *Music Trivia* game contains over 400 questions about the music, the piano, and the composers. There's also a "Guess That Song" game that plays a piece at random for you to guess. This is an excellent program for learning about music and the composers who created some of the best-loved classic pieces.

Title: **Play It By Ear**   *Media:* **Floppy disk**
Publisher: **Ibis Software**   *List price:* **$99.95**

Another self-paced, interactive training software package from Ibis, *Play It By Ear* is especially useful for developing your musical ear.

The software can help you master the subtle sounds of single tones, intervals and chords by providing a variety of self-paced exercises in a realistic learning environment. It features an on-screen piano keyboard or guitar fret-board, and you can select from six levels, or create your own custom exercises.

Its key features include letting you choose from a variety of interactive melodic and harmonic exercises with topics covering note, chord and interval recognition, chord and interval naming, pitches, scales, modes, and much more. You can track your progress with the computer's personal score keeper—you can select a progress graph or post-exercise summary, you can even print out a report if you wish.

Appropriate for beginning through advanced levels, *Play It By Ear* is fun and challenging in a graphically attractive environment. A 64-page manual complete with glossary and tutorial is also included.

Whether you're a student, hobbyist, musician, or music enthusiast, *Play It By Ear*'s self-paced training sharpens your musical senses and helps you develop your ear in a pleasant and painless manner.

Title: **Power Chords**   *Media:* **Floppy disk**
Publisher: **Howling Dog Systems, Inc.**   *List price:* **$99.95**

Whether you're a guitarist, keyboard player, or just have an "ear" for music, *Power Chords* opens up a new world of graphical music making. The most unique thing about this program is that it takes a guitarist's perspective on tune-smithing rather than the usual route of looking at it from the point of view of a keyboardist.

The program is very easy to use and it lets you work with chords and graphic patterns to create songs complete with chord, drum, bass, and melody parts. No knowledge of music notation or MIDI is required to use the software, although having such knowledge will permit you to really "push the envelope" of the program's capabilities.

Power Chords can use any MIDI sound module or drum machine, and it uses any MIDI interface or sound card supported by Windows. Special support is included for Roland GS format and General MIDI sound modules, so you can get the best sounds possible from these devices.

Full song arrangements can easily be created from chords and patterns, and you can audition any chord or music pattern by simply clicking on it. A built-in scripting language can also be used to create or run interactive lessons or demos.

Power Chords is a refreshing way to compose, edit, and play MIDI music that's easy to learn, fun to use, and powerful enough to produce highly-complex musical compositions.

Title: **PowerTracks**   *Media:* **Floppy disk**
Publisher: **PG Music, Inc.**   *List price:* **$29.00**

Known for packing the biggest bang for the buck in its products, PG Music does it again with *PowerTracks*, a full-featured MIDI sequencing program for the incredibly low price of just $29.00.

By no means a stripped-down package, *PowerTracks* provides lots of professional-level features including 48 track recording, independent track looping, Track/Bar and Event List Windows, and more. The editing commands include copy, cut, paste, replace, and undo in addition to percentage quantize, slide, length, fill, transpose, and more.

PowerTracks also provides synchronization to MIDI or MTC/SMPTE standards and support for multiple MIDI ports. The program also features a MIDI metronome and a selectable timebase from 48 to 480 PPQ.

The program is compatible with any MIDI interface or sound card supported by Windows 3.1. As a special bonus, the DOS version of *PowerTracks* is also included in the package free.

Indeed, *PowerTracks* may not have every bell and whistle there is, but it provides all of the essential elements a good sequencer should have, and it puts it all together in an easy-to-use package at an amazingly low price.

PowerTracks may be all the sequencer power many sound card users will ever need, although it is certainly up to handling the demands of the more ambitious MIDI musician as well.

Title: **RhythmAce**   *Media:* **Floppy disk**
Publisher: **Ibis Software**   *List price:* **$99.95**

RhythmAce is an excellent, self-paced, interactive rhythm training software package from Ibis that's ideal for musicians of any age and skill level.

The program helps you to learn, practice, and play rhythm with its huge variety of interactive exercises. You sharpen your abilities as you keep the beat on the keyboard, mouse, or MIDI instrument. *RhythmAce* is rich in user feedback and, since your responses are displayed beneath each exercise line, you know instantly how well you are doing.

Three exercise modes are provided. In Reading mode, the program displays the notation and you play it back. In Dictation mode, a rhythmic phrase is played and then you type the notation on the screen. In Custom mode, you enter your own rhythmic notation, and *RhythmAce* drills you (this is perfect for use with existing material).

You can select single or two-handed rhythms from 12 different skill levels. You can also control the time signature, notation values, tempo, and more. An optional audible metronome keeps time.

You can choose from classical or jazz-oriented libraries, and each contains hundreds of rhythms to form an infinite number of exercises.

Developing a good sense of rhythm is one of the most important musical skills, and *RhythmAce* is invaluable for that purpose.

Title:	Sequencer Plus Gold (DOS)	*Media:*	Floppy disk
Publisher:	Voyetra Technologies	*List price:*	$299.95

Voyetra's *Sequencer Plus Gold* is one of the oldest and most-used MIDI sequencers for PCs in the DOS environment. As of this writing, the Windows version was nearing completion and will be available by the time you read this. Since all of the DOS version's features will be included in the Windows version as well, I'm including it here in the interests of completeness.

Sequencer Plus Gold integrates a powerful MIDI sequencer, Universal Librarian, and MIDI Data Analyzer into what may be the ultimate tool for musicians who can't afford to compromise. Over 2,000 polyphonic, independently-controlled tracks are supported as well as multiple MIDI ports, multichannel, and multitrack recording.

Professional SMPTE/MTC time code support with an accuracy of 1/100th frame, sub-frame offset and song location pointers are other noteworthy features of this outstanding package, as well as full mouse support and a built-in metronome that plays through the PC speaker or as MIDI notes. There's also a "tap tempo" mode for recording in free-form without using a metronome. On-screen volume, pan, and velocity scaling controls permit sculpting the sound while composing, and it also features a jukebox mode that plays a list of songs automatically.

With all these features and more it's no wonder why the DOS version has been the choice of many professional musicians and it's a safe bet that the Windows version will be, too.

Title:	Soloist	*Media:*	Floppy disk
Publisher:	Ibis Software	*List price:*	$99.95

With *Soloist* you can learn to play virtually any instrument and have fun doing it— all you need is your PC, a sound card, and this excellent software program.

Just plug a microphone into your sound card and select your instrument and skill level from the *Soloist* control panel. The program composes a custom exercise just for you. Then you simply sing or play your instrument into the mike, and *Soloist* tells you if you've played the right note and gives you points for your progress.

Soloist is also incredibly diverse. In the game mode you can progress through 36 levels of instruction, or you can use *Soloist* to practice any level or simply explore. When you're exploring you can play or sing and *Soloist* names the note and shows you where it's located on the grand staff.

As a special bonus, *Soloist* also has a built-in chromatic tuner (a $50 value) that you can use for tuning your instrument.

A well-written, easy-to-understand 32-page manual is supplied and it includes a tutorial to help get you started. You can use any instrument from acoustic guitar to piano, saxophone, clarinet, violin, trumpet, flute, electric keyboard, harmonica, or even your own voice, and the program works with any SoundBlaster or 100% compatible sound card.

Like all of the other Ibis software products reviewed in this lesson, *Soloist* is an excellent and fun way to learn music.

Title:	Sound Forge 2.0	*Media:*	Floppy disk
Publisher:	Sonic Foundry	*List price:*	$179.95

Sound Forge is a digital sound editing software package from Sonic Foundry that is particularly rich in special effects—highly useful for adding special touches to your digital sound files.

In addition to being able to record and play back WAV sound files, *Sound Forge* gives you an arsenal of industrial-strength tools to modify and manipulate the sound data. For example, the Effects menu provides choices that include DC Offset, Delay/Echo, Distortion, Fade, Flange, Flip, Insert Silence, Pan, PreDelay/PreEcho, Resample, Reverse, Smooth, Volume, Noise Gate, and Loop sample. As you can see, several of the effects features (such as flanging and pre-echo) are entirely unique capabilities of this program and aren't available on other software products.

Ease-of-use is another area that *Sound Forge* 2.0 excels in, with all program features and functions instantly available from either the icon toolbar or the drop-down menus which support submenus for extended choices.

While this package is an ideal choice for anyone with a sound card working under Windows, it is particularly well-suited for those with heavy-duty sound applications in mind such as multimedia presentations, producing radio spots, narratives for video, or other professional uses. The rich features and effects processing *Sound Forge* 2.0 provides makes it a sure winner.

Title: **Sound Impression**   *Media:* **Floppy disk**
Publisher: **Asystem**   *List price:* **$109.00**

Sound Impression is a program that was designed with the needs of sound authors in mind, and an entire kit of essential "sound smithing" tools are provided, all tied-together with an easy-to-use graphical interface that runs under Windows.

Professional-level .WAV recording, editing, and mixing capabilities are provided, along with OLE (object linking and embedding) support for .WAV, MIDI, and CD sound.

The program provides a graphical interface that looks just like a rack-mounted stereo system you'd find in someone's living room. The CD, MIDI, and Wave rack components actually look and feel like a stereo and, thanks to the multitasking capabilities of Windows, they can be used at any time.

The outstanding features of *Sound Impression* are its ability to support up to 16 Wave editing sessions simultaneously, full support for any Windows-compatible sound card, comprehensive on-line help, and a 16-track Wave composer. With *Sound Impression* even the most complex and ambitious multimedia sound tracks using multiple tracks are a cinch to produce.

Multiple editing views and windows are available so you can instantly switch from one section or track to another without losing your place or train of thought. A rich palette of special effects tools makes it easy to "dress up" your sound files and give them the extra touches that separate amateur productions from those of true professional caliber.

Title: **Studio for Windows 3.1**   *Media:* **Floppy disk**
Publisher: **Midisoft**   *List price:* **$249.95**

This latest version of *Studio for Windows*, a music editing and authoring tool aimed at amateur musicians and multimedia enthusiasts alike, gives PC users the ability to record, edit, play back, and print music using MIDI. *Studio for Windows* was the first Windows application available to combine MIDI sequencing, true real-time notation, and music score printing all in the same program.

A new mixer view has been added to version 3.1 that contains the controls used for recording, arranging, and playback. The mixer view can best be described by saying it looks like a cross between a graphic equalizer and a tape recorder, and this arrangement makes many basic operations highly intuitive.

The mouse is used to select instruments for each track, adjust the chorus, reverb, panning, and volume levels. Individual tracks can also be muted, set for solo, or set for recording. A counter that displays the beat, measure, and ticks and controls for adjusting the master tempo, master volume, master reverb, and master chorus are all provided as well.

The notation capabilities of *Studio* have been improved significantly with version 3.1 also. The resolution in the score view has been increased from 16th notes to 64th notes and triplets (three notes occurring in the time of two notes) are also supported. A wider range of time signatures is also supported by this version. It is an excellent, easy-to-use package.

Title: **SuperJAM!** *Media:* **Floppy disk**
Publisher: **Blue Ribbon SoundWorks Ltd.** *List price:* **$129.00**

The Blue Ribbon SoundWorks hails *SuperJAM!* as "music software for the tone-deaf and talented alike," which is a fairly accurate description of who can effectively use this product. Even if you don't have any musical talent at all, you'll soon be amazed at the excellent music that you can produce with this software product.

The trick of the program is its ability to write music in an unlimited number of styles. Using *SuperJAM!*'s expert features, you can create your own chords, rhythms, and melodies whether you read music or not. You can invent drum tracks, design sections, and combine musical styles at the touch of a button. In fact, you can compose an entire song without ever touching an instrument.

The program has everything you need already built into it, including an interactive on-screen keyboard and the new Eas-O-Matic Music-Maker for instant melodies and chord progressions.

SuperJAM! works with any Windows 3.1-compatible sound card or MIDI instrument, and it can write to MIDI file format for use with MPC-compatible software and other applications that can read and use MIDI files.

The Eas-O-Matic feature is really noteworthy, since it prevents you from entering any "sour" notes. Overall, *SuperJAM!* is an easy, versatile, and creative music program that can turn anyone into a composer in just a few minutes.

Title:	**Synergy**	*Media:*	**Floppy disk**
Publisher:	**SynApps Software Inc.**	*List price:*	**$99.95**

Synergy is a combination of nine Windows utilities. *Eclipse* is a mouse shortcut utility that permits creating action buttons for virtually any Windows program or combination of programs. *Psychic* analyzes how you work and which operations are more prevalent. It then tries to "guess" which file you want or which feature you're most likely to access (based on past experience) and the program has it ready and waiting for you. *SynApps Script Language* (SSL) is a flexible macro language utility for creating complex scripts of mouse, keyboard, and filing operations. *Picasso* facilitates creating, editing, and managing Windows icons. *File Fetch* searches and finds files based upon a wide variety of user-selectable attributes. *LaunchPad* executes tasks or programs at any predetermined time from within Windows. *SynAppShot* permits grabbing "screen shots" and manipulating them. Effects include rotation and stretching.

Audition is a sound utility that manages and plays sound even if you don't have a sound board installed. The program provides and installs a PC speaker driver and routes all of the Windows event sounds, as well as any .WAV sound files, through the PC's speaker for playback. *FX* is a real fun utility that lets you add special effects to Windows events such as opening a file, resizing a window, and so forth. A rich assortment of custom sound files are also included for your use and amusement.

Title:	**Trax**	*Media:*	**Floppy disk**
Publisher:	**Passport Designs**	*List price:*	**$99.00**

Trax is a complete MIDI music recording studio for PCs running Windows 3.1. The package supports the SoundBlaster, MediaVision, and other AdLib compatible sound devices in addition to the Miracle Keyboard from Software Toolworks.

Trax permits composing, editing, and playback of multi-track recordings through the sound card or an attached MIDI device. The sequencer section of the program features 64-track capability and you can punch in and out to correct playing errors, adjust the meter, tempo, and beat for each measure using the conductor track, and a record filter is also provided for selecting which MIDI events/tracks to record.

The song editor section graphically displays track data by measures, and permits scrolling through tracks and measures. Cut, copy, paste, clear, and mix editing functions are all supported as well as complete regional editing control that lets you alter the velocity, quantizing, duration, and transposition.

The step editor greatly simplifies "cleaning up" duration values and other incidentals which may have been less than perfect when the original track was recorded.

Trax is easy enough for the musical novice to use, yet it is sophisticated enough to have a place in a professional composer/arranger/musician's bag of tricks as well. An assortment of musical selections is also included as part of the package, and the software is exceptionally well-documented.

Title:	Trycho Tunes	*Media:*	Floppy disk
Publisher:	Trycho Music International	*List price:*	$15.95-$119.95

You don't have to be a musician or MIDI composer to enjoy MIDI music, and that's what *Trycho Tunes* is all about—MIDI music at the touch of a button. All of your favorite hits, from pop to rock, from country to standards, you'll find them all with *Trycho Tunes* Performance Sequences, which are heralded as the most widely-used MIDI sequences in the world.

Trycho Tunes are available for most popular software and hardware-based sequencers, and setting up the software for any combination of MIDI equipment is easy thanks to the included MIDImap that provides song key, tempo, and suggested patch settings.

All of the *Trycho Tunes* sound very close to the original hit versions of the songs, since all essential instrument components of the original artist's recording are recreated (as much as possible). Of course, all of the *Trycho Tunes* sequences playback through the Media Player accessory in Windows or any sequencing software than can read standard MIDI files. General MIDI format is also supported.

Trycho Music has an extensive library of sequences available, and single-song packs sell for $15.95, triple-song packs are $21.95, and sequence songbooks range in price from $39.95 to $119.95. Trycho also sells the tunes on audio cassette so you don't need a sequencer and MIDI device to enjoy the music. *Trycho Tunes* are among the best MIDI sequences I've heard yet.

Title: **The Turtle Tools for Multimedia**   *Media:*   **Floppy disk/CD-ROM**
Publisher: **Turtle Beach Systems**   *List price:* **$89.00**

The name of the product succinctly tells you what it is and what it does: *Turtle Tools* is a set of five must-have tools/utilities and a WAV sound file collection that make working with sound and multimedia a much more pleasant and productive activity. The six elements consist of:

WaveTools—a Wave audio recording, editing and playback application.

Midisoft Session—a scaled-down version of Midisoft's *Recording Session* sequencer software for developing or editing MIDI musical compositions.

KeyPlayer—a handy utility which permits you to play and record music using just your PC keyboard—perfect for those aspiring musicians who don't own an external MIDI keyboard.

MIDI Tune-up—a very useful MIDI file editor for non-musicians that lets you graphically change tempo, key, instrument, and other settings.

SoundAttach—a neat tool for attaching MIDI and/or WAV sound files to all windows actions—even randomly, if you wish!

SoundBank—a collection of over 300 sound effects and musical pieces supplied on CD-ROM in four different WAV formats and Redbook audio for professional quality.

It would be fair to compare *The Turtle Tools for Multimedia* to the Swiss Army knife: a convenient, easy to handle package that has a load of useful features—a truly incredible value!

Title: **WAVE for Windows**   *Media:*   **Floppy disk**
Publisher: **Turtle Beach Systems**   *List price:* **$149.00**

Turtle Beach calls *WAVE for Windows* "the word processor of sound," and that's a fairly accurate description of what the package is and, in effect, what it can do.

WAVE has all of the features of a high-end tape recorder in that it affords you the ability to work with 8- or 16-bit monophonic or stereophonic sound with sampling rates of 11.025, 22.05, or 44.1 kHz. Cut-and-paste editing makes it easy to manipulate sound clips visually, and three types of sound pasting are provided. A gain adjustment permits changing the volume of all or part of a file, thus making it easy to create perfect fade-ins and fade-outs. To take the "oops" out of your mixing sessions, a full "undo" function is also included.

Other outstanding features and capabilities include several different ways to view your sound for visual analysis, waveform drawing, cross-fading, digital equalization (it provides a 4-band parametric equalizer with sliders—worth the price of the package alone), sound mixing, time compression and expansion, and much, much more.

Sound file import and export capabilities are also excellent with the package, and exotic capabilities including reverse, invert, DC offset, zoom-in, zoom stack, and position marking are also supported by this package.

If you're serious about working with WAV files, *WAVE for Windows* is a package you should consider as required equipment.

Title:	WinSong	*Media:*	Floppy disk
Publisher:	Softronics	*List Price:*	$79.95

WinSong is a composer, sequencer, and jukebox in one package. Moreover, it performs all of these tasks amazingly well and easily at a price that's sure to make it attractive to lots of Windows 3.1 users who are interested in getting more from their sound cards.

Using the composer section is as easy as pushing a button (from those provided on the Graphical menu) to select the musical symbol you want (such as note or rest). Once selected, you merely drag-and-drop it onto the staff. As *WinSong* plays your song back, the musical notation horizontally scrolls on the computer display so you see the notes as they are being played.

The sequencer portion of *WinSong* is a full-featured 64-track MIDI sequencer that provides all of the usual editing features as well as a built-in metronome, loop and mute modes.

The included *JukeBox* utility is a song-playing program that permits you to tell the program which songs you would like to hear and the order you'd like them played in. Your song list can include anything from Jingle Bells to Bach, and you can have anywhere from one to one hundred songs on the jukebox play list.

While *WinSong* doesn't have every feature available on some of the dedicated and more expensive packages, it does deliver a solid value with these three utilities, and, since these are the applications that most Windows users will want, *WinSong* makes an ideal choice for exploiting sound and MIDI under Windows.

Title:	**World of Music Sampler**	*Media:*	**Floppy disk**
Publisher:	**Midisoft**	*List price:*	**$24.95**

Midisoft's *World of Music Sampler* is a series of products designed to provide both entertainment and educational value to musicians and non-musicians alike. Each product in the series contains a library of music accompanied by a booklet providing a wealth of interesting information about the pieces contained on the software.

The *World of Music Sampler* contains one or two pieces from each of the 15 World of Music products. Some of the greatest music of all time—compositions from Back, Mozart, Scott Joplin, and a host of others—are contained on the *Sampler*.

All of the included sound files are Type 1 MIDI files and they are set up to conform to the General MIDI standard. These files can be used with Midisoft's other products or with any other sequencer capable of reading Type 1 MIDI files. The music can be played through any MIDI-compliant device including sound cards supported by Windows.

Since the files are provided in MIDI format, you can modify them, cut-and-paste sections or re-orchestrate the instrument assignments as you desire, and the accompanying booklet contains biographical information about the composers and gives valuable insights on their work. You also get complete MIDI set-up information so, regardless of what kind of equipment you have, you'll be able to make these sequences sound great in just a few minutes. At less that $1 per tune, it's a great musical value.

APPENDIX A:
Glossary

This glossary provides definitions of audio, MIDI, and musical terms as they apply to personal computers.

8-bit/16-bit sound   This refers to the dynamic range of the sampled sound, with 16-bit having double the amount of sound data of 8-bit sound. Eight-bit sound provides 48 dB of dynamic range, whereas 16-bit increases the range to 96 dB, or double that of 8-bit. Since more sound information is involved, 16-bit sound requires more memory and more disk space for storing the sounds than 8-bit sound does, but it provides much better quality.

A

acceptance level   A tolerance level outside of which a voice template will not be considered for recognition purposes. (See *recognition threshold*.)

acoustic   Also *acoustical*. Pertaining to sound or the science of sound. In musical usage, it refers to nonamplified instruments as opposed to electronic or amplified instrumentation, such as an acoustic guitar versus an electric guitar.

acoustic model   A pattern or template of the sound pattern of a word or phrase that is the average of spoken samples taken from a broad range of speakers. Acoustic models are usually used for broad-based recognition systems that use limited vocabularies and do not normally require training by individual speakers.

action button   An area of the screen in a graphical user interface environment that usually looks like a button or pad. Clicking on the button with the mouse causes an action (such as continue, quit, or retry) to start, hence its name.

ADC   An abbreviation for *analog-to-digital converter*, which is a special chip and supporting circuits that converts analog information such as sound into digital data that can be processed and stored by the computer.

ADPCM	An acronym for *adaptive differential pulse code modulation*, an algorithm for compressing audio data so that it requires less memory and disk space. The amount of compression is shown in ratio format, as 4:1, 3:1, and so forth. The ratio numbers indicate how much compression has been applied to the sample. For example, a 2:1 ratio means that the compressed sound is only half the size of the original uncompressed sample. A 3:1 ratio compresses the sound to one-third of its original size, and so on.
aftertouch	A type of keyboard touch sensitivity that permits the player to control the sound after the key has been pressed or while it is being held down. Aftertouch permits adding additional dynamic expressiveness to the music.
algorithm	A formula or equation that consists of rules or processes for solving a specific problem. Different algorithms are commonly used for compressing sound information in digital files.
alias distortion	Audio distortion that occurs when the resolution of the sampling is insufficient to represent the sample accurately. Simply put, aliasing occurs when the sample rate is too low to accurately capture the sound being sampled. For example, severe alias distortion results when music is recorded using a 4-bit sampling rate, taking the form of static, fuzzy sound and background hiss, as well as "clipping" the higher frequencies.
ambient noise	Acoustic noise in a room or other location, sometimes referred to as *room noise*. Any unwanted background noise picked up by a microphone and any acoustic coloration that influences sounds, brought about by the acoustic properties of a room in which a recording is being made or replayed, is described as ambient noise.
amplitude	How much a sound wave rises above and dips below the median line of a waveform. The amplitude determines the sound's intensity or volume.

applet

An informal term used to describe a small application or utility program (that is usually a component of a larger application or utility) running under the Windows graphical environment.

attach

The process of linking one type of data seamlessly to another, as in the attachment of a sound file to a word processing document. When an item, such as a voice file, is attached to a document, the voice file becomes coupled to the document file, much the same as if the sound file was a Post-It note attached to another sheet of paper.

attenuating adapters

Electronic devices that reduce the amplitude of a signal during its transmission from one point to another. Audio attenuating adapters reduce the signal strength of loud sounds to conform them to the acceptable range of sound cards and other recording devices that require a lower signal level.

B

background noise level

Also called the *ambient noise level*, it refers to any noise extraneous to the spoken command in a voice control system.

breakout box/cable

An assembly (usually an extra-cost optional item) that attaches to the 15-pin joystick connector on an audio card to provide additional input and output connectors. The breakout box or cable typically provides connections for MIDI input, MIDI output, and MIDI thru for attaching external MIDI devices such as keyboards and drum machines. A connector for attaching a joystick is also usually provided as well.

bus/expansion bus

A set of hardware lines (wires) used for data transfer among the components of a computer system. Essentially, a bus is a shared highway that connects different parts of the system and provides the pathways for these parts to communicate and work with each other. In addition to data signals, bus connectors also frequently carry electrical voltage to power the installed devices using the bus.

byte
A unit of information used in computer processing and storage consisting of 8 bits that, by their order, represent a single character.

C

CD-ROM
An acronym for *compact disc read-only memory*. CD-ROM is an optical data storage medium for computers that uses laser light to read the binary information it contains.

channel
Any of the 16 communication paths MIDI provides for data transmission. Each of the channels carries its own separate and distinct messages over the same cable, which makes it possible to play several different musical parts on the same instrument or control different MIDI instruments simultaneously.

codec
An abbreviation for *coder/decoder*, which refers to circuitry on a sound card that converts or codes analog information into digital format and decodes it back again to analog for playback. It can also refer to circuits or software that can compress and expand data.

container document
A document file that has objects that are still connected to the original application that created them. The objects residing in a container document may be text, charts, spreadsheets, bitmap pictures, vector drawings, sounds, video clips, and anything else that can be displayed or controlled by a Windows application.

cycle
One complete iteration of a waveform measured from peak to peak.

D

DAC

An abbreviation for *digital-to-analog converter*, which does the opposite of an ADC. A DAC is a special chip and supporting circuits used to convert digital data from the computer into an analog format (such as sound or music) that can be used by humans or other analog devices (like a stereo system).

daisychaining

A term that describes two or more devices linked together through each other to the same PC. The first device is connected directly to the PC, while the second device is connected to the first. The third device is connected to the second, fourth to third, and so forth. Signals are passed through the "chain" back and forth from the computer to the desired device. To avoid confusion or conflicts, each device in the chain is given its own unique channel for communication and ID number.

daughterboard

A printed circuit board that attaches to another, thus adding additional features or functions to the original device. CD-ROM interfaces and wavetable modules are commonly sold as daughterboard upgrade options for several popular PC sound boards.

decibel

A unit of relative measurement commonly used in audio and electronics technology. Abbreviated *dB*, a decibel is one-tenth of a *bel*, named after Alexander Graham Bell. Measurements in decibels fall on a logarithmic scale, since they always compare the measured quantity against a known reference.

dialog box

A special window displayed by the system or application to solicit a response from the user in a graphical user interface environment. Dialog boxes are commonly used to provide a user with the opportunity to cancel an action or continue with it.

digital   Relating to digits or the way they are represented. For our purposes, digital is synonymous with binary because personal computers store and process information coded as combinations of binary digits (bits).

digitize   The act of converting analog data into digital format for processing and storage by a digital computer. *ADCs* usually perform the conversion, while *DACs* convert digital data back into analog format.

DMA   An abbreviation for *direct memory access*, refers to memory access that does not involve the microprocessor. DMA is frequently employed for data transfer directly between memory and an "intelligent" peripheral device such as a sound card. Numeric designations refer to the particular channel that is set up for communication with the device.

DOS   An acronym for *disk operating system*, the basic instructions that enable a computer system to accept and process commands and perform useful work. (See *MS-DOS*.)

DOS-based   Any application or utility that operates directly from the MS-DOS operating system rather than through an alternate environment or operating system, such as Microsoft Windows 3.1.

DSP   An abbreviation for *digital signal processor*, a chip-based integrated circuit which is used in place of *ADC* and *DAC* circuits.

dynamic range   The span of volume between the loudest and softest sounds, either in an original signal (original dynamic range) or in the span of a sound system's recording capability (recorded dynamic range). Dynamic range is expressed in decibels (dB) and represents the difference between the overload level and the minimum acceptable signal level.

dynamic updating   A means of immediately implementing any changes to the current environment that are made by the user or as a result of a process initiated by the user. Examples of dynamic updating include the immediate addition of a newly-added command to the active words list in an active words list for recognition, or an update of the current disk directory automatically as soon as a file is added or deleted.

E

EISA

An acronym for *extended industry standard architecture*, a bus standard introduced in 1988. EISA maintains backward compatibility with ISA (*industry standard architecture*), in addition to adding many of the enhanced features IBM introduced with its Micro Channel Architecture bus standard including a 32-bit data path.

embed

The process of building an item into another item as opposed to attaching it. An embedded sound, for example, becomes a part of the document file it is embedded in, rather than remaining a free-standing entity that can be unattached.

EPROM

An acronym (pronounced *ee-prom*) for *erasable programmable read-only memory*. EPROMs are nonvolatile memory chips that are programmed after they are manufactured. They provide a convenient and cost-effective way for hardware manufacturers to update the features and capabilities of their products through software upgrades. In audio cards, EPROMs are frequently used for storing wavetable sound and MIDI instrument patches.

event

Refers to any status, system, or control message sent or received over a MIDI channel. These messages play notes and control MIDI equipment.

F

fidelity   Audio quality: the higher the fidelity, the more closely the digitally recorded sound matches the original sound without any added distortion or noise.

FM synthesizer   A chip that contains predefined circuits that can generate sound waves. To synthesize different sounds, one fixed waveform modulates another, thus creating a new waveform with better harmonics (tonal quality) than either of the two waveforms that comprise it by themselves. By varying the modulation and adding more waveforms to the mix it is possible to approximate the sounds of musical instruments. The Yamaha YM3812 and YMF262 are the two most commonly-used FM synthesizer chips.

G

General MIDI   An update and enhancement of the MIDI 1.0 standard, which provides greater compatibility between different manufacturers' MIDI equipment when transferring MIDI song files.

H

harmonic   A tone in the harmonic series of overtones produced by a fundamental tone. The term also describes a wave whose frequency is a whole-number multiple of that of another.

host PC   The main personal computer (in a single-user, non-networked system) that controls and utilizes all other connected devices including drives, printers, monitor, keyboard, mouse, joystick, and more. Since the PC provides the logic, input-output, memory storage, computing, and in many cases the actual operational voltage, the PC "hosts" all of the devices as if they were "guests."

humanize

An effect that introduces slight timing, velocity, and volume variations to a MIDI track to simulate the "feel" of a live performance.

I

impedance

A term that refers to resistance in the flow of an electrical current. Resistance impedes the current flow by converting electrical energy to heat, and it is measured in units called *ohms*. For proper sound recording a microphone's impedance level must be in the acceptable impedance range of the recording device and for proper playback the speakers or headphones must be in the proper impedance range of the playback device.

insertion recording

The process of inserting additional sound material into an existing sound file without disturbing or erasing the current material. Insertion recording is a useful technique for extending the length of sound files created with the Sound Recorder accessory beyond the 60-second maximum file length permitted by the utility.

intensity

The loudness of a sound, determined by the amplitude of the waveform. Also referred to as *volume*, intensity is measured in decibels.

IRQ

An abbreviation for *interrupt request*. An electronic signal that is sent when a hardware device (such as a sound card) or software needs to use the microprocessor. This signal is a special instruction that switches control of the microprocessor to the operating system for the task to be completed.

ISA   An acronym for *industry standard architecture*, the widely accepted (but unofficial) designation for the bus design of the original IBM PC. The ISA specification was expanded to include a 16-bit data path in 1984 from its original 8-bit specification with the introduction of the IBM PC/AT computer.

isolated word   A voice command that has a silent pause before and after it that aids the recognition system in determining the beginning and end of the command for comparison to its internal recognition templates.

K

kilobyte   Abbreviated Kb, K, or Kbyte. It is the equivalent of 1,024 bytes. Kilobytes are usually used to express capacities of RAM, floppy diskettes, files and other measures less than a megabyte (1024 x 1024 = 1,048,576 bytes) in size.

L

layering   The process of repeatedly applying a special effect, such as echo, or increase/decrease speed to augment the effect. For example, layering the echo effect three times produces a triple echo effect.

line-level   A line-level signal is typically output by audio components that do not require preamplification (CD and cassette players, for example). Line-level signals are based roughly on the "standardized" signal intensity sent over a telephone line, and it refers to any audio signal having a maximum intensity between .5 and 1.5 volts.

M

MCA

An acronym for *Micro Channel Architecture*, the design of the bus used in IBM PS/2 computers (except for the Model 25 and Model 30). Micro Channel expansion slots are electrically and physically different from the standard IBM PC/AT (ISA) bus, so accessory or adapter cards for standard IBM-compatible PC's won't work in a Micro Channel machine.

megabyte

The measurement term used to represent 1,048,576 bytes (1024x1024 bytes). Megabytes are used to express large capacities when referring to total system RAM memory, large disk drives, and CD-ROM data capacities. (Abbreviated Mb or Mbyte.)

message

A collective term that refers to the words (or bytes) of MIDI control data. Messages typically consist of one or more words that include a status byte and one or two data bytes.

MIDI

An acronym for *musical instrument digital interface*, a specification developed as a cooperative effort among major manufacturers of electronic musical instruments in the early 1980s with the objective of permitting musical instruments of different brands to communicate with each other. Additionally, several MIDI-equipped devices can be linked together under the control of a PC and software for creating, storing, editing, and playing back music in precise synchronization.

modulation

The variation of some characteristic of a waveform (the carrier wave) in accordance with an information-bearing signal wave (the modulating wave). Demodulation is the process by which the original signal is recovered from the wave produced by modulation. In modulation, the carrier wave is generated or processed so that its amplitude, frequency, or some other property varies. By controlling one of these variables, a modulating wave may impress its information on the pulses of the waveform.

monophonic mode   In monophonic (mono) mode a MIDI instrument assigns incoming channel voice messages monophonically, permitting only a single note to be played at a time. Since the voices are each assigned to different channels, however, playing a chord results in three, five, or more different instrument sounds playing individual notes simultaneously. (See *polyphonic mode*.)

motherboard   The main circuit board containing the primary "system critical" components for a microcomputer system. The components found on the motherboard include the CPU, main memory, controller circuitry required for the expansion bus, and expansion slots, in addition to other components required for the proper operation of these circuits.

mounting bracket   A metal bracket found on virtually every expansion card for IBM-compatible PCs that is used for securing the card in its slot with a screw. Sound boards use this bracket for mounting their I/O connectors (including microphone, line in/out, and joystick).

MPC   An abbreviation for *multimedia personal computer*, it refers to a set of specifications drafted by Microsoft and other major manufacturers and developers that defines the minimum hardware and software requirements for acceptable multimedia production and presentation on personal computers.

MS-DOS   An acronym for *Microsoft Disk Operating System* (pronounced *em-ess-doss*). MS-DOS oversees and supervises the basic tasks and services required to run a computer, including disk input and output, video support, keyboard control, and other essential functions.

multitimbral   A term describing a device's ability to produce more than one instrument sound simultaneously.

N

noise	A sound wave that has irregular, nonrepeating vibrations that usually produces an unpleasant sound.

O

ohms	The unit of measure for electrical resistance. A resistance of one ohm passes one ampere of current when a voltage of one volt is applied.
OLE	An acronym for *object linking and embedding*, a set of application protocols in Windows 3.1 that enables one application to use seamlessly the services of another application. Applications that conform to the OLE protocols enable you to create documents that contain linked or embedded information from documents created by other applications, and such an application is referred to as a container document. (See *container document*.) Unlike normal cutting and pasting, the data in an OLE object can be linked (where the data resides in another, separate document), or embedded (where the data resides in the container document). In either case, the object can be edited only by the application that created it, not the application whose document it currently resides in.
omnidirectional microphone	Also called a *nondirectional microphone*, this type of microphone responds to sound waves reaching it from virtually any angle or direction.
oscilloscope	An instrument in electronics that displays waveforms in graphical format. The display typically shows the horizontal and vertical deflection of the electron beam of a cathode-ray tube. These deflections are, respectively, proportional to a pair of applied voltages.
overtone	A harmonic produced by a fundamental tone.

P

patch A sound data file used for loading desired sound libraries into the sound card's memory. Patch files are usually used with wavetable and MIDI devices.

patch cables A general audio term that refers to any type of audio cable used to connect two or more devices together. The most common patch cables have RCA-type jacks at both ends (like the kind used to connect your home stereo speakers), although some patch cables are outfitted with 1/4 inch phone jacks, 1/8 inch mini-phone jacks, dual-RCA-to-1/8 inch stereo mini-phone, or other special-purpose connectors.

PCM An acronym for *pulse code modulation*, the predominant method for storing *uncompressed* sound in digital format. The audio information is encoded in the waveform signal by varying the amplitude of pulses. The pulse amplitudes are limited to several predefined values.

pin connector Usually a single or double row of brass contact pins on a sound card used for attaching a flat ribbon cable. Pin connectors are frequently used for attaching a ribbon cable coming from a CD-ROM drive, among other uses.

pitch How high or low a tone is, as determined by its position in a musical scale. Pitch is determined by the frequency of the vibration, measured in cycles per second (kHz).

pitch-bending A capability of many MIDI keyboards and other controllers used to simulate the way a guitarist stretches a string to alter the pitch of the note.

polyphonic mode The ability of a synthesizer to play more than one note (chords) simultaneously. In poly mode, all notes are voiced the same and sent via the same MIDI channel. (See *monophonic mode*.)

primary messaging medium
A word processing document, spreadsheet, or database file that is the carrier for any secondary messaging medium such as a sound, graphic, or video file. (See *secondary messaging medium*.)

Q

quantize
Also sometimes called *auto-correction*, this refers to the process of correcting slow and fast timing variations to align the tracks with the tempo beats. Quantizing can make sloppy playing sound tighter, but overdoing it can make the composition sound too rigid and mechanical (which could then be corrected by *humanizing*).

R

RAM
An acronym for *random access memory*. RAM refers to semiconductor-based (silicon chip-based) memory that can be read and written by the microprocessor or other devices in the computer system. RAM is classified as *volatile* (rather than *stable*) memory, since it loses all of its stored data when power is interrupted or removed (the computer is shut off).

recognition template file
A file that contains the voice pattern of an individual. The template is used for comparing current spoken words with those stored in the template for purposes of validating the user's access or for purposes of recognition. Templates of specific spoken commands used for recognition are called *recognition training templates*.

recognition threshold
The limits of a recognition template to recognize a spoken word. Some voice command systems permit adjusting the threshold to widen it for a broader range of recognition among multiple users or tighten it to recognize the precise speech patterns of a specific user.

Redbook Audio
The standard specification for compact disc audio quality (16-bit stereophonic sound at a 44.1 mHz sampling rate) as detailed and agreed upon by Philips, Sony and other major manufacturers. Since these technical specifications were published in a book with a red cover, this specification for audio became known as the Redbook standard.

S

sample
The first step required to convert an analog signal into a digital representation. The analog sound is measured at regular intervals called samples. These values are then encoded to provide a digital representation of the analog signal.

sample size
Also frequently referred to as sample depth or bit resolution, this term indicates the number of bits used per sample to express the dynamic range of the audio frequency; more bits per sample result in higher audio fidelity. 8-bit and 16-bit sample sizes are used for general and music recording, while 4-bit sample sizes are usually only used for recording low-quality digital speech.

sampling
The process of converting analog signals to digital format for use and processing by computers. An ADC is used to sample analog signals (such as sound) as voltages and convert them to the binary form required by the computer. Sampling is affected by two major characteristics: the sampling rate (usually expressed in samples per second) and the sampling precision (usually expressed in bits). An 8-bit sample contains only half as much information as a 16-bit sample.

sampling rate
The frequency that samples of a sound are taken. The higher the sampling rate (the more samples taken per unit of time), the closer the digitized sample will be to the

original sound. The highest sampling rates produce the best quality audio. Measured in kilohertz (kHz), the sampling rate refers to the lowest-possible and highest-possible ranges of sound that can be successfully digitized. According to the *Nyquist Sampling Theorem*, the highest audio frequency that can be reproduced must be sampled at at least twice that frequency. This means that in order to reproduce a 20 kHz tone it must be sampled at 40 kHz.

SCSI
An acronym (pronounced *scuzzy*) that stands for *small computer system interface*. SCSI is a standard high-speed parallel interface as defined by the X3T9.2 committee of the American National Standards Institute (ANSI) that permits devices such as CD-ROM drives, hard disks, and printers to be connected to PCs.

seamless integration
The result of hardware and/or software elements working flawlessly without requiring program adjustments or exceptional effort. Ideally, seamless integration refers to multiple applications all sharing the same resources (such as a sound card and audio files) without conflict or without requiring additional loading on the part of the user.

secondary messaging medium
Any auxiliary data format that acts as a supplement to the primary messaging medium. For example, a word processing document would be considered the primary messaging medium, while its attached or embedded sound file would be the secondary medium. (See *primary messaging medium*.)

SMPTE
An abbreviation for the *Society of Motion Picture and Television Engineers*, SMPTE refers to the synchronization standard designed by video engineers to synchronize different pieces of video and audio mixing equipment together. In MIDI, SMPTE is used to sync sequencers and other MIDI equipment as well as multitrack recording equipment to video, and it is used for creating sound

tracks and other high-end applications. SMPTE is a time-based code that marks the passage of time as hours, minutes, seconds, and frames.

sound bite   An informal term that refers to any small audio segment used in broadcast, recording, or multimedia applications, either by itself or in conjunction with text or graphics.

Sound Blaster compatible   Any internal sound card or external audio device functionally compatible with software applications designed for the Creative Labs Sound Blaster series of sound cards.

sound-on-sound recording   A method by which material previously recorded on one track of a tape may be recorded on another track while simultaneously adding new material to it. The technique is often employed with music to give the effect of one musician playing several different instruments or parts simultaneously.

speaker dependent   Any voice recognition system which depends on matching speech patterns of the speaker against voice templates stored within the system. Speaker dependent systems are trained to recognize and respond only to the voices of specific users rather than the general populace. (See *speech recognition* and *voice recognition*.)

speaker independent   Any speech recognition system which uses averaged acoustic models and responds to any speaker whose voice falls within its preset recognition threshold. (See *speech recognition* and *voice recognition*.)

speech recognition   The ability of a computer to understand the spoken word for the purpose of receiving commands or data input from the speaker. The term speech recognition is generally used to describe systems which are capable of understanding limited vocabularies from a broad range of people, as opposed to voice recognition which is trained to recognize and respond only to the voices of specific individuals. (See *voice recognition*.)

speech synthesis The ability of a computer to produce "spoken" words. Computer speech can be produced either by splicing prerecorded words together, or by combining the individual sounds which make up individual words.

T

timbre Also called *tonal color* or *musical quality*, timbre refers to the sound characteristics that allow us to differentiate one sound from another and refers to the qualities that make sounds unique. For example, timbre is what makes a saxophone sound like a sax instead of a guitar. Timbre is determined by the overtones (subsidiary tones), and the distinctive timbre of any musical instrument is the result of the number and relative prominence of the overtones it produces.

tone In music, a tone is distinguished from noise by its definite pitch, caused by the regularity of the vibrations that produce it. For a sound to be called a tone it must possess the attributes of pitch, intensity, and quality.

training The process of recording the speech pattern of a command, or template, for use in recognition by a voice command system.

trimming The process of removing unwanted portions of the sound file that aren't needed, such as ambient noise or silent periods at the beginning or end of a sound file. Trimming helps sound quality and also reduces the amount of memory and disk space required.

transparent device A device that performs its own tasks, usually while sharing a resource such as a system port, without affecting or impeding the operation of any other component in the system. During use, a transparent device is said to be "invisible" to the user since the usage is occurring without the user's knowledge or intervention.

TSR
An abbreviation for *terminate-and-stay-resident*, a type of program that runs under DOS and remains loaded in memory even when it is not running so that it can be quickly invoked for a specific task to be performed while any other application program is operating.

tympanum
Also spelled *timpanum*, this is the eardrum. It also refers to a membranous external auditory structure in certain insects.

U

unidirectional microphone
A microphone that is most sensitive to sounds arriving at it from one direction, usually from the front.

user interface
The point at which the user and the elements in a computer system connect and communicate. Different types of hardware user interfaces include the keyboard, the mouse, the joystick, and so forth. Software user interfaces include drop-down menus, point-and-click operation, action buttons, and dialog boxes. Voice and speech recognition are also user interfaces that permit the spoken word to cause the computer to execute commands or accept data input.

V

velocity
A synthesizer and MIDI term that means how hard the musical key is pressed or released. For keyboards having velocity control, this can affect the loudness or other tonal quality of the sound.

voice annotation
The capability to add vocal sound bites including questions, comments, emphasis, and auxiliary information by either attaching or embedding them in a document, spreadsheet, or database.

voice control

A blanket term to generally describe any product, application, or situation that can be controlled through spoken utterances and can apply to speech or voice recognition technologies.

voice macro

A series of keystrokes that are entered when a voice control system "hears" and recognizes a spoken command.

voice recognition

The ability of a computer to identify the voice of a speaker as an authorized individual. Voice recognition has several applications in addition to receiving commands and data input. It can also be used as a security medium that only allows access to the system for authorized individuals whose voice patterns, stored in templates, match those of the current speaker. (See *speech recognition*.)

waveform

The mathematical representation of a wave, especially a graph of deviation at a fixed point versus time.

waveform audio

Frequently referred to as *digitized* or *sampled* sound, waveform audio utilizes an ADC to convert the analog sound files into digital format and requires a DAC for playback.

wavetable sound

An audio technology that generates sounds by scanning either entire waveforms or portions of them from sounds produced by real instrument or other analog sources such as the human voice. These digitized samples are called sound *patches* and are loaded into the sound system's onboard memory to make them available for use. Wavetable technology is RAM based rather than being "hard-wired," as are the sound circuits in an FM synthesizer chip.

Windows

The popular name for *Microsoft Windows 3.1*, a multitasking graphical user interface environment that runs on MS-DOS-based computers. Drop-down menus, screen windows, and icons that represent entire programs or specific tasks are all features of Windows. Windows makes most computer tasks simply a matter of pointing with a mouse and clicking one of the mouse buttons to activate that application or utility.

word   The native unit of storage on a particular machine. Depending on the microprocessor, a word can be an 8-bit, a 16-bit, or a 32-bit quantity.

APPENDIX B:

Sources

This appendix contains addresses and phone numbers of hardware manufacturers, software publishers, record companies, and other sources.

Hardware Manufacturers (including sound cards, audio ports, and MIDI devices)

Manufacturer:	AdLib MultiMedia, Inc.
	350 Franqueg Street, #80
	Sainte-Fay, Quebec, Canada G1P 4P3
	(418) 656-8743
Product name:	Gold 1000

Manufacturer:	Advanced Gravis Computer Technology Ltd.
	1790 Midway Lane
	Bellingham, WA 98226
	(604) 431-1807
Product name:	UltraSound

Manufacturer:	Antex Electronics
	161000 South Figueroa Street
	Gardena, CA 90248
	(800) 338-4231
Product name:	Series 3/Z1

Manufacturer:	ATI Technologies, Inc.
	3761 Victoria Park Avenue
	Scarborough, Ontario, Canada M1W 3S2
	(416) 756-0718
Product name:	Stereo F/X-CD

Manufacturer:	Aztech Labs, Inc.
	46707 Fremont Boulevard
	Fremont, CA 94538
	(510) 623-8988
Product name:	Sound Galaxy NX Stereo Pro

Manufacturer:	Covox, Incorporated
	675 Conger Street
	Eugene, OR 97402
	(503) 342-1271
Product name:	Speech Thing
	Voice Master Key
	Voice Master System II
	Sound Master II
	Midi Maestro
	(*see also* Software Product listings)
Manufacturer:	Creative Labs, Inc.
	1901 McCarthy Boulevard
	Milpitas, CA 95035
	(408) 428-6600
Product name:	Sound Blaster 16 ASP
	Sound Blaster Pro
	Sound Blaster Deluxe
	original Sound Blasters
Manufacturer:	DSP Solutions, Inc.
	550 Main Street, Suite J
	Placerville, CA 95667
	(916) 621-1787
Product name:	Port-Able Sound Plus
Manufacturer:	Fostex Corporation of America
	15431 Blackburn Avenue
	Norwalk, CA 90650
	(310) 921-1112
Product name:	X-28H Multitracker Cassette Recorder
Manufacturer:	Key Electronics, Inc.
	7515 Chapel Avenue
	Fort Worth, TX 76116
	(800) 533-6434
Product name:	MIDIator External MIDI Interfaces

Manufacturer: Logitech, Inc.
                 6505 Kaiser Drive
                 Fremont, CA 94555
                 (800) 231-7717
Product name: AudioMan

Manufacturer: Media Vision Inc.
                 47221 Fremont Boulevard
                 Fremont, CA 94538
                 (510) 770-8600
Product name: Pro Audio 16 Basic
                 Pro AudioStudio 16
                 Pro Audio Spectrum 16
                 Pro Audio Spectrum Plus
                 Thunder & Lightning
                 ThunderBoard
                 AudioPort

Manufacturer: Microsoft Corp.
                 One Microsoft Way
                 Redmond, WA 98052
                 (206) 882-8080
Product name: Windows Sound System

Manufacturer: MIDIman, Inc.
                 30 North Raymond Avenue, Suite 505
                 Pasadena, CA 91103
                 (818) 499-8838
Product name: MIDIman External/Internal MIDI Interfaces

Manufacturer: Music Industries Corp.
                 99 Tulip Avenue
                 Floral Park, NY 11001
                 (800) 431-6699
Product name: Novation MM-10X Keyboard Controller
                 Novation MidiCon Keyboard Controller

Manufacturer: Video Associates Labs, Inc.
4926 Spicewood Springs Road
Austin, TX 78759
(800) 331-0547
Product name: MicroKey/AudioPort

Manufacturer: MidiSoft Corp.
P.O. Box 1000
Bellevue, WA 98009
(206) 881-7176
Product name: MIDI Kit
(*see also* Software Product listings)

Manufacturer: Omni Labs, Ltd.
P.O. Box 1220
Baldwin Park, CA 91706
(818) 813-2638
Product name: Audio Master AMS-8000

Manufacturer: Shadow Electronics
distributed by Freed International
1121 East Ocean Boulevard
Stuart, FL 34996
(407) 288-7200
Product name: SH-075 MIDI Guitar Converter

Manufacturer: Sigma Designs
47900 Bayside Parkway
Fremont, CA 94538
(510) 770-0100
Product name: WinStorm

Manufacturer: Software Toolworks, The
60 Leveroni Court
Novato, CA 94949
(415) 883-3000
Product name: Miracle Piano Teaching System for PCs

Manufacturer: Turtle Beach Systems, Inc.
Cyber Center #33
1600 Pennsylvania Avenue
York, PA 17404
(717) 843-6916

Product name: MultiSound
(*see also* Software Product listings)

Manufacturer: Video Associates Labs, Inc.
4926 Spicewood Springs Road
Austin, TX 78759
(800) 331-0547

Product name: MicroKey/AudioPort

Manufacturer: Yamaha Corporation of America
6600 Orangethorpe Avenue
P.O. Box 6600
Buena Park, CA 90622-6600
(714) 522-9011

Product name: Portatone PSR-510 Synthesizer
CBX-T3 PC/MIDI Tone Generator
QY-20 MIDI Sequencer/Tone Generator Module

Sound, Music, and MIDI Software (reviewed in Lesson 11)

Publisher: Asystem
1414 Magee Avenue
Berkeley, CA 94703
(510) 525-4311

Product name: Sound Impression

Publisher: Big Noise Software, Inc.
P.O. Box 23740
Jacksonville, FL 32241
(904) 730-0754

Product name:	Cadenza for Windows Ver. 2
	MIDI MaxPak
Publisher:	Blue Ribbon SoundWorks Ltd.
	1605 Chantille Drive NE, Suite 200
	Atlanta, GA, 30324
	(800) 226-0212
Product name:	SuperJAM!
Publisher:	Compton's New Media
	2320 Camino Vida Roble
	Carlsbad, CA 92009
	(619) 929-2500
Product name:	Jazz: A Multimedia History
Publisher:	Cool Shoes (Inter-Galactic) Software
	P.O. Box 2359
	Kernersville, NC 27285
	(919) 722-0830
Product name:	Drummer 2.0
Publisher:	Covox, Inc.
	675 Conger Street
	Eugene, OR 97402
	(503) 342-1271
Product name:	Voice Blaster
	(*see also* Hardware Product listings)
Publisher:	Dr. T's Music Software
	100 Crescent Road
	Needham, MA 02194
	(617) 455-1454
Product name:	Composer Quest
	Dr. T's Sing-A-Long

Publisher: First Byte
19840 Pioneer Avenue
Torrance, CA 90503
(310) 793-0610

Product name: Monologue for Windows

Publisher: Five Pin Press
P.O. Box 550363
Dallas, TX 75355-0363
800-726-6434

Product name: 260 Instant Drum Patterns

Publisher: Future Trends Software, Inc.
1508 Osprey Drive, Suite 103
DeSoto, TX 75115
(214) 224-3279

Product name: EZ Sound FX

Publisher: Howling Dog Systems
Kanata North Postal Outlet
Box 72071
Kanata, Ontario Canada K2K 2P4
(613) 599-7927

Product name: Mr. Drumstix' Music Studio
Power Chords

Publisher: Ibis Software, Inc.
140 Second Street, Suite 603
San Francisco, CA 94105
(415) 546-1917

Product name: Interludes Series
RhythmAce
Play It By Ear
Soloist

Publisher: Metatec Corp.
7001 Discovery Boulevard
Dublin, OH 43017
(614) 761-2000

Product name: Best of MIDI Connection Vols. 1 & 2
Best of Sound Bytes, Vol. 1
Nautilus Monthly Magazine on CD-ROM

Publisher: Microsoft Corp.
One Microsoft Way
Redmond, WA 98052
(206) 882-8080

Product name: Microsoft Musical Instruments
(*see also* Hardware Product Listing)

Publisher: MidiSoft Corp.
P.O. Box 1000
Bellevue, WA 98009
(206) 881-7176

Product name: Multimedia Music Library
Music Mentor with Recording Session
Studio for Windows 3.1
World of Music Sampler
(*see also* Hardware Product listings)

Publisher: Passport Designs, Inc.
100 Stone Pine Road
Half Moon Bay, CA 94019
(415) 726-0280

Product name: MusicTime
Trax
Master Tracks Pro-4
Encore

Publisher: PG Music, Inc.
266 Elmwood Avenue, Unit 111
Buffalo, NY 14222
(800) 268-6272

Product name: Band-In-A-Box
PowerTracks
The Pianist

Publisher: Prosonus
11126 Weddington Street
North Hollywood, CA 91601
(818) 766-5221
(805) 494-9996

Product name: Mr. Sound FX
MusicBytes

Publisher: Softronics
5085 List Drive
Colorado Springs, CO 80919
(719) 593-9540

Product name: WinSong

Publisher: Sonic Foundry
1110 East Gorham
Madison, WI 53703
(608) 256-3133

Product name: Sound Forge 2.0

Publisher: Sound Sources Unlimited, Inc.
2985 East Hillcrest Drive, Suite A
Westlake Village, CA 91362
(805) 494-9996

Product name: AudioClips Collections

Publisher: Soundtrek
3384 Hill Drive
Duluth, GA 30136
(404) 623-0879

Product name: Jammer Pro 2.0

Publisher: SynApps Software, Inc.
2009 178 Avenue NE
Redmond, WA 98052
(206) 562-3015

Product name: Synergy

Publisher: Trycho Music International
2166 West Broadway Street, Suite 330
Anaheim, CA 92804
(909) 696-3577

Product name: Trycho Tunes

Publisher: Turtle Beach Systems
Cyber Center #33
1600 Pennsylvania Avenue
York, PA 17404
(717) 843-6916

Product name: Turtle Tools for Multimedia
WAVE for Windows
(*see also* Hardware Product listings)

Publisher: Twelve Tone Systems, Inc.
P.O. Box 760
Watertown, MA 02272
(800) 234-1171

Product name: Cakewalk Professional for Windows

Publisher:	Voyetra Technologies
	Five Odell Plaza
	Yonkers, NY 10701-1406
	(800) 233-9377
Product name:	AudioView
	MusicClips Collection Bundle
	Sequencer Gold Plus
Publisher:	Wolfetone Multimedia Publishing, Inc.
	1010 Huntcliff, Suite 1350
	Atlanta, GA 30350
	(404) 992-7500
Product name:	Magiclips Music

Game Software Products (in Lesson 7)

Publisher:	Access Software
	4910 West Amelia Earhart Drive
	Salt Lake City, UT 84116
	(801) 359-2900
Product name:	Amazon Guardians of Eden
Publisher:	Amtex Software Corp.
	P.O. Box 572
	Belleville, Ontario Canada K8N 5B2
	(613) 967-7900
Product name:	Eight Ball Deluxe
Publisher:	Broderbund Software, Inc.
	500 Redwood Boulevard
	P.O. Box 6121
	Novato, CA 94948
	(415) 382-4400
Product name:	Prince of Persia II

Publisher: Dynamix, Inc.
1600 Millrace Road
Eugene, OR 97403
(503) 343-0772

Product name: Betrayal at Krondor

Publisher: Electronic Arts
1450 Fashion Island Boulevard
San Mateo, CA 94404
(415) 571-7171

Product name: Populous II

Publisher: I-Motion
1333 Ocean Avenue, Suite J
Santa Monica, CA 90401
(310) 576-1888

Product name: Alone in the Dark

Publisher: LucasArts Games
P.O. Box 10307
San Rafael, CA 94912
(415) 721-3300

Product name: X-Wing

Publisher: New World Computing, Inc.
20301 Ventura Boulevard, Suite 200
Woodland Hills, CA 91364
(818) 999-0606

Product name: Might and Magic: Clouds of Xeen
Might and Magic: Darkside of Xeen

Publisher: Spectrum Holobyte
2490 Mariner Square Loop
Alameda, CA 94501
(510) 522-3584

Product name: Chess Maniac 5,000,000,001

Publisher: Virgin Games
18061 Fitch Avenue
Irvine, CA 92714
(800) 874-4607

Product name: The 7th Guest
Monopoly Deluxe for Windows

Record Companies of Artists Interviewed (in Lesson 9)

Company: American Gramaphone Records
9130 Mormon Bridge Road
Omaha, NE 68152
(402) 457-4341

Albums by John Archer/Checkfield:
    Water, Wind and Stone
    Distant Thunder
    Through The Lens
    View From The Edge

John also appears on:
    Day Parts/Sunday Morning Coffee
    Day Parts/Party
    Day Parts/Dinner
    Day Parts/Romance

Company: Capitol Records
1750 North Vine
Hollywood, CA 90028
(213) 462-6252

Albums by Les Paul (with Mary Ford):
    The Legend and the Legacy (4-CD boxed set)
    Les Paul with Mary Ford (selections from set)

Company: Narada Productions
                 1845 North Farwell Avenue
                 Milwaukee, WI 53202
                 (414) 272-6700

Albums by Jay Chattaway:
                 Space Age (from the PBS TV series)

Albums by David Arkenstone:
                 Valley In The Clouds
                 Island (with Andrew White)
                 Citizen of Time
                 In The Wake Of The Wind
                 Chronicles

Company: Private Music
                 9014 Melrose Avenue
                 West Hollywood, CA 90069
                 (213) 859-9200

Albums by Suzanne Ciani:
                 Seven Waves
                 Velocity of Love
                 Neverland
                 History of My Heart
                 Pianissimo
                 Cafe Luna
                 The Private Music of Suzanne Ciani

Company: Silver Wave Records
                 P.O. Box 7943
                 Boulder, CO 80306
                 (393) 443-5617

Albums by Fowler & Branca:
                 The Face On Cydonia
                 Etched In Stone

Miscellaneous Listings

Name: American Society of Composers, Authors, & Publishers (ASCAP)
ASCAP Building, One Lincoln Plaza
New York, NY 10023
(212) 595-3050

Specialty: ASCAP is the oldest performing rights licensing organization in the U.S.,
founded so that creators of music would be paid for the public performance of their
works, and users (licensees) could comply with the Federal Copyright Law.

Name: Broadcast Music International (BMI)
320 West 57th Street
New York, NY 10019
(212) 586-2000

Specialty: BMI, founded in New York in 1940, exists to protect the rights of over
120,000 songwriters, composers, and music publishers, and to distribute royalties
to them for those performing rights.

Name: The Guitar Guy
2008 Highway 37
Toms River, NJ 08753
(908) 270-8686

Specialty: Paul "Unk" Unkert, the proprieter, is a master luthier who builds, restores,
and customizes acoustic and electric stringed instruments. Vintage and classic
instruments are also bought, sold, repaired, and traded.

Name: National Association of Independent Record Distributors (NAIRD)
P.O. BOX 568
Maple Shade, NJ 08052
(609) 482-8999

Specialty: NAIRD is a trade association which was formed in 1972 to establish
channels and generally promote the independent recording industry. To improve
communication between record labels and distributors, the organization hosts an
annual convention, publishes a membership directory and a newsletter.

BIBLIOGRAPHY

Print Media

Graf, Rudolf F. *Modern Dictionary of Electronics*. Howard W. Sams & Sons Co., 1977.

Woodcock, Joanne, et al. *Computer Dictionary*. Microsoft Press, 199.

Benford, Tom. *Welcome To...CD-ROM*. MIS:Press, 1993.

Benford, Tom. "MIDI: Musical Instrument Digital Interface." *ComputerCraft* Magazine, September, 1991.

Tway, Linda. *Welcome To...Multimedia*. MIS:Press, 1992.

Eiche, Jon F. *What's a Synthesizer?* Hal Leonard Publishing, 1987.

Eiche, Jon F. *What's MIDI?* Hal Leonard Publishing, 1990.

Starr, Greg R. *What's a Sequencer?* Hal Leonard Publishing, 1990.

Freff. *What's a Sampler?* Hal Leonard Publishing, 1989.

Optical Media

Microsoft Multimedia Bookshelf. (CD-ROM/1992 Edition), Microsoft Corporation.

INDEX

The Author Wants To Hear From You!

I'm always interested in feedback from my readers and I'd love to hear from you. In addition to hearing your comments on this book, I'll add your name to my mailing list to keep you updated of other projects I'm working on that might be of interest to you. You'll also have the opportunity to purchase autographed copies of my first book, *Welcome To...CD-ROM*, or my upcoming audio music album on CD as well as other special offers for my readers.

Your Name: _____

Address: _____

City: _____ State: _____ Zip: _____

(The following is optional information to establish reader demographics):

Phone: _____ Sex: _____ Age: _____

Fill in, clip or photocopy and mail to:　　Tom Benford c/o CPTS
　　　　　　　　　　　　　　　　　　　　　2329 Highway 34 - Ste. 201
　　　　　　　　　　　　　　　　　　　　　Manasquan, NJ 08736

===

Now in Production: Tom's debut album, *Some Things I've Done...*

A great collection of tunes for listening, working or working-out to!

The CD alone - $15.95 (plus $2.05 S&H).

The CD with companion 3.5" high-density diskette *with* the MIDI files for all the tunes and technical notes on the album's production - $20.95 (plus $2.05 S&H).

An album of original instrumental compositions written and performed by Tom Benford, produced entirely with PCs and General MIDI gear! This album is *not available in stores*, but <u>autographed copies of the CD can be ordered directly from Tom Benford</u>. A companion 3.5" high-density diskette containing the actual MIDI files for all of the tunes on the album is also available with the purchase of the album. <u>**To order:**</u> autographed CD album only, $15.95; autographed CD *plus* MIDI song disk combo, $20.95. **Please add $2.05 S&H** to all orders. Send cash, check or money order only -- sorry, no C.O.D.s or credit cards.

INSTALLATION NOTES FOR USING THIS CD-ROM

All computer data files are located on Track #1, and can be accessed using a CD-ROM drive installed on an IBM-compatible PC. Tracks 2-9 are AUDIO TRACKS which can be played on any audio compact disk player. You can also play these files on your computer's CD-ROM drive using the Windows Media Player accessory (the appropriate CD AUDIO drivers must be installed in Windows) or the CD player utilities usually provided with sound cards. The files and software demos should be copied to floppy diskettes from the CD-ROM for installation, since many of these programs will need information about your particular computer and sound card configuration to operate properly. If you need additional help on formatting floppy diskettes and copying files, refer to the MS-DOS user's guide that came with your computer. Here are concise instructions for using these programs:

CAKEWALK: Format two floppy diskettes using the DOS format command. Insert diskette #1 in your floppy drive (e.g., drive A), and copy the contents of the *Cakewalk\Disk1* subdirectory from the CD-ROM onto the floppy using the following form:

> **copy x:\Cakewalk\Disk1*.* A:**

substituting the drive letter of your CD-ROM drive (e.g., D) for x. When the copy is completed, replace the floppy with diskette #2 and repeat the procedure, using the following form:

> **copy x:\Cakewalk\Disk2*.* A:**

again substituting the appropriate drive letters. When this copy is completed, insert floppy diskette #1 in your drive (e.g., drive A), and start Windows. From the File menu of Program Manager select **Run**. In the command line box, type **A:\setup.exe** and follow the on-screen instructions and prompts from there. If you have a problem installing or need help, call *Twelve Tone Systems* technical support at (617) 924-6275.

HWLNGDOG: There are two program demos in this subdirectory, so you'll need two floppy diskettes. Copy the contents of each subdirectory of the CD-ROM onto freshly-formatted floppy diskettes, respectively, using the following form:

> Diskette 1   **copy x: \HWLNGDOG\MRDRMSTX*.* A:**
> Diskette 2   **copy x: \HWLNGDOG\POWRCHDS*.* A:**

substituting the appropriate drive letters for your CD-ROM and floppy drives.

To install the MR. DRUMSTIX demo, read the README.TXT file that was copied onto diskette #1 and follow those instructions. To install the PowerChords demo, read the README.TXT file that was copied onto diskette #2 and follow those instructions. If you have a problem installing or need help, call *Howling Dog Systems* technical support at (613) 599-7927.

IBIS: There are six program demos contained in this subdirectory; five will run from DOS, and one (NP4WINDW) will run from Windows. Copy the contents of each subdirectory onto individual newly formatted floppy diskettes, and follow the installation instructions contained in each of the README files for each respective program. If you have a problem with installing or need help, call *IBIS* technical support at (415) 546-1917.

JAMMER21: Copy the contents of this subdirectory onto a freshly-formatted floppy diskette. Insert the floppy diskette in your drive and type **A:\INSTALL**. When the installation is finished, type **README** at the prompt for additional information on configuring/using the program. If you have a problem with installing or need help, call *Soundtrek* technical support at (404) 632-0879.

MAXPAK: Copy the contents of this subdirectory onto a freshly-formatted floppy diskette. Insert the floppy diskette and start Windows. Insert the floppy diskette and start Windows. From the File menu of Program Manager select **Run**. In the command line box type **A:install.exe** and follow the on-screen instructions and prompts from there. If you have a problem installing or need help, call *Big Noise Software* technical support at (904) 730-0754.

NAUTILUS: The Nutcracker Suite can be run directly from the CD-ROM, or, if you prefer, you can copy all of the files contained in this subdirectory to your hard drive (about 28MB of space will be required if you copy). To run it from the CD-ROM, start Windows. From the File menu of Program Manager select **Run**. In the command line box type:

x:\NAUTILUS\TBOOK.EXE NUTCRKR.TBK

substituting the letter of your CD-ROM drive (or your hard disk, if you copied the files) for x. The program may take a couple of minutes to load if you are running it directly from the CD-ROM drive. If you have a problem installing or need help, call *Nautilus* technical support at (614) 766-3150.

PROSONUS: Assorted MIDI, music (.WAV), and sound effects (.WAV) files are located in the respective subdirectories of Prosonus. These files can be accessed and used directly from the CD-ROM using the Windows Media Player accessory or the utilities provided with your sound card. Of course, you can also copy these files to your hard disk if you desire. *Prosonus* can be contacted at (818) 766-5221.

SNDFORGE: The Sound Forge demo can be installed on your hard disk directly from the CD-ROM. Start Windows and select **Run** from the File menu in Program Manager. In the command line box enter:

x:\SNDFRGE\setup.exe

substituting the letter of your CD-ROM drive for x. See the README.TXT file for additional information after the installation is completed. If you have a problem installing or need help, call *Sonic Foundry* technical support at (608) 256-3133.

SUPERJAM: Copy all files from this subdirectory onto a newly-formatted floppy diskette. Insert the floppy diskette and start Windows. Select **Run** from the File menu in Program Manager. In the command line box enter:

A:\setup.exe

See the README.TXT file for additional information on using the program and configuring it for your sound card. If you have a problem installing or need help, call *Blue Ribbon Sound Works* technical support at (404) 315-0212.

VOYETRA: An assortment of MIDI files are located in this subdirectory, and these files can be accessed and used directly from the CD-ROM using the Windows Media Player accessory or the utilities provided with your sound card. Of course, you can also copy these files to your hard disk if you desire. *Voyetra* can be contacted at (800) 233-9377.